THE RED AIR FORCE AT WAR

MiG Menace Over Korea
The Story of Soviet Fighter Ace Nikolai Sutiagin

YURI SUTIAGIN AND IGOR SEIDOV

Translated and Edited by Stuart Britton

Pen & Sword
AVIATION

First published in Great Britain in 2009 by
PEN & SWORD AVIATION
an imprint of
Pen & Sword Books Ltd
47 Church Street
Barnsley
South Yorkshire
S70 2AS

ISBN 978 1 84884 038 6

Printed and bound in the UK by
MPG Books

Pen & Sword Books Ltd incorporates the imprints of
Pen & Sword Aviation, Pen & Sword Maritime, Pen & Sword Military,
Wharncliffe Local History, Pen and Sword Select, Pen and Sword
Military Classics, Leo Cooper, Remember When,
Seaforth Publishing and Frontline Publishing.

For a complete list of Pen & Sword titles please contact
PEN & SWORD BOOKS LIMITED
47 Church Street, Barnsley, South Yorkshire, S70 2AS, England
E-mail: enquiries@pen-and-sword.co.uk
Website: www.pen-and-sword.co.uk

Contents

List of Illustrations

Editor's Preface

This English translation is an abridged version of Igor Seidov's and Yuri Sutiagin's *Groza 'Seibrov': Luchshii as Koreiskoi voiny* [The Menace to 'Sabres': The Top Ace of the Korean War] (Moscow: Izdatel'stvo 'Iauza' 'Eksmo', 2006), which is dedicated to the story of the Soviet ace Nikolai Sutiagin. The original book contains material that, while interesting in its own right, was not pertinent to Nikolai Sutiagin's life and combat record and was therefore excluded. Due to length considerations, in other places I have had to summarize the original Russian and selectively excerpt from some of the long orders and reports, which were presented verbatim in the original.

This book provides a revealing view into the operations of a Soviet fighter regiment during the war – its men and their training, its equipment, and its successes and failures in combat. However, the authors place this analysis within the context of a larger discussion of the Soviet Air Force and its role in the Korean War.

There has been a long-running debate about the number of aerial combat victories scored by each side during the Korean War. Seidov and Sutiagin present the Russian side of this debate. However, the authors openly acknowledge that the records on both sides may be inaccurate, so they do not pretend to hold the absolute truth on the subject. They note whenever American records differ from the Soviet records and recognize that some of the Soviet 'kills' may have in fact returned to base, albeit in a damaged condition. They also speak objectively about other matters in the book, such as training crashes, disciplinary problems in the 17th IAP [Fighter Aviation Regiment] and weaknesses of the MiG-15.

The authors do recognize the declining effectiveness of the Soviet fighter regiments as this period came to a close, as improved variants of the F–86 arrived and the US 51st Fighter Wing switched over to the Sabre. As Seidov and Sutiagin reveal, fighter regiments arriving later from the Soviet Union had a more difficult time than the 17th IAP and its brother regiments experienced. The authors also criticize Stalin's policy of rotating entire regiments and divisions through Manchuria during the war, which in their view was inferior to the American policy of rotating individual pilots and led to unjustifiable losses.

I wish to acknowledge the assistance of James Gebhardt, who is himself a translator of many books on the Soviet Armed Forces and its Air Force, and Boris Kavalerchik, a native speaker of Russian and a specialist on the Red Army's armor. Both stood by to help me with particularly knotty matters of translation and understanding. I also want to thank one of the authors, Igor Seidov, who was always quick to reply to my requests for elucidation or elaboration. As always, any mistakes in translation are my own. For the most part, I have used the Library of Congress system of transliteration. One exception is with the Soviet 'Yak' fighters and bombers. I have opted to use the letter 'Y' at the start of the name, rather than the Library of Congress 'I', to avoid any possible confusion with the Russian abbreviation for the Fighter Aviation Regiment, which is 'IAK'.

I also want to extend my sincere gratitude to the staff at the Air Force Historical Research Agency at Maxwell Air Force Base in Alabama. I especially want to thank Lynn Gamma and Kevin Burge, who always stood by with information and maps to assist me with identifying some of the Korean locations mentioned in the original book. In many cases, direct transliteration of those names did not produce recognizable locations found in English-language sources. We did not succeed in identifying every location; some of the smaller villages in that secretive country could not be ascertained from their Russian names or located on any available maps. In those cases, I used the context of the passage in question to identify the area of the location and a larger, known town in that area, and then used that known location with the phrase 'in the area of ...'. Of course, that is also an expression that the authors used in many instances!

Finally, I want to thank Artem Drabkin, project coordinator of the *Ia pomniu (I remember)* website at http://www.iremember.ru, which is a vast repository of stories, memoirs, and photographs submitted by Red Army veterans. Mr. Drabkin passed along the manuscript for Seidov and Sutiagin's book and arranged for the rights with the Russian publisher for an English translation of it.

Stuart Britton

Authors' Preface

More than fifty years have passed since the end of the war between South and North Korea with the participation of international forces of the United Nations (UN) on one side, and the Chinese People's Volunteers (CPV) on the other. The participation in this war of Soviet servicemen, primarily pilots, was long a secret to the majority of citizens of the Soviet Union, up until the time of perestroika and glasnost. The results of the aerial conflict in the skies above Korea have still not been fully assessed, since the calculation of victories and losses in this air war by our researchers and official government agencies differs from that on the American side.

It is well known that the pilots of two Soviet air divisions – General Lobov's 303rd (later commanded by Colonel Kumanichkin) Fighter Aviation Division (*istrebitel'naia aviatsionnaia diviziia* – IAD) and Colonel Kozhedub's 324th IAD – fought most successfully in Korea. However, it has turned out that of the five aviation regiments that comprised these two aviation divisions, the combat record of the 303rd IAD's 17th Fighter Aviation Regiment (*istrebitel'nyi aviatsionnyi polk* – IAP) is known least of all, because the pilots of this aviation regiment left behind no written recollections, as did S. Kramarenko (of the 176th Guards Fighter Aviation Division [GIAD]), and E. Pepeliaev and B. Abakumov (of the 196th IAP). Moreover, an unenviable fate lay in wait for the 17th IAP at the end of the 1950s – it was disbanded, leaving only the 18th GIAP and the 523rd IAP as part of the 303rd IAD.

Meanwhile, despite its 'provincial' status (from 1945 on, the aviation regiment was based in the Soviet Far East), the 17th IAP fought no worse than the other famous 'parade' regiments of the aforementioned divisions, which came to the war from the Moscow area and often participated in ceremonial flyovers and aerial shows. The 17th IAP ranked second according to the number of kills registered over the enemy, while at the same time suffering the least number of losses. In addition, other notable records of this air war belong to the 17th IAP: the top Soviet ace of the war, Nikolai Sutiagin (twenty-two victories), served in its ranks; the flight of Captain Dokashenko shot down more enemy planes than any other flight; and Captain Dokashenko himself once managed to shoot down three American F-86 'Sabre' fighters in one battle.

The present book, without pretending to offer a complete account of the war, is offered to the reader in order to fill in the gap in existing literature about the 17th IAP and its pilots in the air war in Korea. At the same time, our primary focus will be on Nikolai Sutiagin. Nikolai Vasil'evich himself left behind no memoir or personal recollections. The material for this book is based upon documents from the Russian Federation's Central Archive of the Ministry of Defense [TsAMO], the diary of his wife R.O. Sutiagina, and the reminiscences of his colleagues.

The book contains the story of the making of Nikolai Sutiagin as a pilot, whose talent shone brightly during the air battles over Korea, and of his further fate and service in the Soviet Air Force. The story of N. Sutiagin in the Korean air war is presented against the backdrop of a general description of the combat operations of the 17th IAP of the 303rd IAD.

The authors of this book excuse themselves to the readers for the overabundance of 'dry' texts from archival documents in their work! Of course, it would be more interesting to read the lively tales of veterans of this war, but as it turned out, for long years they were completely forbidden to speak or write about the given subject. Only in 1993 was the seal of secrecy partially removed from the documents relating to this war, and more importantly, veterans of the war could finally begin to speak and write about their experiences in it.

However time spares no one, and by this time many Korean War veterans have already passed on, including the main hero of this narrative, Nikolai Vasil'evich Sutiagin, and many of his former comrades in the regiment. Now only documents can have something to say about how our pilots fought in the skies of Korea and how they gained their victories, albeit through the dry language of dispatches, reports and orders.

The authors have sought to supplement the documental narrative with excerpts from the recollections of those people who were close to Nikolai Vasil'evich, who knew him personally, or who fought together with him in the Korean air war. With this work, the authors of the book wanted to honor the combat service and accomplishments of our fathers and grandfathers, who honorably did their military duty in this long secret war.

The authors are grateful to all the Korean War veterans, as well as their family members and close friends, who helped us in every possible way. Without their help, much, which they saw with their own eyes, would have vanished without a trace and would never have reached our reader. Our enormous thanks to them for this! We are especially grateful to Diego Zampini (Argentina) and Nikolai Bodrikhin for their help in creating this book.

Igor Seidov
Yuri Sutiagin

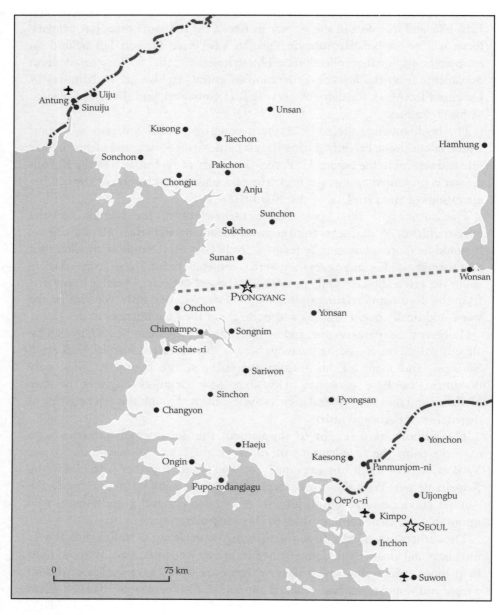

The Korean peninsula during the war.

Chapter One

The Making of an Air Warrior

Nikolai Sutiagin was born in the village of Smagino on the banks of the P'iana River, about 120 kilometers south-east of Nizhegorod (formerly Gor'ky) on 5 May 1923. His father, Vasilii Alekseevich, was a middle-class citizen who had a small farm, and later became a decorated sapper in the Red Army during the Second World War. As the first child, his parents came to rely upon Nikolai to help with the hard labor around the farm and to look after his younger siblings. Nikolai grew up as a strong and healthy son, with a solid sense of personal responsibility and diligence.

In 1934, when Nikolai was eleven years old, he moved to the city of Gor'ky to live with his grandfather, in order to help the family. Life in the city was not easy for him – in addition to his middle school studies, he took jobs wherever he could find them. For a time, he even earned some money on the side by taking small parts in productions put on by the city's Opera Theater. Nikolai had a decent singing voice, and some people even began to believe that an acting career lay ahead for him.

In the 1930s, the network of flying clubs was growing rapidly in the country, as young men and women were enthusiastically signing up in large numbers in order to emulate famous aviators and national heroes such as Baidukov and Chkalov, and the many Soviet combat fighter pilots who distinguished themselves in dogfights over Spain during the Spanish Civil War. In 1939, when Nikolai reached sixteen years of age, he joined the *Komsomol* (Young Communists), which gave him access to flying lessons at one of these clubs. In addition to classroom study of flight theory, aerodynamics and navigation, the students were able to make training flights. They trained on the standard Soviet trainer of those years, N.N. Polikarpov's U-2 biplane, which was cheap to produce and simple to operate and maintain. By 1953, over 33,000 U-2s had been built.

Nikolai quickly became one of the best students, and he seemed destined to become a combat pilot. However, around the time of his call-up for military service, Nikolai was strongly influenced by the popular film *The Tractor Drivers*, which glorified the Soviet armored forces. Sutiagin decided to enroll in a tank specialist school, but his application was rejected because of his height. At 5 feet 10 inches, Nikolai was too tall to serve in tanks, which were designed for much shorter men. Although perhaps disappointed, Nikolai didn't hesitate with his next decision, and at the beginning of March 1941 he enrolled in the Chernigov Military Aviation School for Pilots (VAShP).

In connection with the rising military threat, the number of aviation schools and academies in the Soviet Union had been expanding enormously to accelerate the training of pilots. Among the new aviation schools was the Chernigov VAShP, which had been created by order of the People's Commissar of Defense on 6 November 1940 with five squadrons of I-15bis biplane fighters. The school completed its formation in February 1941, and the first detachment of students began their theoretical studies that month. Those students with previous flying club experience began training flights right away.

The outbreak of the war in June 1941 disrupted the training schedule. School instructors, staff, and I-15bis fighters were repeatedly drawn into active combat duty. Flight training and aerial gunnery practice labored under acute shortages of equipment, spare parts, and fuel and lubricants. The rapid German advance twice forced the relocation of the school, first to Rostov in September 1941, then to the cities of Kyzyl-Arvat and Kazandhik in Turkmenistan in November 1941. Through all of this, Nikolai Sutiagin continued his training, and on 7 November 1941 he took his military oath.

Kyzyl-Arvat was a small city, with a population in those years of approximately 50,000 people. The land around the city is arid and flat like the steppe, bounded by mountains to the north and deserts to the south, and with the exception of the occasional dust storm, the weather is ideal for year-round flying. However, shortages continued to restrict the students' hours in the air and living conditions were less than ideal due to the near absence of building materials, which forced the majority of students to live in dugouts or tents. The school's airplane park counted altogether 175 planes (well below its authorized strength of 304 planes), consisting of a mix of UT-1, U-2, UT-2, UTI-4 types, plus several each of I-16, Yak-1 and Yak-7 fighters. Nevertheless the Chernigov VAShP finally had a stable location and could begin to turn out a steady stream of pilots for the Red Army. Already by 1 April 1942, over 2,000 students had passed through the school, though shortages in aircraft, fuel, and spare parts throughout 1942 meant that the school was unable to meet its graduation targets.

Back in 1942, training flights took place in very difficult conditions: the summertime temperatures reached 50 degrees C. (122 degrees F.) and higher; therefore, training flights began at sunrise, ended at 11:00 AM–12:00 PM, and resumed at 5:00 PM. Students diligently studied the parts of the airplane, the theory of flight, how to handle an airplane in flight, tactics, navigation, topography, meteorology, and the silhouettes of their own and enemy airplanes. To be honest, the theoretical training was less than desirable – the primary emphasis was on the practical side of flight training: in flying weather they flew, and in poor weather not suitable for flying, they studied the parts of the airplane. To study the experience gained by combat pilots in the war, they made use primarily of articles published in the newspapers *Red Star* and *Stalin's Falcon*.

Nikolai Sutiagin was a good student and flew with confidence, training on UT-2 and UTI-4 types. By the time of his graduation at the end of August 1942, he had conducted 495 training flights with a total flying time of 83 hours and 36 minutes (including his time with the flying club). The *Komsomol* reference for the student Nikolai Sutiagin declared that '... he showed both initiative and discipline'. His graduation certificate read in part: 'Superbly disciplined. Carries out orders conscientiously and precisely. Possesses a good standing within his unit.'[1]

To his deep disappointment, Sergeant Sutiagin didn't wind up at the front – almost all the pilots who graduated in July–August 1942 were sent to the Far East in exchange for the flight staff there, who in turn were transferred to the front against Germany. Most of the pilots from the Chernigov VAShP's 7th Aviation Squadron, in which Sutiagin trained, were placed under the command of Major Khoderov and then assigned to one of the Maritime District's reserve regiments.

In the reserve aviation regiment, the young pilots polished their piloting technique, practiced flying in various formations and analyzed their combat applications – after all, aerial combat was practically not taught at all in any of the aviation schools. However, Sergeant Sutiagin did not have long to brush up on his skills.

In the 582nd Fighter Aviation Regiment in the Far East

In October 1942, Nikolai Sutiagin was assigned to the 582nd IAP with the 9th Air Army's 249th IAD. The 9th Air Army had been formed in August 1942 with the assignment to protect the Soviet Union's Far Eastern airspace.

Within just a month, however, in connection with a reorganization of the 582nd IAP, Nikolai was reassigned to the 5th IAP in the same aviation division, where he joined the 1st Aviation Squadron in Novo-Nikol'sk. There, he embarked upon a crash course to master the I-16 fighter in a short period of time. The fact that on 3 December alone, Sergeant Sutiagin conducted eleven training flights with an instructor over the airfield speaks of the intensity of the training. On 4 December, regiment commander Major Manaseev graded Sutiagin's flying skills and gave him an overall evaluation of '4' (out of a possible '5'), and approved him for independent flights in the I-16 fighter.[2] The next day the commander of the 1st Aviation Squadron, Senior Lieutenant

Didenko, conducted another inspection of Sutiagin's piloting skills. He observed, 'With retracted landing gear, he forgot to release the speed brakes in turns,' and 'his hand is a little unsteady on the control stick,' but noted that Sutiagin would quickly eliminate the indicated mistakes. Soon Nikolai was reassigned to the 2nd Aviation Squadron.

In the very same 5th IAP, another pilot with the family name Sutiagin was serving: Nikolai's own uncle, Aleksandr Alekseevich, who was only a few years older than his nephew and with whom he had previously lived at their grandfather's in Gor'ky. At one time, Nikolai was even posted to his uncle's flight. Flight commander A. Sutiagin sometimes deliberately lowered his nephew's flight evaluations, so that Nikolai could make additional training flights. At that time, units didn't have enough fuel and lubricants, and flying time was limited. However, Nikolai's best friends in the regiment were pilots Boris Ivanov and Sergei Bychkov.

Colonel (ret.) Boris Ivanov recalls:

> I got to know Sutiagin in the autumn of 1942, when we arrived at the 5th Aviation Regiment of the 9th Air Army, which was based in the Maritime District. What sort of man was Sutiagin? He was tall, well-built, with a round, freckled face. Nikolai stood out on any assignment and in any company. At the time, no one supposed that he would become our first jet ace. But in conversation among ourselves, we didn't refer to him as anything other than 'Ace'. Why, you ask?
>
> We weren't in combat, but we were at the front, where from day to day we anticipated a Japanese attack, so combat training was feverish. And in this, Sutiagin had no equal in flying technique, and he was a superb shot. He never missed the aerial target.
>
> Any serious business in the 5th IAP started with his name. He became part of that team of pilots, who were ready to accept the most difficult assignments. I remember how in 1944 the Yak-9 was coming out, and we had just mastered the Yak-7B. They began to form a group of pilots who would have the first opportunity with the new Yaks, and the first name on the list was Sutiagin's.

It was in the 5th Aviation Regiment that Nikolai met his future wife Raia [diminutive version of Raisa], who was serving as an armament mechanic in his squadron. Raisa Onufrievna Baranova was born on 10 August 1921, and had been mobilized for service in the Red Army in May 1942. She was sent to the Far East, where she took a sixth-month course for master armament mechanics in the 56th School for Junior Aviation Specialists in Vozzhaevka. The girls were often called upon to help harvest vegetables, unload coal and cut trees, so their preparation in the school was less than desirable.

When Raisa graduated in November 1942, she was sent to the 5th IAP's headquarters in Novo-Nikol'sk. There they offered Raisa a position in the headquarters as a clerk, but she requested duty as a technician. She was assigned to the 1st Flight of the 3rd Aviation Squadron. At first Raia was troubled by her lack of preparation, but she quickly picked up the necessary skills. The work was physically demanding, dangerous and required long hours. The flight crews headed to the airfield at 6:00 AM each day and labored until 7:00 PM, readying airplanes for sorties. In February 1943 there was a fatal incident, when technician Nadia Omel'chenko accidentally shot her friend Katia Chernous while they were reloading machine guns. Nadia was in the cockpit, while Katia was standing in front of the plane's right wing. Thinking they were reloading the right outboard machine gun, Nadia flicked the switch for the right inboard machine gun and pressed the trigger to empty it of its remaining rounds. A bullet struck her friend in the head.

At the Sukhaia River and in Pokrovka

At the beginning of June 1943, Raia was transferred to the 2nd Aviation Squadron based at the Sukhaia River. It is there that she became acquainted with Nikolai Sutiagin, and their gradual courtship began. The airfield was located to the west of Vladivostok, on the shore of Peter the Great's Harbor; the city of Vladivostok was clearly visible from the shoreline next to the airfield. Here, many of the pilots had their first bird's-eye view of the Pacific Ocean, and they frequently had to fly over it. According to the pilots, flying over the sea at that time, without good navigational instruments, was not a pleasant sensation. There was often a haze or fog, and when the coastline faded from view, it had a strong psychological effect on the pilot. As a result, many of the pilots had a natural desire to cling to the coastline.

As Raisa noted in her diary, the area was unusually beautiful, with the sea on one side and a forest preserve that teemed with game surrounding it on the other sides. Trout could be found in the Sukhaia River itself, so the region was a paradise for hunters and fishermen, but the area bristled with pillboxes and anti-aircraft positions to protect the airfield, while military patrol boats plied the waters of the harbor. The situation in the Far East was tense, as the Japanese frequently violated Soviet airspace and territorial waters. From time to time, alarms and expectations of Japanese attack kept the fighter regiments on a high state of alert, and pilots would spend all day sitting in their cockpits. The constant air patrols kept the ground crews busy.

In between periods of high alert, the regiment would return to routine combat training. Yet even this did not come without cost. Two training accidents in 1943 took the lives of two pilots in the 5th IAP, Senior Lieutenant Fomichev and Senior Lieutenant Karov, who both crashed in their I-16 fighters.

In April 1944, the 2nd Squadron moved to Novo-Nikol'sk in order to trade in their outdated I-16s for the new Yak-7B. However, instead of returning to Sukhaia River, on 18 April the 2nd Squadron relocated to Pokrovka, because the field at Sukhaia River was unsuitable for the new Yaks. Moreover, that summer the Sukhaia River airfield was often hampered by fog and drizzle – conditions totally unsuitable for flying.

After flying the plane, many pilots considered the Yak-7B to be one of the best fighters of the war, on a par with the LaGG-3 and MiG-3, as it was easy to fly and aerodynamically stable.

It was around this time that Raisa Baranova began to notice the attention paid to her by Nikolai Sutiagin. He often lingered around his plane while Raisa cleaned his machine guns, and made sure to be at the airfield whenever Raisa had sentry duty there. Initially, she hadn't been particularly drawn to the quiet and modest village fellow, but gradually his reliability, helpfulness and sense of responsibility won her over. Of course, she also knew of his reputation as a superb pilot, which didn't hurt his chances.

By October 1944, Nikolai Sutiagin was now flying as a lieutenant and flight commander. He had repeatedly demonstrated his superior flying skills and good marksmanship in training and competitions. Over the two years he had been with the 5th IAP, Sutiagin had received fourteen commendations from command for his successes in combat training.

In November 1944, the commander of the 9th Air Army Major General Vinogradov inspected the readiness of the 5th IAP and its preparations for the winter. He especially commended the regiment commander and the commander of the 3rd Aviation Squadron in his report. For the year 1944, the 5th IAP was recognized as the finest regiment in the division. The total flight time for the regiment for the year was 1,164 hours, an average of 53 hours and 17 minutes for each pilot. The regiment had staged 999 mock dogfights. There had been, however, two non-fatal crashes and five mechanical failures, and one incident when a pilot became lost while flying.[3]

On 5 December, the regiment went into its winter quarters. The pilots and ground personnel had to live in canvas tents, and it was a constant struggle to ward off the cold. With the slower pace of operations in the winter, commanders now had time to write annual personal reviews for each pilot. This is what regiment commander Major Manaseev and the 2nd Aviation Squadron commander Senior Lieutenant Olenitsa wrote about flight commander Lieutenant N.V. Sutiagin on 8 January 1945:

At work and in everyday life he is polished, cheerful and tactful. When following the orders of higher command … he is persistent and exacting. He renders great assistance to his squadron commander in forging an iron military discipline in the unit.

As a pilot he is well-trained. He has good piloting technique. He flies confidently and boldly. There are no incidents of pilot error in his record.

… In studying the experience of the current war, he takes particular <u>interest in successful aerial combat tactics as described by Guard Colonel Pokryshkin, and he uses them in his own combat-training missions.</u> [Emphasis in the original.]

Conclusion: Meets the responsibilities of flight commander.[4]

On 1 January 1945, the 5th IAP had forty pilots on its roster, thirty-six of which had been trained on the Yak-7B. The regiment with a staff of thirty-two crews was capable of conducting a combat mission in simple meteorological conditions.

Preparations for War

In March 1945, the 2nd Aviation Squadron transferred from Pokrovka to Novo-Nikol'sk in order to take part in army-level maneuvers. This was by now a rehearsal before the start of combat operations against Japan. In the meantime, fascist Germany was in its death throes as the Red Army closed upon Berlin from the east, and the Allies were breaching the Rhine River to the west.

Raia was regularly following the events on the Soviet-German front. From day to day she waited for news about the end of the war with Germany. Nevertheless, when it came, the news of the long-awaited victory took her by surprise. In her diary, she wrote:

> 9.05.45 The war is over! What can be greater than that? I was on duty at the headquarters. Someone called: 'Tell the commander to prepare some people for a meeting in honor of the end of the war with Germany.'
>
> Oy! … and I dropped the receiver. Boundless joy. I picked up and dropped the phone several times and ran out into the street, to listen to the honks and celebratory gunfire that drifted to us from the city of Voroshilov.

The entire staff of the regiment celebrated. There were meetings in all the squadrons. Speakers poured scorn on German fascism and expressed their pride for our glorious Red Army, navy, and air force, and for our people, who had secured victory through their hard work behind the front. They also swore that the borders of the Far East would be vigilantly defended from any encroachments by Japanese militarism. They vowed to remain alert, since the hotbed of war in the Far East remained.

On 27 May, the regiment received new airplanes: Yak-3 fighters. The flight staff began to master it, flying from dawn to dusk. For once, the regiment was given unlimited fuel for this. The ground crews had to clean the weapons and service the planes in darkness. The Yak-3 was one of our best fighters of the war. With the aim of lightening the plane as much as possible, the Yak-3 had only the minimal necessary amount of instruments and on-board equipment that would enable it to fight in daytime in good weather. The compulsory piece of equipment was a radio that provided two-way communications.

All the runways of the Maritime District's airbases were grass. In the Far East, bands of torrential rains pass through regularly, every three years. The rivers leave their banks, bridges are carried away, and the dirt roads and grass airfields dissolve into muck, knocking them out of service. Flight operations must halt for 20–30 days at a time. Such was the case in July 1945. In the neighboring 582nd IAP, while checking the landing strip for operational readiness, the airplane of deputy regiment commander Captain Platov nosed over when it landed. Regiment commander Major M.M. Kriukov's UT-2 broke up while landing when flying in for a meeting with the 249th IAD's commander, Colonel Kondrat.

When the commander of the 9th Air Army, now General P.M. Sokolov, learned of the wreck of two of the division's airplanes, he immediately demoted Captain Platov to flight commander. Sokolov relieved Colonel Kondrat of command and appointed Colonel T. Mikhailov in command of the division.

Through the summer of 1945, the 5th IAP continued its intensive flight schedule. Pilots with combat experience against the Germans arrived to share their knowledge of aerial combat and to lead tactical exercises. As Raia noted in her diary on 22 July 1945, 'The guys never leave the cockpits of their planes … Every day, troop trains are heading toward the border. Many frontline units have arrived from the West. We will be fighting …'

Nevertheless, the intensive training didn't proceed without losses. In June 1945, the 3rd Aviation Squadron lost two pilots, Konovalov and Romanenko, when their planes crashed. At the beginning of July, there was another plane crash, which killed pilot Petrov. Raia confided in her diary:

> Today we had an accident. Petrov crashed … we had just left the

canteen when Lida came running up to meet us: 'Ladies, one of our men has crashed ... I saw myself how the airplane plunged to the ground.'

We started running for the airfield. I was frightfully worried. The thought flashed through my mind: 'What if it is Nikolai?' Planes were taxiing off the runway, and we tensely observed which pilots were returning. My agitation didn't subside until I recognized Kolia [Nikolai]. I immediately heaved a sigh of relief. 'What does this mean, love?' ... 'This year, some bad sign has fallen over our regiment. This is the third crash in the past month ... and what fine men are being killed!'

In the middle of July, the division command offered to send away the families of officers to relatives living beyond the anticipated war zone. The 5th IAP relocated to border airfields, where the planes were dispersed and camouflaged. Slit trenches were dug for the flight staff, round the clock sentries were established in the squadron and flight areas, and the regiment began to live a front-line existence. Pilots increased their study of the airfields in Manchuria and Japanese aircraft types, their mission to escort ground attack light bombers, and aerial combat tactics. From day to day, everyone anticipated the onset of combat operations, and everything was made ready for it.

A hard fight was anticipated. By the summer of 1945, the Japanese had constructed more than twenty airbases and 133 airfields in occupied Manchuria and Korea, with an estimated operational capacity of more than 6,000 aircraft. The Imperial Japanese Army Air Force in eastern China, Manchuria and Korea included the 2nd and 5th Air Armies. Soviet intelligence estimated that between these two air armies, the Japanese had 600 bombers, 1,200 fighters, and approximately 200 reconnaissance and auxiliary airplanes.

About this time, an incident occurred that nearly ended Nikolai Sutiagin's flying career, almost before it had started! From Raisa's diary we know that on 28 July 1945 there was a wedding celebration in the 5th IAP's 2nd Aviation Squadron, and the celebrants, Sutiagin among them, had gotten drunk. On the way back, a sentry stopped Nikolai and another of the party-goers. An argument erupted, Nikolai broke away and ran, and the sentry opened fire – but fortunately missed. Raisa reports that everybody returned from the party totally intoxicated, hardly able to stand on their feet. The next morning it was the squadron's turn for sentry duty, but it was in no condition to serve this responsibility and the regiment command had to dismiss the squadron from duty. It was a major incident within the entire 9th Air Army, but one with strangely little repercussion. The pilots likely avoided severe punishment because of the nearness of war.

On 7 August, the 9th Air Army was assigned to the 1st Far Eastern Front, which was deployed along the eastern boundary with Manchuria and Korea. The task of the 1st Far Eastern Front in the upcoming offensive, labeled Operation August Storm, was to break through the enemy's fortifications along the Mulichen and Mutanchiang Rivers. The specific responsibility of the 249th IAD was to support the offensive of the 25th Army in the direction of Hunchun and Wanching by escorting the ground attack light bombers of the 251st Assault Aviation Division.

For combat fighter pilots eager to test their mettle against an adversary, Operation August Storm was a disappointment. Unknown to the Soviets, the Japanese had withdrawn the bulk of the serviceable bombers and fighters to bases in southern Korea and Japan prior to the offensive, leaving behind mostly reconnaissance aircraft, a few obsolete fighters, and a lot of grounded aircraft in various states of disrepair. On the first day of the offensive, 9 August 1945, there were only four encounters with the enemy in the air along the entire sector of the 1st Far Eastern Front. All were reconnaissance aircraft. Fortunate fighter pilots from the 147th IAD intercepted three of the reconnaissance flights and shot down two of the Japanese R-98 reconnaissance planes. Airmen of the 32nd IAD intercepted another Japanese R-98 and downed it.

Due to inclement weather (the first day of Operation August Storm was marked by heavy rain and thunderstorms), the 5th IAP was able to launch only one sortie. The fighters met no resistance in the air, but came upon a Japanese column and shot it up. This became the general pattern as Operation August Storm unfolded. As forces of the 1st Far Eastern Front advanced into the depths of Manchuria, capturing Japanese airbases and their garrisons along the way, the regiments of the 249th IAD flew missions to strafe retreating Japanese columns and knots of enemy resistance hunkered down in permanent fortifications.

Between the start of the offensive on 9 August and the Japanese capitulation on 2 September 1945, Nikolai Sutiagin conducted only thirteen sorties, several of which were not in his Yak-3 fighter, but in the Polikarpov PO-2. Three of these sorties were 'free hunt' and reconnaissance sorties with a total flight time of 1 hour and 51 minutes. Sutiagin had no opportunity to test his skills in combat against a Japanese pilot, but his combat work was still noticed by his superiors. In August 1945, Lieutenant Sutiagin received his first honor for combat excellence: the Order of the Red Star.

The Road Home ... through Korea

After Japan's surrender, the 5th IAP returned to its previous base at Novo-Nikol'sk, but it was not there for long, as the higher command decided to transfer aviation units to Korea, which had been liberated from the Japanese. However, with the war now over, demobilization on a massive scale was set to happen, firstly of the female service personnel. Raisa was set to return home to Belorussia, but Nikolai insisted that she remain with him and marry him.

On 24 September, the flight staff departed for Korea; the 5th IAP now had the mission to monitor and defend the airspace of North Korea. The plan was for the ground crews and support services to follow them. While the pilots flew their planes to Singisiu, the technical staff traveled by ship from the port of Pos'et to Wonsan. From here, the staff traveled by train to Singisiu, but when they reached it, they found that the pilots had flown to Port Arthur. It took more than a month for the rear administrative and support services to catch up with the flight staff, which complicated flight operations for the regiment in the interim.

The order for the demobilization of the women arrived in Port Arthur. Most of the women headed home by steamship, but Junior Sergeant Raisa Baranova remained behind: on 1 November 1945, she became the wife of Lieutenant Nikolai Sutiagin. They wanted to throw a wedding party for all their friends on 7 November, for which the entire regiment was waiting, but on 6 November the entire flight staff flew to Dairen (Dalian). The ground staff followed them. In Dairen, the young wives settled comfortably into apartments. Wrote Raisa Sutiagina:

> I never anticipated that Nikolai would be so thrifty and concerned with the household. He has already acquired almost everything necessary for the apartment ...
> 2.12.45 Nikolai is a wonderful friend. It seems that I have fallen in love with a true husband. He is tender, affectionate and caring ...

Soon, the mass demobilization of men from the army was pending, even for the pilots. In October 1945, a special review of the flight staff was made to decide the fate of each pilot. The review of the period from December 1944 to October 1945 for flight commander Lieutenant N.V. Sutiagin, dated 11 October 1945, described Sutiagin as 'decisive and bold', 'energetic', and fond of taking the initiative. It recommended that 'he be kept in the Red Army in fighter aviation or as a test pilot'.[5]

Nikolai was lucky – they kept him in the air force, without which he could not even imagine his future life in peacetime. In January 1946, his wife Raisa began work as a schoolteacher. Time passed quickly in Dairen, yet far from her homeland, Raisa's mood worsened. She badly wanted to continue her own education, but this would only be possible back in the Soviet Union. By May 1946, she was confiding in her diary of 'a hellish boredom. Cards, neighbors, books'.

Only a month later her hopes were realized when the regiment received an order to return to the Soviet Union; however, the transfer did not go smoothly for Raisa Sutiagina. Once again, the pilots flew on ahead, leaving their families behind to travel by steamship, but Nikolai forgot to fill out the necessary forms for Raisa to receive his pay in his absence. They had to wait a whole month for the steamship to arrive. Raisa was forced to sell the family radio and other household items in order to purchase food.

For Nikolai, the time in Korea had not been a waste: he studied this tiny country thoroughly from the air, and he could easily orient himself above the complex topography. This familiarity with the future theater of combat operations would play an extremely useful role five years later, when he had to engage in dogfights over North Korea.

After the return to the Soviet Union, the regiment resumed combat training: flights, studies, gunnery practice, and familiarizing itself with its latest equipment – the American P-63 Kingcobra obtained through Lend–Lease. Our pilots respected the Kingcobra for its easy handling and for its comfortably spacious cockpit, from which the pilot enjoyed a wide field of view. The aircraft also had good instruments and an excellent gunsight. Although the Kingcobra arrived in time to play some role in Operation August Storm, perhaps its main contribution would come several years later, when the Soviet Air Force was making the transition to jet fighters. The point was that the Kingcobra had a tricycle landing gear, just like the new Soviet jet fighters, the MiG-9 and MiG-15. All Soviet piston-engine fighters had tail wheels. So the Kingcobras were used to instruct Soviet pilots in the new procedure for taking off and landing with a tricycle landing gear.

There were also major changes in Sutiagin's family life within months of the return to the Soviet Union. In November 1946, Raisa gave birth to their first child, a daughter named Galina.

For those pilots who remained to serve in the regiment, the pace of training grew from year to year. Thus, if Sutiagin had logged 73 hours on 135 flights in 1946, then in 1947, he logged 171 hours on 205 flights and in 1948, 161 hours on 265 flights.

In April 1947, in connection with the disbanding of the 5th IAP, Lieutenant Sutiagin was transferred to the 190th IAD's 17th IAP of the 9th Air Army's 2nd Combined Corps. His future victories in Korea would be connected with this aviation regiment.

'Personally disciplined, but ...'

Evidently, Sutiagin's relations with his direct superior in the 17th IAP, squadron commander Senior Lieutenant N.I. Maslennikov, did not go smoothly. The performance review for flight commander N.V. Sutiagin, written by his commander in December 1947, contains some curiously contradictory statements. The report acknowledges Sutiagin's 'excellent flying skills' and 'fine aerial combat technique', and recommends his promotion to senior lieutenant and the position of deputy squadron commander. However, while calling Sutiagin 'personally disciplined', it points to 'incidents of lack of discipline, arguments with his commanding officer, and insubordination in the matter of flight training for the younger pilots'. The report states that Lieutenant Sutiagin 'enjoys practical authority in the aviation squadron and the aviation regiment', but he 'does not give sufficient help to his squadron commander in instilling firm military discipline in the squadron'.[6]

The squadron commander brings serious accusations to bear on Sutiagin, but at the same time considers him worthy of promotion to a higher rank and position. Of course, it is easy to call any foot-dragging by a subordinate 'arguments' from the superior's point of view, especially in the matter of training new pilots. Also, Nikolai Sutiagin never kowtowed before superior commanders and always defended his position, even if this brought him trouble.

Here is how one of his fellow pilots in the 17th IAP, Aleksei Nikolaevich Nikolaev, remembers Sutiagin:

> I knew Nikolai Vasil'evich Sutiagin quite well. We served together in the same regiment for several years. He was a very fine comrade, responsive, seasoned and calm. You could lay a lot on his shoulders in everything, and he wouldn't let you down. He was physically strong and loved sports, especially basketball. However, he wasn't in favor among the higher command – especially after one brawl with some tankers. He was an excellent pilot; he handled his plane beautifully and was a superb shot.

With some delay, in April 1948 Lieutenant Sutiagin received his promotion to senior lieutenant.

After his return to the Soviet Union following the war, Nikolai Sutiagin had applied repeatedly for admission to the Military Air Academy, but without success. Lieutenant Colonel Manaseev, his former regiment commander in the 5th IAP, had written in a performance review of Sutiagin's desire to study at the Academy, and formally recommended him for promotion to deputy squadron commander and for admission to the Academy's command school. However, in those years, admission to the Academy was a privilege reserved almost exclusively for Heroes of the Soviet Union from the Great Patriotic War. In 1949, Sutiagin finally did gain admission to the Air Force Academy, but he wasn't there long. In April of that same year, he was appointed to fill a deputy squadron commander position in the 17th IAP back in the Far East.

Not long after his return to the 17th IAP, another incident tarnished Sutiagin's reputation and left a formal reprimand in his personnel record. On January 5 1950, Sutiagin was accused of drunken brawling with officers from a different unit. While the file is silent on details of this incident, the family chronicle has the following to say:

> In January 1950, Nikolai received a leave of absence and was traveling with his wife and young daughter aboard the Vladivostok–Moscow train toward his destination. Here we need to mention that one of Nikolai's favorite pastimes was the card game 'Preference' – a traditional way that many officers relaxed. On the train, Nikolai naturally found some fellow card-players, and spent the days playing cards in another car, leaving his young wife unaccompanied in their sleeping compartment. Two officers from a different unit, traveling in the same car, began to flirt crudely with Raisa and to harass her. When a neighbor informed Nikolai about what was going on, he immediately rushed back to his sleeper, and without stopping to deliberate, drove them from the compartment with punches. The other side put up no resistance and retreated, and with that it seemed the matter was closed.
>
> However, when Nikolai returned from his leave, he found a complaint waiting for him at unit headquarters, filed by the suffering officers. It turned out that both men were officers of the Special Department [military counterintelligence], who claimed that Nikolai had attacked them without provocation in a drunken rage, seemingly eager to start a brawl. Sutiagin's word meant nothing against such testimony, so Nikolai received the full treatment from his superiors, and a formal reprimand was entered into his personnel record. All because of a card game!

Mastering Jet Technology

On 4 October 1950, the 17th IAP joined the 303rd IAD of the 54th Air Army and relocated to the Voznesensk airbase. The 303rd IAD, which had recently arrived from the West, had a storied combat history and was considered one of the best fighter divisions in the air force. Alongside the 17th IAP, two other regiments were part of the 303rd IAD – the 18th GIAP and the 523rd IAP.

That same week in early October, the 17th IAP began to re-equip with new jet aircraft. Along with other pilots, N. Sutiagin in the month of October passed the classroom instruction and was graded out on the MiG-15 and UTI

Yak-17 trainers with a general evaluation of 'excellent'. He conducted his first independent flight in the MiG-15 on 31 October, and by 13 November he was already authorized to train other pilots of the squadron from the rear cockpit of the UTI Yak-17 trainer. In the ensuing months, he conducted the following number of flights in the MiG-15: in November, eighteen; in December, five; in January 1951, sixteen; in February, twelve; and in March, three.

Meanwhile, the situation on the Far Eastern borders was heating up. War had erupted on the Korean peninsula, and provocations from the American side were becoming more frequent.

On 25 December 1950, the 17th IAP restaged from the Voznesensk airbase to the base at Vozdvizhenka, where it continued to train on the new jet fighter. However, mastering any new technology, especially in aviation, is fraught with risk, and the first jet aircraft suffered from many teething problems that took a sad toll on the lives of the pilots. The 17th IAP was no exception: on 30 December 1950, a MiG-15 crashed, claiming the life of its pilot, Lieutenant N. Savitsky, a senior pilot in the 1st Aviation Squadron.

At the time of the crash, Sutiagin was commanding the 1st Aviation Squadron. Blame for the accident – as usually happens in such cases – was placed on the commander, who had not ensured accident-free flight operations while training on the MiG-15. The divisional Party Committee therefore decided to sustain the previous Party reprimand 'for brawling' in his personnel file. Of course, this was just a trifle, compared to the death of a squadron pilot; however, a feeling of resentment over the matter lingered within Nikolai Sutiagin. One can only guess at the role all this played in the future, but it is clear that Nikolai had a strong desire 'to rehabilitate' himself, and was looking for the opportunity to do so.

Chapter Two

In China the Regiment Prepares for Battle

The 'Unknown War': Key Actors and Performers

Soviet involvement in the Korean War stemmed from repeated requests by the North Korean and Chinese governments in the late summer and autumn of 1950 for Soviet jet fighters to provide air cover over the North Korean territory adjacent to China. At the time, the North Korean People's Army (NKPA) was experiencing particularly great difficulties in getting supplies and reinforcements to its frontline units. Movement of men and material was virtually impossible in daylight hours because of the enemy's overwhelming superiority in the air.

The small North Korean air force, equipped with aircraft of Soviet design and manufacture such as the piston-engine Yak-3, Yak-9, Yak-11, La-9, and La-11 fighters and Il-10 ground attack planes, had been decimated by the more experienced American pilots in their piston-engine P-51, F4U and F-82 fighters, and especially the F-80C jet fighters that escorted B-26 and B-29 bombers on their missions (see Appendix).

The fledgling Chinese People's Liberation Army Air Force (PLAAF) was then only beginning to familiarize itself with the MiG-9 and MiG-15 jet fighters it had received from the Soviet Union. Thus, the Chinese government had no air cover for the build-up of its Chinese People's Volunteer (CPV) 13th Army Group along the Yalu River or for its planned offensive into North Korea.

Stalin was wary of becoming entangled in the Korean conflict, even though he was happy to lend material support to the Chinese and North Korean militaries. In addition, two Soviet IADs were already present in China: Lieutenant General Pavel F. Batitsky's 106th IAD, which was defending Shanghai against Chinese Nationalist air attacks; and Major General Ivan M. Belov's 151st GIAD, which had arrived in north-eastern China in July 1950 with a rather vague order to cover the CPV 13th Army Group in Manchuria north of the Yalu River and to train Chinese pilots to fly the MiG-15. However, the Chinese government wanted a larger and clearer commitment from the Soviet Union before it launched its planned counteroffensive across the Yalu.

Evidently, the rapid approach of US ground forces to the Yalu River in October–November 1950 pushed the Chinese to begin their offensive despite the absence of a promise of Soviet air cover. In addition, the fact that American bombers were striking almost freely throughout the depth of North Korea and were threatening the strategic bridges over the Yalu River prompted Stalin to commit additional Soviet fighter aviation regiments to Manchuria, though it is still not clear that he intended for them to become involved in combat over Korea. However, the Americans were targeting the North Korean town of Sinuiju, which lay just across the Yalu River from the complex of airfields around Antung which was to base some of the Soviet fighter regiments in Manchuria (and indeed, on one occasion accidentally attacked Antung itself), which perhaps made a clash between Soviet fighters and UN aircraft inevitable.

On November 14 1950, on Stalin's personal instruction, the 64th Separate Fighter Aviation Corps [from this point on, the authors refer simply to the '64th Fighter Aviation Corps', abbreviated as IAK] was organized to command the operations of the Soviet fighter aviation regiments in Manchuria. Major General of Aviation I.V. Belov became the corps commander. The 64th IAK itself came under the umbrella of the Operational Group, commanded by Colonel General of Aviation S.A. Krasovsky, which oversaw all Soviet aviation and anti-aircraft units on Chinese territory. The basic task of the 64th IAK was to protect the strategic bridges across the Yalu River and the Suiho power plant; later, its mission was extended to protect the irrigation dams, communications, supply lines and airbases on the territory of the PDRK within 75 kilometers of the Chinese–Korean border from enemy air attacks.

Depending on the period, the fighting strength of the 64th IAK consisted of two or three fighter aviation divisions, two anti-aircraft artillery divisions, and one aviation-technical division. The number of personnel in the corps fluctuated during the course of combat operations. At the end of 1951, the combat units and formations of the corps had a total of around 13,000 men. Altogether with the support services and auxiliary units, the corps totaled 26,000 men.

A total of twelve aviation divisions served in the 64th IAK at various times during the war. The first were regiments of the 28th, 50th, and 151st IAD, and from December 1950, the 324th IAD. In March 1951, the 303rd IAD replaced the 50th IAD.

The United States Air Force, as the primary air force of the UN armed forces, was the main antagonist of the 64th IAK. Its Far East Air Force (FEAF) had 1,172 airplanes at the start of the war, but this number grew continuously as the war progressed. By the end of 1951, 1,440 combat aircraft were operating against the NKPA and the CPV. FEAF controlled the subordinate Fifth Air Force in Japan, which in turn commanded several wings of tactical bombers, fighters, and reconnaissance and transport aircraft. A specially created Provisional Bomber Command controlled several bomber wings, which operated over the front as well as against targets in the deep rear.

Each USAF wing consisted of two or three squadrons of fighters, fighter-bombers, or bombers. Each squadron had an authorized strength of twenty-two aircraft. Thus, an American air force wing of three squadrons was similar in strength to a Soviet aviation division of two-regiment composition.

The USAF's basic jet fighter in the Far East at the outbreak of the war was the Lockheed F-80C Shooting Star, a straight-wing fighter that carried the standard armament for American fighters of six .50 caliber (12.7mm) machine guns. Designed as a fighter-interceptor, it proved inferior to the MiG-15 and was later employed as a fighter-bomber. The F-80C Shooting Star equipped the 8th Fighter-Bomber, the 49th Fighter-Bomber, and the 51st Fighter-Interceptor Wings.[1]

With the appearance of the MiG-15 over the Yalu River in November 1950, the USAF quickly rushed two additional fighter wings to Korea, each equipped with a different fighter, in the hope of finding a counter to the MiG-15. The 27th Fighter-Escort Wing, which had fifty Second World War veterans on its flight staff, was considered one of the very best in the USAF. It flew the F-84E Thunderjet, which was another straight-wing jet fighter that began production in May 1949. The F-84 had been designed to escort B-29 bombers on their missions, but it also proved to be plainly inferior to the Soviet MiG-15. While the F-84E continued to provide close escort to bombers in 1951, it increasingly was used in a ground attack role.

However, FEAF had also put in a specific request to the USAF High Command for F-86 fighters. Accordingly, the 4th Fighter Wing, with its 334th, 335th and 336th Fighter Squadrons arrived in theater and began flying missions in December 1950. It also had many combat veterans of the Second World War on its flight staff, but its fighter, the F-86 Sabre, was quite comparable to the Soviet MiG-15 in performance. Flown by experienced pilots, the Sabre was always a serious threat to the MiG pilots, and the MiG versus Sabre dogfights over the Yalu River have become one of the classic duels in military aviation history.

The primary target for American air strikes from November 1950 on became the bridges and roads across the Yalu River between China and North Korea, over which flowed the supplies for the North Korean and Chinese armies. For this purpose, B-29 strategic bombers in large groups, covered by F-80 and F-84 fighter escorts, conducted attacks on the bridges across the Yalu, while the B-26 tactical bombers interdicted the roads in Korea, especially at night, since the bulk of the Chinese forces moved along the roads only after the sun set.

In the spring of 1951, the 324th and 303rd IAD were leading the struggle against the American air attacks directly, while the 151st IAD at this time was operating in the second echelon in corps reserve, covering rear areas in China, and serving as a source of reinforcements for the two frontline divisions whenever they took on massed enemy formations. An additional detached regiment, the 351st IAP, conducted nighttime combat operations, but in daylight hours it remained on duty at lower levels of alert in reserve. Units of the 151st IAD and the 351st IAP operated out of the base at Anshan.

Three-time Hero of the Soviet Union and famous ace of the Great Patriotic War, Colonel Ivan Nikitovich Kozhedub, commanded the 324th IAD. The 176th Guards and 196th Regiments of this division, which had been based before this in Moscow, were considered elite units in the Soviet Air Force and were personally supervised by Vasily Stalin, Joseph Stalin's son, who commanded the air force of the Moscow Military District. These regiments were the first in the country to make the switch to the new MiG-15 jet fighters, and regularly conducted parade flyovers at Moscow ceremonies.

The 303rd IAD under the command of Major General of Aviation Georgii Ageevich Lobov had been previously based in Iaroslavl' and Kostroma and also frequently took part in parade flyovers. This division included the 177th IAP, the 523rd IAP, and the 18th GIAP, all of which flew MiG-15s. Back in June 1950, this division had transferred to the airbase at Vozdvizhenka in the Maritime District under the strictest security, where it prepared for combat operations. Its 177th IAP was transferred to the 50th IAD, which was to become the first to conduct combat missions in Korea. In return, in the month of October 1950 the 303rd IAD received the 'local' 17th IAP from the 190th IAD; this regiment was still only preparing to retrain on jet planes. While the pilots of the other regiments of the 303rd IAD continued to prepare for battle, they concurrently trained the pilots of the Far Eastern aviation regiments on the new jet technology.

A Special Mission

In March 1951, the 17th IAP in which Nikolai Sutiagin was serving began to prepare for its assignment to Manchuria. At this time, the air war between North and South Korea, or more accurately, between Soviet and American pilots was in full swing. Not all the pilots were anxious to return to war, especially those who had passed through the Great Patriotic War, and who had families and had become accustomed to peace-time life. After all, they would be fighting for a different country; but a refusal would mean the end of their flying careers, and everyone understood this.

In the middle of March, the regiment received an unexpected order: to replace the Soviet markings on their planes with North Korean markings; disassemble the planes; load them onto trains; and head to China. Soon an additional order arrived: the flight staff was to turn in all their personal documents, including their personal identification papers, and their Party and

Komsomol membership booklets. Their families were issued with payment vouchers and told that their men were being sent on a government mission. It was recommended for wives with children to go and stay with relatives. Nikolai's wife Raisa decided to move back in with her mother. She saw Nikolai off at 12:00 noon on 27 March 1951.

Before leaving for China, the entire flight staff of the division gathered at the officers' club in Vozdvizhenka. There the commander of the air army, General Senatorov, informed them on the status of combat operations in Korea, gave the assembled officers a few parting words, and shook the hand of each pilot as he left.

At the end of March, the following roster of officers from the 17th IAP left on the special assignment to China:

From Regiment Command:
Flight personnel:
Lieutenant Colonel Ivan Semenovich Parshikov – Regiment commander
Major Boris Vasil'evich Maslennikov – Regiment deputy commander
Captain Nikolai Ivanovich Maslennikov – Regiment navigator
Major Ivan Vasil'evich Vorob'ev – Deputy regiment commander for aerial gunnery
Ground personnel:
Major Mikhail Vasil'evich Danilov – Regiment chief of staff
Captain Ivan Andreevich Shul'gin – Regiment deputy chief of staff
Major Mikhail Vasil'evich Krylov – Deputy commander for political affairs
Lieutenant Colonel Ivan Pavlovich Kisliuk – Secretary of the Party Bureau
Captain Pavel Vasil'evich Purgin – Regiment senior engineer
Squadron Flight Rosters:
1st Squadron
Captain Stepan Savel'evich Artemchenko – Squadron commander
Senior Lieutenant Nikolai Vasil'evich Sutiagin – Deputy squadron commander
Senior Lieutenant Vasilii Fedorovich Shulev – Deputy squadron commander for political affairs
Lieutenant Alekhin Ivan Mikhailovich – Pilot
Senior Lieutenant Sergei Stepanovich Bychkov – Flight commander
Lieutenant Aleksandr Sergeevich Shirokov – Pilot
Senior Lieutenant Nikolai Nikolaevich Kramarenko – Senior pilot
Lieutenant Vladimir Nikolaevich Makarov – Pilot
Senior Lieutenant Fedor Georgievich Malunov – Flight commander
Senior Lieutenant Nikolai Filippovich Miroshnichenko – Flight commander
Captain Mikhail Fedorovich Osipov – Pilot
Senior Lieutenant Aleksei Afanas'evich Ostankov – Pilot
Senior Lieutenant Nikolai Iakovlevich Perepelkin – Senior pilot

2nd Squadron

Major Sergei Grigor'evich Ivanov – Squadron commander

Captain Nikolai Pavlovich Mishakin – Deputy squadron commander

Senior Lieutenant Vasilii Fedorovich Ankilov – Deputy squadron commander
for political affairs

Captain Ivan Nikolaevich Morozov – Flight commander

Senior Lieutenant Evgenii Naumovich Agranovich – Pilot

Senior Lieutenant Aleksei Andreevich Komarov – Senior pilot

Senior Lieutenant Dmitrii Leonti'evich Polianichko – Pilot

Senior Lieutenant Pavel Petrovich Gostiukhin – Pilot

Lieutenant Boris Andreevich Kordanov – Pilot

3rd Squadron

Major Ivan Alekseevich Chugunov – Squadron commander

Captain Viktor Alekseevich Blagov – Deputy squadron commander

Senior Lieutenant Aleksandr Vladimirovich Bykov – Deputy squadron
commander for political affairs

Senior Lieutenant Aleksei Nikolaevich Nikolaev – Pilot

Senior Lieutenant Nikolai Grigor'evich Dokashenko – Flight commander

Senior Lieutenant Vladimir Mikhailovich Khvostantsev – Senior pilot

Senior Lieutenant Boris Dmitrievich Kukhmakov – Senior Pilot

Lieutenant Aleksandr Timofeevich Bozhko – Pilot

The 1st Squadron of the 17th IAP had three flights, while the 2nd and 3rd Squadrons each had two flights. The regiment numbered thirty-three pilots, 104 officers, 123 sergeants, and twenty-nine privates; altogether, 289 men. The regiment was equipped with thirty-one MiG-15bis jet fighters.

Of the thirty-three pilots in the regiment, nineteen were veterans of the Great Patriotic War, eight had flown in the brief war with Japan, and only six men lacked any combat experience. The average age of the pilots in the squadrons was twenty-eight to twenty-nine years, while the pilots in the regiment's command staff averaged thirty-three years of age.

The 17th IAP's command also had the following members:

Major of Medical Services Vikentii Mikhailovich Pozdniak – Senior doctor

Major Veniamin Pavlovich Goriainov – Chief of communications

Captain Leonid Aleksandrovich Eliseev – Radar station chief

Captain Evgenii Vasil'evich Grigor'ev – Chief of chemical services

Captain Ivan Fedorovich Pronichkin – Chief of objective control means[2]

Senior Lieutenant Anastasii Vasi'evich Kuznetsov – Assistant chief of staff for
special communications

Sergeant Nikolai Paramonovich Astakhov – Chief of physical training

The most experienced pilots in the regiment were Captain Artemchenko,

Captain Blagov, Major B.V. Maslennikov, Captain N.I. Maslennikov, Captain Mishakin, Major Ivanov, and Senior Lieutenant Bykov. All were veterans of the Great Patriotic War, each with several Orders and medals for combat distinction.

Captain Artemchenko had been the deputy commander of the 3rd Squadron for a long time. He was a very experienced, excellent pilot, who had fought bravely in the Great Patriotic War, but shortly before the war's end, he had been shot down over East Prussia and taken prisoner by the Germans. Though he was a prisoner literally for just a few days, the experience had deeply affected him. He was almost in a state of panic prior to the regiment's departure, fearing that because he had been a prisoner, they would forbid him to go to China and demobilize him. However, everything turned out all right for him.

The Regiment's forward team, headed by deputy commander Major Maslennikov, left the aerodrome at Vozdvizhenka for China on 23 March 1951. The team included Major Vorob'ev, pilots Polianichko and Alekhin, and a technical staff consisting of the officers Kurchavin, Smirnov, Gorbunov, Shtykov, and Kotel'nikov, and twenty-six sergeants and privates. The forward team's task was to prepare the airfield to receive and accommodate the rest of the regiment.

On 28 March 1951, the remainder of the regiment crossed the national border into China in two groups: the first group consisted of thirty-one officers and thirty-eight sergeants, while the second group had sixty-four officers and eighty-eight sergeants. After crossing the border, the military servicemen received the order to remove their shoulder boards and undo their tabs.

On 30 March, the personnel of the regiment arrived by train at the Mukden-East station as part of the 303rd IAD. Upon arriving at the Chinese airfield at Mukden, which was located about 200 kilometers from the border with North Korea, the men immediately began to reassemble their planes. They also received Chinese uniforms without any signs of rank – blue cotton trousers, a drab jacket with a turned-down collar, a forage cap, and shoes.

A.N. Nikolaev, a pilot in the 3rd Squadron, recalled:

> We were all dressed in a Chinese uniform. It was difficult to distinguish ranks and titles, which simplified things between superiors and subordinates, and this was very good. There were not those same formalities, which usually happen in military life. After all, we were at war, and this was leaving its mark on our day-to-day existence.

The 17th IAP spent the next several days unloading equipment from the trains and re-assembling the MiGs. Thirty-one planes and thirty-two wing assemblies had been shipped. By 5 April, pilots were checking out the MiGs on short test flights, and the next day the 1st and 2nd Squadrons became operational with a strength of eighteen crews.[3]

At Mukden the 17th IAP was assigned to further training and, in case of a call from the 64th IAK command post, to protect the air bases at Antung and Singisiu from attacks. The 324th IAD and the Corps headquarters were based at Antung, while the North Korea air force used the base at Singisiu.

The personnel were housed in well-furnished barracks at Mukden. The pilots were given a separate building, where accommodation was arranged by squadron – four to five men in each room, though all conveniences were located in the common corridor. However, the barracks were damp, which adversely affected the pilots' health in the springtime – especially those who suffered from chronic respiratory problems.

In view of the heightened strain on the flight personnel, the dampness of the accommodation, and the large amount of dust at the base, some pilots developed conjunctivitis, rhinitis, or middle ear infections. Most of the patients with these problems were treated on an outpatient basis, but two required in-patient treatment at the medical post. The pilots were transferred to a dry, three-story residence, and their health was more closely monitored. For prophylactic purposes, pilots were given nose drops consisting of a 2 per cent solution of ephedrine with adrenaline before flights. The floors of their rooms were mopped with a 2.5 per cent bleach solution. The mechanics and technicians received gauze masks to protect them from dust in order to prevent upper respiratory problems.

The pilots received daily check-ups at the airfield and back at their barracks, while monthly medical examinations were conducted at the medical post. Permission for the pilots to fly each day was noted on the operational schedule. The technical staff suffered little illness.[4]

The pilots and ground staff received nutritious meals. The pilots ate three meals a day, and received an extra breakfast on days of combat duty that was provided before the duty shift or else delivered to the airfield. The servants in the mess hall were Chinese who didn't know the Russian language, which made communication difficult. On doctors' instructions, the entire flight staff used only boiled water from the kitchens that were located on the base.

An Unsuccessful Debut for the Far Easterners and Its Consequences

While continuing the flight training program and making preparations on the ground, the regiment also stood by for combat duty. Operating from a rear airbase, the 17th IAP with thirty pilots and twenty-eight MiG-15 planes was to protect the city of Mukden from enemy reconnaissance and any possible enemy air attack. In addition, it had to be ready (according to the command's plan) to reinforce the operations of our air force in the region of Antung. The pilots of the regiment didn't have to wait long for such an order to arrive.

On 12 April 1951, an order came from the command post of the 64th IAK to scramble a group to go to the assistance of regiments of the 324th IAD, which were contending with a large formation of B-29 bombers and escorting fighters in the region of Antung. Between 09:30 and 09:32 in the morning, the 2nd Squadron, which had been standing by at readiness level No. 1 was scrambled, as well as an additional group from the 523rd IAP led by Major Danilenko. The 1st and 3rd Squadrons of the 17th IAP remained at readiness levels No. 2 and No. 3, respectively, and never took off.[5] The commander of the 2nd Squadron, Major Ivanov, led his formation of eight MiGs to the region of the air battle.

The target of the bombers was the railroad bridge across the Yalu River near Sinuiju. Forty-eight B-29 bombers and eighty escorting jet fighters were taking part in this mission. The bombers were flying in three groups, with each group arranged in the standard American 'combat box' formation of high, lead, and low squadrons. The first group, which contained a bomber armed with a radio-controlled, 5,400 kg (12,000 lb) Tarzon bomb, made its bomb run along the length of the bridge, while the second and third groups made their runs at a 30–35° angle to its span. Fighters of the 324th IAD tangled with two of the bomber groups at a distance of 45–30 kilometers from the bridge and hindered their bombing runs. Only the remaining group managed to bomb the bridge, as a result of which several bombs fell in the vicinity of the target. The radio-controlled Tarzon bomb exploded 150 meters from the bridge and did no damage to it.

Arriving in the vicinity of Antung to help, the leaders of both groups from the 303rd IAD established contact with the 324th IAD command post and, since by this time the battle was already winding down, received the order to return to their bases. However, when the order arrived, Major Ivanov departed at high speed in the wrong direction, leaving his bewildered group scattered in his wake. Major Ivanov, plainly disoriented, strayed 100 kilometers from the correct flight path back to base and simultaneously descended to an altitude of 2,000 meters, which complicated tracking the planes on the radar screens.

Major Ivanov's wingman that day was the squadron's deputy commander, Captain Mishakin, who was also the 2nd Squadron's navigator. When Mishakin saw Major Ivanov veer off course, he started to pursue him to bring him back on course, but Mishakin failed to monitor his instruments and also became disoriented.[6]

It should be noted that it was rather easy to lose one's way over the Korean terrain, especially on the first few flights. The terrain is mountainous and quite rugged, with few landmarks. Only coastal features and the few major cities, such as Pyongyang, Antung and Anju stood out as landmarks. It is not surprising that pilots on their first combat sortie could not correctly find their current location in the air, when most of their attention had been devoted to searching for hostile planes.

Only thanks to the skillful efforts of Lieutenant Colonel Kumanichkin, who at that time was the temporary acting commander of the 303rd IAD and was present at the division's command post, was the 2nd Squadron successfully landed at several airbases in China. The pilots Ivanov, Mishakin, and Gostiukin made a landing at the Mukden-East airbase; Morozov at Antung; and Antipov, Agranovich, Kordanov, and Komarov at Liaoyang. The pilots made no use of their radio navigation instruments.

The first combat flight was an embarrassing failure, which led to some discomforting conclusions: the 17th IAP was not ready to conduct combat operations; it had not yet mastered formation flying in elements and flights; and the squadron commander did not demonstrate that he was capable of handling the group in battle. The reaction of the commander of the 303rd IAD followed swiftly.

In an order issued on the following day, General Lobov filed a request with the 64th IAK commander to remove Lieutenant Colonel Parshikov from his post as regiment commander. The order also placed chief of staff Major Danilov under ten days of house arrest for the regiment's inadequate readiness for combat operations and for failing to brief the pilots before the mission. Major Ivanov was warned about being unfit for his position, and regiment navigator Captain Maslennikov received a reprimand. Only the radar station crew that guided the scattered planes to safe landings received a formal expression of gratitude for its outstanding work. The group from the 523rd IAP also performed more successfully.

On the whole, the battle on 12 April was a success for the corps: ten B-29s and four F-84s had been shot down. A few more Superfortresses had crashed upon landing at their airbases, so the enemy's real losses were even greater. Although the Americans claimed in turn to have shot down seven MiGs on this day, all forty-four of our MiG-15s from the 324th IAD that participated in the battle returned to their airbases. Two of the planes were damaged. Senior Lieutenant Iakovlev from the 523rd IAP, who received a wound to his face from fragments of his shattered cockpit canopy, had been forced to make a belly landing.

The Americans mourned their losses from this engagement for almost a week after the 12 April battle. This day became known as 'Black Thursday' and the American B-29 strategic bombers failed to make an appearance in 'MiG Alley' (the name give to the area in north-west North Korea between the Yalu and Chongchon Rivers, where most of the air battles between the Communist and UN pilots occurred) for some time afterwards.

The judgment that the 17th IAP was unready for combat operations was corroborated by the regiment's next combat mission on 16 April, when at 12:47 Major Ivanov led eight MiGs to reinforce a battle against enemy bombers and escorting fighters in the area of Antung at an altitude of 8,000 meters. The groups failed to make contact with the adversary, which withdrew in a southerly direction. Lieutenant Colonel Parshikov and Major Krylov had received serious admonitions from General Krasovsky, but a ChP [a Russian acronym derived from *chrezvychainoe proisshestvie* which translates directly as 'extraordinary occurrence', but means any major incident or accident] that occurred three days after the disastrous first mission decided their fate.

On 15 April, a 'settling of scores' between officers of the 1st and 3rd Squadrons occurred in the regiment during a supposedly fraternal dinner. This brawl within the regiment was the final straw for regiment commander Lieutenant Colonel Parshikov and his deputy for political affairs Major Krylov; on 18 April they were removed from their positions. On 4 May, Parshikov and Krylov received demotions and were returned to the Soviet Union to Voroshilov-Ussuriisk to serve in an infantry regiment. Upon the men's departure, the command even withheld some of Major Krylov's pay as punishment for a minor shortfall in the regiment's political education materials.

On 19 April, Captain Grigorii Ivanovich Pulov, a deputy regiment commander who was also the flight inspector for piloting technique and flight theory in the 523rd IAP, was named to assume command of the 17th IAP. Pulov was a veteran of the Great Patriotic War and had been credited with one personal victory against the Germans. Senior Lieutenant Ivan Iakovlevich Alimpiev, who headed the division's Party School, became the 17th IAP's acting deputy commander for political affairs, and served in this role for two months, until Lieutenant Colonel Ivan Ivanovich Iasyrev arrived on 25 June 1951 to assume the position.

Meanwhile, the regiment was given additional time to train for combat operations, and there were no more combat sorties prior to 14 June. The pilots kept busy by training intensively for combat. They had plainly not logged enough hours in the new jet fighters: back in the Soviet Union, each pilot had only 15–20 hours flying the MiG-15 before leaving for China.

The pilots practiced flying in formation in elements, flights, and full squadron formations. The leader would carry out complex maneuvers both in level flight and in climbs and dives with no warning to the rest of the group before starting his maneuver. The other pilots would have to keep their place in formation while executing the maneuver, and not lose the leader. These training sessions helped the pilots learn to hold a compact formation and to be successful in later air battles with the enemy.

Nevertheless, on the first few missions, though the full squadron might have launched to do battle, the pilots often straggled back to base one by one. However, as the pilots gained experience and grew accustomed to combat, they began returning to base in elements or full flights.

While training at Mukden, the pilots also practiced flight navigation and made gunnery runs at ground targets at a range on the other side of the city, although they never had an opportunity to operate against ground targets in combat.

On 19 April, a new officer arrived to take command of the 17th IAP's 3rd Squadron. This was Captain Mikhail Nikolaevich Shcherbakov from the 18th GIAP – an experienced pilot, a veteran of the Great Patriotic War who had earned two Orders of the Red Banner and the Order of the Patriotic War.

Combat Training Comes at a Price of Blood

On 24 April, the outgoing commander of the regiment, Lieutenant Colonel Parshikov, left to undergo hospital treatment. Since Captain Pulov was still preparing to assume the position, acting command fell to Parshikov's assistant, Major Vorob'ev.

The next day, a pilot in the 3rd Squadron, Senior Lieutenant Boris Dmitrievich Kukhmakov, was killed in a crash when his MiG-15bis No. 121087 went down during a mock dogfight. The cause of the disaster remained unknown, but the most likely reason for the crash of Kukhmakov's jet was the exceeding of the fighter's red line of Mach .88 during the training dogfight, and an ensuing spin.

At speeds close to the maximum, MiG-15 pilots often encountered flight instability, and a particularly dangerous phenomenon known in Russian as a *valezhka* – a sudden loss of lift under one wing, which would unexpectedly flip the plane onto its side or back. The jet would become nearly uncontrollable, and the result, especially with inexperienced pilots, could be a very dangerous spin. In the Soviet Union, for safety reasons, training flight airspeeds had not exceeded 700 km/hr, so the pilots had never encountered this phenomenon. However, dogfights require the pilot to use all the possibilities of his plane, and the pilots began conducting training flights at top speeds. Each plane had its own individual characteristics, so each jet had to be checked specially to determine the particular speed at which this dangerous phenomenon would arise. This practice was called 'driving the plane into a *valezhka*'. At the time of the accident, pilots were aware of the problem and were working out the techniques necessary to bring the plane out of a *valezhka*. Such training, unfortunately, didn't proceed without victims.

Here's what A.N. Nikolaev, a former pilot in the 3rd Squadron remembers:

Arriving in Mukden in the People's Republic of China in the spring of 1951, we started intensive flight training in MiG-15 jets. There was a great need for this. We had very, very little previous experience at the controls of these planes. But serious and important work lay ahead of us. One day, having already conducted two training flights, my leader Senior Lieutenant Kukhmakov turned in his jet for routine maintenance work. The new regiment commander, Captain Pulov, gave his own plane to Kukhmakov for a third flight. We flew off in a flight of four to the training area to conduct a two versus two mock dogfight. Once in the zone, having passed Dokashenko's element in a head–on run, my leader began a left turn, and then went into a vertical dive. I, of course, followed him. Our airspeed quickly increased, so I pulled out of the dive, but he, without responding to my radio inquiries, disappeared into a ball of smoke on the ground. The three of us returned to base without completing the assignment. Soon the Chinese authorities informed us of the crash of our plane – it was my leader, Senior Lieutenant Boris Dmitrievich Kukhmakov, with whom I had flown together for many years.

The cause of his death remained a puzzle for us. His remains were returned to Port Arthur, where they were buried in a Russian military cemetery. He was an experienced pilot who handled his plane well, and was an excellent shot. If he had managed to participate in battles, I am deeply convinced that he would have scored many victories. Soon Senior Lieutenant Kotov from the 523rd IAP was named to take his place.

Next there occurred a few careless mishaps in the 17th IAP, as well as in other units of the 303rd IAD, which didn't reflect well on the pilots and ground crews. In the 523rd IAP, Captain Popov left his parachute on the wing of his aircraft. While towing the plane to its revetment, the parachute slipped off and fell beneath one of the plane's wheels. The MiG was damaged and required factory repair. General Lobov ordered the pilot to pay for the cost of the repairs.

On 30 April, flight commander Senior Lieutenant Malunov made a very rough landing – his MiG bounced several times. He corrected for the error clumsily and almost crashed his plane. He received a formal warning from the division commander about being unfit to fly.

However, General Lobov didn't only punish the men; he also encouraged the pilots and technical personnel. Thus, on 30 April in honor of the approaching First of May holiday, the division commander paid compliment to a large group of servicemen through a personal order. Among others, pilots of the 1st Squadron were singled out for their success in combat training: Captain Artemchenko received a valuable gift, a rifle, while Senior Lieutenant Sutiagin received just an expression of gratitude.

The failures of the regiment on its initial combat missions and the fatal crash of a pilot in training had an adverse affect on the morale in the regiment. Some of its members began to express disgruntlement. From a political report by the regiment's temporary acting deputy commander for political affairs Senior Lieutenant Alimpiev to the division's chief of the political department:

> On the evening of April 30 outside the barracks housing the sergeant staff in the presence of a group of sergeants and officers, Senior Sergeant Sh., an armorer in Captain Artemchenko's crew, expressed unhealthy attitudes while in an intoxicated condition, consisting of the following (uncensored expressions): 'They have brought me here free of charge just to pour out my blood', that he 'refuses to subordinate himself to anyone else and that he will live, just as he pleases'.
>
> Senior Sergeant Sh. was arrested on the spot and placed in the guard house under ten days of strict arrest.[7]

Others tried to drown their sorrows and concerns in liquor. Drinking bouts became more frequent in the regiment, especially after paydays, though the sale and consumption of alcohol had been strictly forbidden by the division commander. The results were typical. For example, on 29 April the chief of the PARM-4 (regimental aviation repair shop), Senior Lieutenant-Technician G., became intoxicated and created a scene in the garrison at the Mukden-East airbase in Mukden. He fired several shots from a pistol next to the officers' club, then fired at and wounded a pig belonging to the Chinese commandant. He was arrested and placed in confinement, and then turned over to the Officers' Honor Court.

There were also cases of secrecy leaks: pilots and technicians sent letters back to their wives via passengers aboard transport planes returning to the Soviet Union. In Vozdvizhenka, the wives found out about the dismissal of the 17th IAP's commander and deputy commander for political affairs. The division commander threatened in an order to turn the authors of these contraband letters over to a military tribunal, but the matter never went that far.

Between 4 and 8 May, the pilots and technical staff of the regiment were tested on their knowledge of the operation and maintenance of the MiG–15bis with the VK–1 engine. Pilots who received even just one mark lower than 'good' on any of the three exams were grounded. The majority of pilots passed the test successfully. Senior Lieutenant Sutiagin received a top score of '5' on Operation of the Airplane and Engine, a '4' on Weapons, and a '5' on Special Equipment. The following pilots failed the exam: Shcherbakov on Weapons; Captain Maslennikov on Operation of the Airplane and Engine and Special Equipment; Ankilov on Weapons and Special Equipment; and Bykov, Dokashenko, Nikolaev and Khvostantsev on all three! Those who had failed the first exam faced a repeat exam on 18 May. Incidentally, these results did not reflect in any way on the later combat results of these pilots – those same 3rd Squadron pilots Bykov, Dokashenko, Nikolaev and Khvostantsev all fought well enough.

Attention toward the pilots' physical training was also strengthened:

- The pilots' daily schedule now included an hour of physical training
- Supervision over the pilots' morning exercise routine was strengthened
- As part of the exercise program, pilots took part in gymnastics, track, basketball, or handball, depending upon the individual needs of the pilot.

It is true, however, that once the regiment began combat operations, neither the pilots or the maintenance personnel were up for physical exercise and sports – the physical burden of their combat work was already more than enough.

The 18th GIAP, as the best prepared regiment, was the first of the division's units to begin active combat service. On 6 May, this regiment together with a base security unit transferred to Antung, and began joint combat operations with the 324th IAD on 8 May.

The 18th GIAP's first air combat occurred on 20 May, when ten MiGs from the 3rd Squadron led by the squadron commander Captain Antonov encountered eight F–86 planes. In truth, neither side fired in this encounter. It was not until 1 June when flight commander Senior Lieutenant Evgenii Mikhailovich Stel'makh opened the combat score of the 303rd IAD, but he himself perished in the action. Stel'makh was a veteran of the Great Patriotic War who flew fourteen combat missions over Korea before this eventful, but fatal mission.

In his final combat, Senior Lieutenant Stel'makh shot down a B–29 bomber, and his cannon shells then left another one burning. At that moment, however, he was jumped by enemy fighters. One F–86 pilot fired a long burst that managed to sever his MiG–15's elevator control cable. Stel'makh made the decision to eject from his plane. Unfortunately, all of this was occurring in an area where enemy guerrilla groups were operating. Enemy guerrillas fired at the pilot as he was descending in his parachute, wounding him three times. When he landed, the bleeding Stel'makh entered his final and unequal combat. A nearby unit of Chinese Volunteers fought their way through to the spot of the tragedy, but it was already too late. Having fired off his two clips of cartridges, Stel'makh saved the last bullet for himself ... (another version of his death has it that Stel'makh came down amid North Korean forces, which mistakenly took him to be an American and began to fire at him. Having no way to identify his nationality and deciding that he was surrounded, Stel'makh began to blaze away from his pistol and died in the ensuing exchange of fire).

This was the division's first combat loss. On 1 June, the division's Political Department issued a leaflet dedicated to Senior Lieutenant Stel'makh's exploit. On this same day, the future ace of the 18th GIAP Senior Lieutenant Lev Shchukin scored his first victory, shooting down an F-51 Mustang. Shchukin would go on to score fifteen victories in Korea, and twice had to eject from his own crippled MiG.

This regiment's next success took place on 6 June, when sixteen MiG-15s under the command of Lieutenant Colonel Smorchkov, a Second World War veteran who had scored two victories against the Germans, pounced on four F-80 Shooting Stars, shooting down one and forcing the other three to ditch at sea. The victories were credited to Smorchkov, Os'kin, Shchukin (his second), and Maznev.

However, the 17th IAP suffered another loss in May, though again not in combat. On 11 May at 09:30 during a training flight south-east of Mukden, MiG-15bis No. 121086 went down, killing a pilot of the 2nd Squadron, Senior Lieutenant Nikolai Kuz'mich Kotov. Kotov had just arrived in the regiment on 29 April from the 523rd IAP as a senior pilot.

This was the same Senior Lieutenant Kotov who had distinguished himself back in December 1950, when the 523rd IAP, then still in the Soviet Union, was patrolling Soviet airspace. On 26 December 1950, an American reconnaissance B-29 had penetrated Soviet airspace, and a pair of MiGs from the 1st Squadron (leader, Senior Lieutenant S.A. Bakhaev; wingman, Lieutenant Kotov) had been scrambled with the orders to intercept the intruder and to force the plane to land or to shoot it down. Our pilots shot the Boeing down over the mouth of the Tiumen'-Ula River after a brief battle. Later, Major S. Bakhaev, who had scored thirteen victories in the Great Patriotic War against Germany, would shoot down eleven more planes in Korea and receive the title Hero of the Soviet Union.

However, on this ill-fated day in May 1951, Lieutenant Kotov took off in tandem with the unit commander. After conducting Exercise No. 103 of the Fighter Aviation Course of Combat Training RS-1950, the leader Major Pulov went into a descending left turn at an altitude of 2,000 meters with a bank angle of 45–50° and an airspeed of 700–750 km/hr. During this turn, wingman Senior Lieutenant Kotov began to slide from the right side of his leader to the left side and, without leveling out his plane, fell out of the formation in a steepening dive. Kotov made no response to his leader's command to pull out of the dive, and the plane, tilted to the left and in a leftward spin, went almost vertically into the ground and exploded.

News of the accident was reported to the division, the corps, and to the headquarters of the Air Force Operational Group. The investigatory commission that studied this flight accident came to the following conclusions:

ORDER

Of the Commander of the AF OG No.057 from 18.05.51

'On the disaster of a Senior Pilot of the 17th IAP 303rd IAD Senior Lieutenant Kotov N.K. and on measures to prevent flight accidents'

[...]

It has not been possible to establish the real cause of the crash because of the aircraft's complete destruction and the lack of any sort of attempt by the pilot to communicate about the emergency by radio or to eject.

This investigation has established the following:

1. Pilot Kotov on the day of his death had not been scheduled to fly on the given assignment and therefore Commander Pulov did not conduct any preflight preparations or preflight briefing with him.
2. The plane in which Kotov suffered the disaster was not his own.
3. The plane's mechanic, Technician-Lieutenant Pereverzentsev, was not the one who took possession of the plane from the previous mechanic on 8.5.51, and did not fill out the requisite documents on the plane's transfer, while the regiment headquarters never issued an order on the assignment of this plane to Mechanic Pereverzentsev.
4. On 9.5.51 while making flights in this airplane, the inspector of piloting controls Major Pravotorov and the regiment navigator Captain Maslennikov noted that the plane pitched strongly and that the aileron control was stiff (indicating hydraulic control problems). The plane's mechanic made repairs to the plane, but a test flight to check the plane's balance was necessary, which was reported to the regiment commander, Captain Pulov.

Captain Pulov, against all good judgement, disregarded the reports of the mechanic and the engineer of the regiment, Captain Purgin, and issued the plane to Pilot Kotov on 11.05.51 without first checking it out on a test flight.

5. A subsequent inspection of all the regiment's aircraft revealed a number of extreme violations of the rules of technical maintenance and the presence of eight to fifteen defects in each plane – play in the elevators and in the flap hinges, odors in the oxygen, and others.

6. Ducking his responsibility, division commander Major General Lobov rather than analyzing the preconditions for the disasters in the division and ensuring a high degree of readiness of the units, chose a false path, a path of shunning the 17th Regiment, as if he had no connection with it whatsoever, whereas the regiment had joined the division in October 1950.

   On 12.5.51, the second day after the disaster, though he had no right to do so, division commander Major General Lobov reported to the War Minister [Voennyi Ministr] that all faults in his division stemmed not from his leadership, but originated within a regiment that he did not think belonged to him. He seemed to forget that Kotov had become a pilot of the 17th IAP only on 29 April of this year, and before this had been in the 523rd IAP of the very same division, and that both the mechanic of the regiment headquarters flight, in which both accidents occurred, and the regiment commander himself are long-time members of the 303rd IAD.

7. Aircraft maintenance is unsatisfactory not only in the 303rd IAD, but also in other divisions of the corps. For example, on 13 May of this year in the 176th IAP of the 324th IAD there were four failures of the Bu-1 hydraulic actuators.

   The chief engineer of the Corps, Colonel of Aviation Technical Services Voronin, present at this time in the 324th IAD, failed to organize the study of the manual on the operation and repair of the Bu-1 hydraulic actuator, relying instead on the presence of aviation industry representatives for the Bu-1 in the units of the corps, and removed himself from supervision over this device.

All the above taken together justifies the conclusion that Comrade Kotov's fatal crash occurred as a consequence of the following:

1. The most flagrant violations of flight regulations, of the 1943 Manual for the Engineer-Aviation Service, and of the orders that govern flight operations by the commander of the 17th IAP Captain Pulov.

2. The superficial leadership of the units on the part of the commander of the 303rd IAD Major General Lobov, who overrates himself and who gave no practical, daily assistance to his units.

3. The low level of the organization of the technical repair service in the regiment on the part of the senior engineer of the Aviation Regiment Captain Purgin.

4. The likely failure of the hydraulic aileron controls, with which the pilot was unable to cope while flying the plane.

I ORDER:

[...]

4. The declaration of a reprimand to the commander of the 17th IAP Captain Pulov for the flight accident, which resulted in the death of the pilot and the loss of a plane.

  Captain Pulov deserves harsher punishment. This measure is being limited in consideration of his previous fine work as regiment commander and the relatively short period of time in his current position.

5. By order of a deputy of the Air Force High Command, the senior engineer, Captain of Aviation Technical Service Purgin has been removed from his current post.

6. The declaration of a reprimand to the chief engineer of the 64th IAK Colonel of Aviation Technical Service Voronin and the senior engineer of the 303rd IAD Lieutenant Colonel Nesterov for their weak leadership of the Engineer Aviation Service.

7. The declaration of a reprimand to the commander of the 303rd IAD Major General Lobov for his weak oversight of the 17th IAP's flight operations.

8. To call the attention of the commander of the 64th IAK Major General Belov to improving the leadership of the Corps' units and to more effective supervision.

COMMANDER, AF OG KRASOVSKY
CHIEF OF STAFF, AF OG PROSTOSERDOV
DEPUTY CHIEF OF STAFF, AF OG KISILEV[8]

Other possible explanations for the cause of Kotov's crash were the pilot's loss of consciousness or his possible delirium. The quality of the on-board oxygen in the planes was simply not monitored, as a result of which the oxygen canisters equipping the airplanes in this case had been filled with oxygen that had a strong odor (as noted in the later inspection of the regiment's planes, but not mentioned in Krasovsky's order) of 1,1 dichloroethane – a common degreaser, but also formerly used as a surgical inhalational anesthetic.

Elementary safeguards regarding the security of the planes and their sealing [*plombirovka*] were violated in the most flagrant fashion.[9]

As a result of Kotov's accident, there were a number of changes and consequences. As noted in Krasovsky's order above, senior engineer Captain Purgin was removed from his post for being insufficiently exacting toward his subordinates, and for the mistakes he permitted in the organization of the engineer-aviation service. Several other junior officers received similar judgments. Squadron engineer Captain Cherednichenko was removed from his post for repeated mistakes by the technical staff which put planes out of service, for the poor organization of technical training, and for his poor knowledge of the planes and equipment. The technician of the Headquarters flight, Technician-Lieutenant Bubnov was dismissed from his post for poorly supervising the authorization of planes for operational use and for the absence of technical documentation within the flight, given five days of arrest, and then transferred to a different unit. For unsatisfactory work in maintaining his planes, Technician-Lieutenant A.I. Pereverzentsev was also removed from his post and sent back to the Soviet Union.

The sixth point of the findings in the above cited order from the commander of the Operational Group is interesting. From it, it is possible to draw the conclusion that the 303rd IAD commander General Lobov had his own 'favorites' in the division, and that the 17th IAP wasn't among them. Remember, the 17th IAP was the new regiment in the 303rd IAD, and unlike the other regiments in the 303rd IAD, it was from the Far East and had not seen service against the Germans. Later, when the 17th IAP had proven itself in battle, and had even surpassed its fellow regiments in the number of aerial victories, Lobov's attitude toward it improved.

The general himself enjoyed the authority and respect of his subordinates. Here's how the former deputy commander of the 523rd IAP, Major Grigorii Ul'ianovich Okhai describes him:

> G.A. Lobov was a solidly built man of above average height. He was strong-willed, principled, demanding, but fair. He loved to fly. Whenever he flew on a combat mission and we were part of his group, we always tried to cover him against any possible enemy attack. He engaged in battle courageously and fought skillfully, using all the flight and tactical capabilities of the plane. He knew well how to organize and handle the division's flight operations, using excellently prepared, large-scale plans.

The Elimination of Shortcomings. Training Continues.

On 22 May, Captain Grigorii Iosifovich Papulov, a veteran of the Great Patriotic War and a senior technician of a squadron in the 18th GIAP, arrived in the 17th IAP to assume the role as the unit's senior engineer in replacement of the cashiered Captain Purgin. Captain Papulov energetically took to eliminating the shortcomings in the organization of the engineer-technical service.

The regiment was staffed with thirty ground crew teams, with a mechanic, technician and a driver on each team. The unit was also fully staffed with armorers and specialists. The senior technical staff consisted of three squadron engineers, eight flight technicians, three senior special equipment technicians, three senior armaments technicians, a radio technician, and a technician for oxygen equipment.

The following men made up the senior technical staff of the 1st Aviation Squadron:

Captain of Technical Services Boris Ivanovich Vorob'ev – Squadron engineer
Senior Lieutenant N.N. Baranov – Squadron adjutant
Captain G.G. Berketov – Senior technician for armaments
Technician-Lieutenant S.F. Salo – Senior technician for special equipment
Malyshkin – Senior electronics mechanic
Plenkin – Electronics mechanic
Tret'iakov – Senior radio mechanic
Bezmenov – Senior instruments mechanic
Chernykh – Instruments mechanic
Kniazev – Radio supervisor
Shornikov – Instruments supervisor
Pakhomov – Parachute packer

Simple inexperience was a major source of the problems with the regiment's technical services. Most of the technical staff had been retrained on the MiG-15bis only by March 1951; moreover, the aircraft technicians had arrived straight from school in December 1950 and therefore lacked established work routines or experience in working on the unit's complement of planes.

The squadrons' senior armaments technicians had arrived in the unit just before the departure to China, and therefore they were not familiar with the MiG-15's weapons and did not know how to repair them. The flight-level technicians Efimov, Mikhailov and Bubnov had also been promoted to their positions from among the group of aircraft technicians immediately prior to the departure, and therefore had no experience in leadership at their new level. Maintenance and repair work on the MiG-15bis was done without confidence, as a result of which the flight-level technicians were not respected by their subordinates or their commanders, which undermined the quality of the work done to ready the planes for missions.

All this placed the question in front of the regiment's command and the senior engineer of how to bring the collective together, improve its work, and to organize the technical training. Over this period, the senior engineer-technical staff committed several errors in their work:

1. Technical training was poorly organized; technical analysis of the work was almost completely absent; defects and failures of the equipment during operation received little study, and their causes were not reported to the entire technical staff; and training aids (blueprints, schematics) for the airplane, engine, weapons system, and special equipment were lacking.

2. The senior engineer-technical staff superficially and haphazardly inspected the aircraft; for example, the regiment's engineer in the month of April inspected only eight of the regiment's thirty-one aircraft. The squadron engineers also paid little attention to post-flight inspections, and the norm for inspections was not fulfilled. Although aircraft technicians did in fact inspect their own planes, they still had little experience in this work, and their inspections were done hastily and superficially. As a result of this, MiGs that had defects were approved for flights.

3. Technical documentation (the keeping of log-books, workers' notebooks, notebooks of transfers into and out of the repair shop, and personnel duty records) was neglected or completed late. Even elementary notes about the work performed on the aircraft were lacking, and the record of completing scheduled work was not monitored.

4. Disorganized, cluttered work stations and toolboxes led to the poor organization of work on the planes.

5. The service battalion's supply of needed items like lubricants, rags and spare parts to the regiment on days of scheduled missions and during work on the planes was unsatisfactory. The absence of a regimental storeroom hindered the squadron engineers and flight technicians from supervising the work on a MiG and ensuring its rapid return to operation, since they were often forced to run to the technical warehouse for safety wire, rags, grease, and other basic parts and assemblies necessary for putting the plane back into operation.

6. The routines of the duty officers on duty at the parking areas were

inadequate and lacked proper controls, planes were left unsealed, and the exchange of planes between the duty officers at the parking areas and the technicians in the repair shops was being handled carelessly. All this taken together led to cases in the regiment where MiGs were rendered unserviceable through the fault of the technical staff. Thus, for example, plane technician A. broke a cockpit canopy; one plane was damaged and put out of operation by technicians while towing it to the start line; and one plane was put out of operation while filling the oxygen canisters.

The Chief Engineer of the Air Force Operational Group issued Special Directive No. 1 on 18 May 1951, which noted all the shortcomings in the Regiment's engineer-aviation service and gave instructions to correct them.

The leadership of the 17th IAP and the head of the engineer-technical service, Captain Papulov, took energetic measures to eliminate these problems: the entire flight and technical staff underwent training exercises based on the 1943 Manual for the Engineer-Aviation Service and testing on their understanding of the planes, equipment and their duties; an equipment inspection commission worked to identify faulty equipment; proper documentation procedures were put into place in the hangars, repair shops and on the parking aprons, and log-books were checked for completeness and accuracy. In addition, a new system of technical analysis of the planes and equipment was enacted, which summarized the results after each day of flight operations or repair on the aircraft. Equipment malfunctions were tracked for each MiG, whether it was being used by the unit, or on loan to another unit.

The efforts of the leaders of the engineer-technical staff bore fruit – the skill of the technicians and mechanics grew significantly, the average turnaround time for a plane between flights decreased steadily, and the number of potential causes of flight accidents diminished. Between 2 April and 11 June, the ground crews and technical staff made possible 1,027 training flights with a total flight time of 512 hours and 42 minutes, and sixteen combat sorties with an aggregate flight time of 18 hours and 12 minutes.

Of the twenty-nine aircraft that remained in the regiment after the two air crashes, three of the jets lacked hydraulic controls. They proved difficult to handle in dogfights, so combat operations in them ceased. This left only twenty-six planes in the regiment, so in the July–August period of 1951, the regiment received three more MiGs.[10]

In the month of May 1951 a new problem for the 17th IAP arose – a mass outbreak of typhoid fever among the local population. Our military servicemen all received vaccinations against typhus. This helped, but several pilots were nonetheless put out of action by the disease. Two pilots of the 1st Aviation

Squadron, Lieutenants I.M. Alekhin and V.N. Makarov, had to be hospitalized. Replacements for them were needed urgently.

On 15 May, flight commanders Senior Lieutenant Nikolai Stepanovich Volkov, who would ultimately go on to score seven victories in Korea, and Senior Lieutenant Georgii Tikhonovich Fokin arrived in Mukden. Replacements had to meet certain criteria. Some pilots were rejected because of health problems, others for family reasons. In the 523rd IAP, for example, they turned down a Jewish pilot who, on the one hand had a good record, but on the other hand had an aunt who lived abroad. The aunt tipped the scales against him. However, the primary criteria for selection were the level of the pilot's training and the presence of combat experience. Therefore, young pilots primarily remained in the Soviet Union. On 30 May, another pilot, Senior Lieutenant Nikolai Aleksandrovich Savchenko, arrived in the 1st Aviation Squadron from his position as a senior pilot in the 18th GIAP.

Around this time, a certain Colonel Dziubenko arrived at one of the Mukden airfields with an elite group of test pilots, whose wingmen were all experienced pilots from active units – deputy commanders of squadrons and flights. One of the group's orders was to force one of the newest American fighter jets, the F-86 Sabre, to make a landing at one of the Soviet or Chinese airbases. The test pilots gave several lectures in the regiments of the 303rd IAD on the subject of the flight characteristics of the MiG-15bis at high speeds. These lectures were quite informative and helped the division's pilots learn how to handle the MiG at high speeds. They acquainted the pilots with such dangerous phenomena as the *valezhka*, and the reversed reaction to movements of the rudder. This elite group then flew to the base at Antung, where regiments of Kozhedub's 324th IAD were already operating. The deputy commander of the 303rd IAD, Lieutenant Colonel Kumanichkin, also flew with the group to Antung in order to study their combat operations. However, Dziubenko's group was unable to fulfill its orders to force a Sabre to land, and Dziubenko himself was killed on one combat mission. The group was then dissolved; the test pilots returned to the Soviet Union, while their wingmen were reassigned to the divisions then operating in Manchuria; in the future, many of them fought successfully.

Training constantly for combat, the flight staff of the 17th IAP gradually improved their knowledge and skill. Some credit for this indeed belonged to Nikolai Vasil'evich Sutiagin, who through his position dealt precisely with flight tactics and the navigational training of the pilots in the 1st Squadron.

In a recommendation for promoting Sutiagin to the rank of 'Captain' and to the position of deputy commander and navigator of an aviation squadron of the 17th Fighter Aviation Order of Suvorov 3rd Degree Regiment of the 303rd

IAD, signed by squadron commander Captain Artemchenko on 23 May 1951, it was noted:

> Over his time in the regiment, [Sutiagin] has shown himself to be a capable fighter pilot. He retrained on the MiG-15 in a short time and at present flies as part of a group in the squadron that flies exclusively in daytime at high altitudes of up to 13,000 meters in simple meteorological conditions. He knows the MiG-15 airplane and the VK-1 engine well and handles them competently. [He was] a participant of the war with Japan, where he demonstrated his dedication to the Party of Lenin-Stalin and to the socialist Motherland. He is politically mature, and correctly understands the policies of our Party and government. He is an outstanding student of combat training and political education. He possesses good organizational capabilities. He gives a lot of assistance to the commander in the organization of air operations in the flights and in educating the personnel. He is demanding toward himself and to his subordinates, while at the same time he is a sensitive and caring commander-educator. He possesses business-like authority among the personnel and the senior chiefs. Ideologically firm and morally stable.
>
> CONCLUSION: [Sutiagin] is fully suitable for the post of deputy commander and navigator. He is worthy of promotion to the next rank of 'Captain'.[11]

In May, for his years of service, Nikolai received the medal 'For combat service'; but as it turned out, all of his real combat service was still in the future.

Several more incidents occurred in the regiment in the month of May 1951. This time it was the 3rd Squadron that 'distinguished' itself. One MiG-15 was damaged while being towed, through the negligence of a technician. Other units of the division, which were stationed on the airbase, also had their share of incidents. The flavor of those times is given by the following case, which shows up in the chronicle of the 303rd IAD's Political Department.

One day, the paymaster [of Military Unit Field Post 32924] Lieutenant S., while on a business trip into Mukden, visited a Chinese restaurant, where he became drunk. He became acquainted there with an unknown woman of Russian origin, and brought her back to the base in his vehicle. For his demonstrated lack of vigilance, he was turned over to a Junior Officers' Board of Honor.

June began with another incident that involved officers of the 17th IAP.

There were several 'sharp' guys in the regiment, who showed quick wits and initiative in matters of cultural pastimes. However, this everyday story, inoffensive on the whole, turned into the next investigation of 'moral decay' once it came to the attention of the command, with subsequent punishment for the guilty parties and their chiefs.

At the beginning of June, Nikolai Sutiagin, as a military informer (such an unofficial post existed in those days) was appointed to investigate the matter of Technician D., whose misdemeanor consisted of the following.

On 2 June 1951, the chief of the radar service Captain K. and the adjutant of the 3rd Aviation Squadron Senior Technician-Lieutenant D., led by the chief of staff of the [Military Unit Field Post 54954] Captain N., all in an intoxicated state, left the base on their own initiative and drove into Mukden. The purpose of the trip for Captain K. was to find a bearing for an A–6 engine, while Lieutenant D. was seeking shirts and ties for two of the squadron's officers. Captain N. went along, in order to try on a raincoat. Once in the city, as the investigative report states, '… they had more drinks, and then visited a brothel, where they had relations with non-Soviet women, which compromised themselves as officers of the Soviet Army'.

An investigation conducted in the unit established that these officers changed into civilian clothing, left their weapons behind, and took a Dodge 3/4-ton truck. In the store Churin & Co., they purchased beer and cognac, and shared the contents of the bottles among themselves. They became acquainted with a Russian emigrant, a counter-revolutionary White [the label given to all forces that opposed the Bolsheviks in the Russian Civil War], who was a driver for the director of Churin's store. From him, they obtained an address for the location of a brothel in Mukden and the password that would gain them admittance. While at the store, they encountered Captain Shul'gin, the acting chief of staff of the regiment, who had also driven into the city without permission. Shul'gin was the senior officer present, but he took no measures against the drunken subordinates, and made no attempt to prevent a major incident.

Next, the party purchased five more bottles of cognac and anise liquor and spent three hours wandering the market street. Then they began to search for a local resident who could show them the way to the brothel. Captain K., totally intoxicated, tried to take control of the steering wheel of the truck, but the driver prevented him from doing so. A Chinese man in a rickshaw, whom Captain N. hired for 2,000 yuan, led them to the brothel. They spent more than four hours there, where they shared a bottle of vodka with some of the Chinese ladies that worked there. K. paid the first Chinese woman 25,000 yuan, and the second woman 11,000 yuan. Captain N., in his own words, had no relations with the women. Senior Technician-Lieutenant D.

primarily remained outside around the truck. At 20:25 they returned to the base.[12]

The participants in this 'cultural expedition' were turned over to an Officers' Board of Honor. Captain Shul'gin, who had made no effort to intercede to prevent an embarrassing incident, was placed under five days of house arrest. For the actions of their subordinates, Major Pulov and Major Danilov received reprimands, while Major Maslennikov received sharp criticism. Captain K. was transferred to a different unit on 19 July 1951.

Of course, such cases didn't define the situation in the regiment. Between April and June 1951, the regiment's pilots conducted intensive training for combat operations: mock dogfights involving elements against elements and flights against flights. On 11 June 1951, the order arrived for the regiment to move to the new base at Myaogou, 20 kilometers south-west of the Antung airbase.

The Chinese had built the Myaogou airbase in the course of one month, using no earthmoving equipment, but instead large round pans suspended from the ends of a yoke. They carried dirt, crushed rock, and other material needed for the construction in the pans, and they worked barefoot or in slippers – and always at the double through the muck (the airbase was laid out in a swampy area). There were no less than 10,000 people working in this way on the site. The workers laid out a concrete strip that was 2.5 kilometers long and 80 meters wide, with concrete taxiways to the hardened revetments for the MiGs. The airfield was only 10–15 kilometers from the Yalu River.

The two-month postponement of combat for the 17th IAP had not been wasted. In addition to flight training, the pilots studied the terrain, the situation on the ground and the atmospheric conditions, the enemy's tactics, and worked out their own aerial combat tactics.

Chapter Three

Combat Operations, Tactics and Routines in the Korean Air War

The Situation on the Ground and in the Air over the Korean Peninsula

At the time of the 17th IAP's transfer to Myaogou in preparation for combat operations, the situation on the ground in Korea was relatively static. The battles lines stretched along a band of terrain 10 to 15 kilometers north of the 38th Parallel. The enemy was not showing much activity, focusing instead on regrouping its forces and making preparations for a new offensive. Enemy aviation, on the other hand, was launching heavy and concentrated attacks on targets in North Korea, primarily in the region of Sinuiju and Anju. The United States as of 9 May 1951 was operating with eight fighter wings, four bomber wings, and additional wings and groups of Marine aviation, reconnaissance and transport aviation. Altogether, the US air forces in the Korean theater had 1,360 planes and 50,000 personnel in May 1951. England, Australia, Canada and South Africa were contributing another 225 combat aircraft to the UN effort in Korea. Altogether, there were 1,716 aircraft of all types operating against the North Korean and Chinese forces.[1]

Prior to May 1951, enemy bomber aviation had tried repeatedly to attack the railroad bridge across the Yalu River in the vicinity of Sinuiji. However, after suffering heavy losses in the attacks on 7 and 12 April, until 23 October 1951 the enemy concentrated most of its bombing efforts south of the Chongju–Taechon line, operating primarily against railroad stations and crossings in the region of Anju, Usan, Chongju, and airbases in the vicinities of Taechon and Naamsi. Ground attack planes gave support to troops on the battlefield, but simultaneously operated against communications, crossings, bridges, rail lines and roads in North Korea. The enemy fighters covered the combat operations of the bombers and fighter bombers, and sought to neutralize the threat to those operations posed by our own fighters.

Enemy Operational Air Tactics

This material has been taken from the Summary[2] of the results of the 17th

IAP's combat operations, but for a better understanding of the conditions in which our pilots fought and the tactics that they faced, the authors have decided to introduce material from it here before describing those combat operations themselves.

The Operational Tactics of Bombers

In the period between June and October 1951, enemy B-29 bombers systematically bombed targets in the regions of Haksong, Chasan, Anju, Unsan, Sukchon, and Pyongyang, operating against troop concentrations, industrial targets, railroad stations and marshalling yards, river crossings, airfields, and communication lines and facilities. Between four and twenty-four bombers participated on average in each bombing raid, escorted by up to fifty F-80, F-84 and Gloster Meteor IV fighters. The enemy also typically dispatched a screen of thirty or more F-86 fighters well in advance of the bomber group and in the path of our intercepting fighters.

The B-29 bombers, as a rule, approached the target in flights of four planes organized into a box combat formation. If there were several of these flights, then they were arranged into column or line formations, with a distance between the flights of 500–800 meters. The B-29 bombers typically operated at an altitude between 4,000 and 7,000 meters.

The close escort fighters flew in elements or flights both behind the bomber formation at the same altitude, or 600–1,000 meters above the bombers. Because of their greater speed, the fighters maintained position by performing scissors maneuvers, but while doing so never strayed more than 800 to 1,000 meters from the bombers.

The close escort fighters never gave our attacking fighters serious problems. As a rule, if our fighters were determined to reach the bomber formations, they were able to break through to them despite the close escort. The main obstacles to our fighters were the forward screens of F-86 fighters, which frequently tied up our fighters in dogfights before they could reach the bomber formations.

On a typical day, the enemy on average would generate one to three concentrated raids. The B-29 bombers often operated in difficult meteorological conditions, using radar to bomb through cloud cover.

After 23–24 October 1951, when the enemy suffered heavy bomber losses, the B-29s began operating only at night singly, or in small groups of up to twelve bombers. Night bombing missions were conducted in both clear and bad weather using radar targeting devices. Bombing at night, as a rule, was done from an altitude of 7,000 to 8,000 meters. The primary targets of the bombers remained the airfields under construction in North Korea and the railroad bridge across the Yalu River.

The B-26 medium bombers were used only at night, operating to interdict troop movements, targeting individual vehicles, and against river crossings. They also conducted reconnaissance and dropped diversionary groups on the territory of North Korea and China in the area of Antung. They would approach from the direction of the sea at altitudes of 1,500 to 3,000 meters, and in the majority of cases, operated as single planes at these altitudes.

The Operational Tactics of Fighter-bombers

American F-80, F-84 and F-51 fighter-bombers participated in both concentrated attacks and independent strikes in groups of eight to forty or more planes, both with fighter escort and without. The fighter-bombers offered direct support to the ground forces, attacking enemy troops and equipment on the battlefield; interdicted the movement of supplies and reinforcements heading to the front; and attacked railroad stations, bridges, and storage facilities in the deep rear.

Before a concentrated strike in cooperation with bombers or before a massed ground attack, the enemy liked to send ahead a group of four to eight F-80s or F-84s for the purpose of reconnaissance, after which the main group of up to thirty to forty fighter-bombers would arrive 30–40 minutes later.

The fighter-bombers' primary route to targets in the vicinities of Singisiu, Sonchon, Chongju, Anju, Chasan, Unsan, Sukchon, and Uiju was along the western coast of the Korean peninsula at an altitude of 5,000 to 6,000 meters and a speed of 550–600 km/hr. They typically adopted a combat formation of a column of eights, with around 500–600 meters of altitude between the low and high flights, and cruised at a speed of 550–600 km/hr. Upon approaching the target area, the fighter-bombers would drop to 1,000 to 3,000 meters and increase their speed to 900 km/hr. Over the target, they would rearrange themselves into a circle, and groups of eight to sixteen planes would work over individual targets in the area.

If the target was protected by anti-aircraft artillery, the fighter-bombers would normally attack in pairs, but if the target had no anti-aircraft artillery cover, then the fighter-bombers would dive on the target individually. If the target area was situated close to the coastline, then the planes would egress out over the sea, where they would reassemble and repeat their attack procedure. Whenever MiGs appeared, the enemy fighter-bombers would typically quickly head for the sea, but if the target area was not near the coastline, the fighter-bombers would retreat to the south and south-east once the MiGs showed up.

When under MiG attack, the fighter-bombers would form into a circle, consisting of elements at various altitudes, which would weave while gradually drawing off back to their own territory or in the direction of the sea. The UN fighter-bomber pilot's standard reaction to a direct attack on his plane was to try to turn into the attack and meet it head-on. If the combat was occurring at low altitudes, enemy fighter-bombers would hug the deck, using the rugged terrain and the high maneuverability of their aircraft to escape back to their own lines.

However, the fighter-bombers were not totally passive and defenseless opponents. There were occasions when a numerically superior force of enemy fighter-bombers would encounter MiGs on a reverse heading. On these occasions, the enemy planes would readily take the MiGs on in a head-on pass, firing at the oncoming MiGs from various shallow angles of deflection and from long-range, counting upon filling the airspace in front of the MiGs with bullets and getting a few un-aimed bullet hits. When making a pass from behind, our pilots also had to be careful not to overshoot their targets and pull up in front of them, for the opposing pilot would immediately open fire and briefly pursue, before flipping his plane on its back and diving away.

During massed fighter-bomber attacks in the areas of Sonchon, Singisiu and Chongju, their operations would be covered by enemy F-86 fighters. Small groups of fighter-bombers, which operated in the area of Anju and to the south, often did not receive fighter escort.

After suffering heavy losses in June, July and August in the Sonchon–Chongju area, in the middle of September the fighter-bombers shifted their area of operations to the east, to the region of Chongju, Anju, Taechon and Sunchon. The enemy ground attack planes also began receiving fighter cover, both from immediate fighter escorts, and from forward fighter screens.

There were observed cases when the fighter-bombers attempted to confuse our ground control intercept stations by imitating F-86 fighters. They would approach at high altitudes of 7,000–8,000 meters and speeds of 800 km/hr, then with a sharp dive they would emerge over the target area, make one or two runs over the target, and then flee in the direction of the sea or to the south-east.

During the last two months of the 17th IAP's combat operations, encounters with enemy fighter-bombers became rare, since they would leave at the approach of our fighters and refuse combat with the MiGs. Incidentally, the piston-engined F-51, known as the famous P-51 Mustang in the Second World War, was still used in a ground attack role in Korea. However, in the majority of cases it was employed over the front lines and along the eastern coast of the Korean peninsula, as well as in difficult weather. The 17th IAP never encountered the F-51.

The Operational Tactics of Fighters

The primary enemy fighter in the Korean theater of combat operations was the F–86 Sabre. F–86 fighters operated in groups of four, six, eight, twelve, twenty-four and up to forty planes. Their typical combat formation was a four- or eight-ship column.

At the start of the 17th IAP's combat operations and until September 1951, the enemy's fighters flew in compact formations. However, after several months of experience against the Soviet MiGs, they began to adopt looser formations, similar to our own combat formations.

The F–86 fighters were used to set up the fighter barriers that were deployed in advance of the bombers or ground attack planes on our fighters' likely avenues of approach, with the aim of breaking up our combat formations. If the screening F–86 fighters enjoyed a tactical advantage or numerical superiority, then they willingly tangled with our fighters in dogfights. The enemy also used small 'hunter' groups of two to six Sabres, which patrolled our egress routes from a battle and near our airbases. Taking advantage of our pilots' reduced vigilance on the return to base, these 'hunters' would conduct sudden, unexpected attacks.

The F–86 fighters normally flew to 'MiG Alley' in large groups along the western coastline of the Korean peninsula at altitudes of 5,000 to 7,000 meters, until reaching the island of Sinbi-to, where they would climb to 10,000 to 12,000 meters. While doing so, part of the force would form into a circle, while the rest of the force in small groups of six to eight planes flew to the mouth of the Yalu River and mouth of the Songchon River. These small groups had the aim of scattering our combat formations, but without getting involved in a dogfight.

Often, another group of sixteen Sabres would approach the area of combat operations from the east. Before reaching it, they would make a wide swing to the north, waiting for the approach of our fighters in the area of Anju, when they would bank to the left and try to swing in behind our planes.

While all of this unfolded, the planes that had remained circling above Sinbi-to would look for an opportunity to dive onto the rear of our fighter groups as they passed in the direction of Anju – especially if our pilots turned to meet the eastern group of F–86s. In the majority of cases noted in the 17th IAP's operational log, combat began in the Pakchon–Anju–Chongju region, where eight to sixteen additional F–86 fighters would reinforce the fight from the direction of the sea or from the south.

During heavy raids, in order to protect the bombers and fighter-bombers, the majority of F–86 fighters would be located at an altitude of 8,000 to 9,000 meters, with detached flights of four or six planes at a higher altitude of 11,000 to 12,000 meters. The F–86 fighter pilots liked to make use of the inversion layer, where contrails would form: if the contrail level was at high altitude in the vicinity of 12,000 to 13,000 meters, then the F–86 planes flew just below the level, while if the contrail level was below 10,000 to 11,000 meters, then the F–86 jets tried to stay just above it at 12,000 to 12,500 meters. The main F–86 group would detach an element or flight as bait and send it into the inversion layer to create the highly visible contrails, while the rest remained concealed.

If the F–86 fighters held an altitude advantage, then they liked to attack our planes from behind through shallow dives at low angles of deflection, counting upon the element of surprise. If in this case they were at a numerical disadvantage, then after the attack the Sabre pilots would dive away, but if the F–86 fighters outnumbered our MiG–15s, then the F–86s would stay and dogfight. The F–86 planes also liked to attack from below and behind, but after the attack they usually dived away. The F–86 fighter pilots typically opened fire from a distance of 800 down to 200 meters.

If attacked by our fighters from behind, the F–86 pilots would refuse battle. They would try to evade in a steep, descending spiral, or by diving away at top speed in the direction of the sea while using their Sabre's afterburner. If a dogfight continued for more than five or ten minutes, then additional F–86 fighters often arrived to join the action. If, however, the action had already ended by the time of their arrival, then the superior enemy forces would pursue our retreating planes and chase them back to the Yalu River.

In the month of August 1951, a new British fighter, the Gloster Meteor IV appeared in the theater of combat operations. At first, it was used as a fighter and cooperated with the F–86 fighters at an altitude of 8,000 to 10,000 meters. Still the Meteor was no match for the MiG–15, and after experiencing significant losses, the British fighter began to be used as close escort for the B–29 bombers and in a ground attack role.

The Tactical Operations of Our Fighters

Depending on the weather conditions and the combat situation, the Soviets would keep one or more squadrons, even full aviation regiments, standing at readiness level No. 1. Typically, it was these fighters that would get the signal to launch. Upon receipt of the order, the squadron or regiment would take off in an established sequence of pairs. To enable the quickest possible assembly in the sky, take-offs occurred with 12- to 15-second intervals between each pair of jets. Depending upon the given assignment and the situation in the air, the group would either assemble while making a 90° or 180° climbing turn after take-off or those aircraft that launched later would simply have to catch up with the rest of the group.

As a rule, the group commander received the mission by radio from the division command post before take-off, or immediately after take-off. This allowed the group commander to select the appropriate assembly maneuver. It was important for rapid assembly after take-off for the lead group to adopt a speed of not more than 500 km/hr. As soon as the formation had assembled, the squadron commanders would accelerate, in order for the formation to gain altitude as quickly as possible.

After reaching the assigned altitude, while moving toward the combat area with drop tanks, the formation's airspeed increased to 800–850 km/hr. After dropping the spare tanks, the leader would increase airspeed to 900–950 km/hr, and begin the search for the enemy.

Our fighters normally would assume a loose combat formation, echeloned in altitude. Such formations were easy to manage and maintain, allowed for rapid maneuver and mutual support, and provided a greater degree of protection from surprise attack. The commander could flexibly adjust the combat formation, given the tactical situation and the meteorological conditions.

The two-plane element was considered the basic unit of combat formations, though the use of a single plane was considered permissible in very rare situations. It was believed that the pair should never split up in combat under any circumstances, even in the most difficult situations. Such cohesion was obtained by selecting pairs on the basis of the level of the pilots' training, their characters, and the cooperation they displayed in training flights.

While moving toward expected contact and searching for the enemy, the combat formation usually employed a leading pair of planes flying line abreast or at a shallow angle with a set interval between them. This formation provided for the widest view of surrounding airspace. If an element was operating independently, then the interval between the two planes increased to 300 meters, which allowed wider fields of vision. Before the start of an attack and during the ensuing combat, the pair would shift into a 'sharp stagger' (*ostryi peleng* – literally, 'acute bearing') formation, with the wingman dropping back into a sharply staggered position behind and to the right or left of the leader. Whenever the leader changed direction, the wingman had to follow him by the shortest path, literally cutting corners while shifting to the new heading. It was the wingman's job to cover the commander from sudden attacks from behind; to keep watch for attacks from out of the sun or broken cloud cover; to report any spotted enemy planes immediately; to stay alert for signals from the leader; and to maintain formation.

Maneuvering by the leader was not to interfere with the wingman's constant monitoring of the skies. Sharp changes in the direction of flight were permissible only in cases of sudden attack by the enemy. In all vertical maneuvers, the wingman had to remain inside and behind the loop of the leader and keep watch over the airspace outside the loop, while the leader in this situation paid more attention to the airspace within the loop and kept the wingman in his field of vision.

The combat formation for a flight of four planes was built upon the formations of two-plane elements; during assembly and while moving toward the area of anticipated contact, the flight employed the line abreast 'front' formation, but switched to a 'stagger' formation in anticipation of an attack. During changes in the direction of flight, the leader of the rear pair always had to pass behind and if possible below the leading pair.

The responsibilities between the elements within the flight were distributed analogously to their distribution within the pair: the strike element (*udarnaia para*) searched for the enemy and attacked first, while the cover element protected the actions of the strike element from an attack by enemy fighters. If the situation called for it, the cover pair was ready at the command of the flight commander to switch roles and lead the attack. The distances (longitudinal spacing) and intervals (horizontal spacing) of the combat formations were as follows: the 'front', intervals between elements of 300–400 meters, and a distance between them of 25–100 meters; the 'stagger', intervals of 50–100 meters, and a distance of 300–500 meters between the leading element and the trailing element.

The combat formation of the squadron and regiment was built upon the combat formations of the pairs and flights, which were echeloned in altitude and loosely arranged, both laterally and in depth. The most widely used combat formation of the squadron and regiment in combat operations over Korea was either the 'column of flights' or the 'sharp stagger', echeloned in altitude up to 600 meters, with trailing flights following within practical firing range of the flight in front of it. This gave the trailing flight the opportunity to repulse an attack by enemy fighters on the leading flight. The specific combat formations adopted by the squadron and the regiment in each separate case were determined by the enemy's activity and tactical movements, the meteorological conditions, and the decision of the commander.

As a rule, the combat formation of the squadron consisted of one or two flights, which operated as the strike group, while one flight remained at higher altitude as a cover group. In the regiment, usually two squadrons comprised the strike group and one squadron, the cover group. With an increase in altitude, the height advantage of one flight over another decreased by up to 500 meters, and in certain cases the squadrons flew at the same altitude. The nature of the mission – the types of enemy aircraft involved – also influenced the formations, and the combat itself often scattered the formation into separate flights and elements, each involved in its own duel.

The Soviet ace Grigorii Ul'ianovich Okhai relates:

American pilots flew in groups, but only in tight formation; especially the pairs flew almost wingtip to wingtip, even in turns, dives, and climbs. Our pairs flew at a distance from between aircraft of 600 to 1,200 meters, with small differences in altitude of 200 to 500 meters. In a group of squadron size or larger, we flew in a staircase arrangement, which allowed us to maneuver freely. It sometimes happened that you and your wingman would be chasing a formation of four F-86s, flying in compact formation, and when you approached to a distance of 800–1,500 meters, one pair of F-86s would go into a climb, the second pair would roll over and dive away, and if you hesitated for just a moment to think about which pair to follow, then the enemy would already have made his break, and it would be almost impossible to chase him down again.

The Americans covered B-29 bomber groups with a large number of fighters of different types (F-86, F-84, F-80). For example, they'd send out 120–150 fighters for just nine B-29 bombers. The F-86, which had greater speed, always flew as the high group, and when they received word that MiGs were approaching, the Sabres would fly on ahead of the bombers in order to tie us up in dogfights before we reached the B-29s. The remaining fighters of the covering force stuck with the B-29s. Our leaders would respond by leaving behind small groups of fighters to duel with the Sabres, while the remaining force would break through to the bombers at high speed.

The search for the enemy in the air was an important element of our fighter tactics. The long-range search for the enemy planes was done with the help of Ground Control Intercept (GCI) radar facilities. It would begin from the moment our group had taken its general flight heading toward the area of the anticipated clash with the enemy. Only the group commander had two-way communications with the GCI controllers, who kept him informed about the enemy. The remaining pilots only overheard the information about the enemy and mentally pictured the enemy's location, heading, and altitude in relation to them.

The GCI controller fed the following data to the group commander in his messages about the enemy: the number of enemy planes, type, altitude, location and heading. Having this data, the commander could outline a plan for the forthcoming battle and make timely adjustments to the battle plan that had been worked out on the ground, and arrange his forces. The group commander, based on the situation (meteorological conditions, position of the sun, information about the enemy), chose the direction from which to enter the indicated zone in order to engage the enemy aircraft.

The immediate search for enemy airplanes was made visually by all the pilots during the entire flight, from the moment of climbing into the cockpit until the plane taxied into the apron area after landing. The first pilot to spot the enemy planes was obliged to report it immediately, giving his call sign and heading, the location of the enemy, and the enemy's number and type. For example, 'This is 241, bearing straight ahead, below and to the right, eight Sabres.'

While the combat unfolded, the group commander kept the pilots informed about the enemy's location and altitude, and issued the command to disengage from the battle. The group commanders also monitored the radio during a battle, so that overexcited pilots didn't clog the air with excessive chatter as planes started going down in smoke and flames. The pilots were given a firm instruction not to overuse the mike even if their planes were experiencing mechanical problems (inability to retract landing gear, a failure in the hydraulics system, and so forth); instead, they were to briefly report to the commander about the problem, and then make an independent decision about whether or not to abort the mission.

While attempting to spot the enemy, the group commander paid special attention to the airspace in front of him, while the commander of the rear flight (or squadron) kept careful watch over the airspace behind, in order to prevent a surprise attack. Any plane detected in the sky was treated as hostile until its identity had been fully established. Due to certain similarities between the MiG-15 and the F-86, sometimes our pilots mistook enemy planes for their own, and vice versa. There were even cases of mistaken MiG attacks on our own planes.

There were several distinct characteristics of the F-86 that distinguished it from the MiG-15. The horizontal stabilizers were positioned below the tail (the MiG-15's were higher), the tail's silhouette resembled a boot, and the drop tanks were positioned closer to the fuselage. The F-86 was noticeably larger than the MiG-15, and its canopy was more convex. In pursuit and during escape from battle, F-86 pilots frequently employed an afterburner, which would generate a dark trail of smoke behind the fighter. The afterburner was operated only in short bursts, lasting for only two or three seconds.

Bursts of anti-aircraft artillery fire and bomb explosions were a great help in the search for enemy aircraft, since they revealed the location where enemy fighter-bombers were operating. At high altitudes, the enemy planes left contrails that were visible from great distances, therefore it was not recommended for our groups to fly in the contrail level.

Characteristics of jet combat

Air combat in Korea was characterized by the large number of planes involved, the swiftness and impetuousness of attacks, the rapid maneuvering for position, the fleeting nature of the battle, and the widespread use of radar facilities. The primary characteristics of jet combat were:

- Air combat, as a rule, took place at speeds of the order of 1,000 to 1,050 km/hr. The parameters of combat increased significantly, and the engagements covered a large amount of space in both the horizontal and the vertical planes. Jet squadrons frequently dueled with enemy aircraft over an area of 10 to 15 kilometers and within a 4,000 to 5,000 range in altitude.
- Air combat might occur at any altitude, from nap of the earth flight to the aircraft's operational ceiling. The average altitude for dogfights was in the neighborhood of 6,000 to 10,000 meters. Dogfights at altitudes less than 5,000 meters significantly increased fuel consumption, which decreased the remaining time available for flight and combat.
- Aerial combat at altitudes above 11,000 meters placed special demands on maintaining a combat formation, so intervals and distances between planes and groups in the formation had to be reduced, while maneuvering in the horizontal and the vertical planes had to be restricted. Combat at these altitudes also quickly raised the threat of exceeding the plane's red line in airspeed.
- Jet combat was quick and decisive. After making an attacking pass at such high speeds, the target plane receded so quickly that the attacking pilot often lost sight of it, forcing him to make a new search for it in order to make a second attack. Therefore, pilots sought to shoot down an adversary with the first pass.
- Battle at such high speeds and with such rapid changes in altitude placed heavy physical demands on the pilots, which required great physical exertion from them.

The flight was considered the most suitable unit for independent operations against small groups of enemy planes. The flight commander was given a great deal of leeway in making the decision whether or not to launch an attack on enemy planes, as long as he first reported to the squadron commander about his decision.

If one pair in the flight was sufficient for conducting a successful attack, the other pair could provide cover against surprise attacks by enemy fighters. If the flight encountered organized groups of fighter-bombers and bombers, then it was necessary for the entire flight to break up the enemy's formation with the very first attack, and then to split into separate elements to focus upon destroying isolated or crippled bombers that had dropped out of the formation.

Once groups flying as part of a regiment-sized formation arrived in the designated combat area, they opened the battle at the signal of the commander. The groups' success in battle depended upon receiving complete information on the situation in the air from the ground radar service, which enabled a commander to choose a battle plan and combat formation corresponding to the situation, and to begin the combat under the most advantageous conditions. Once the battle started, the group's success depended upon close cooperation among the separate flights and elements and the accurate execution of the group commander's orders.

Aerial combats with different types of airplanes had their own characteristics, which our pilots had to take into consideration. Attacks on F-86 fighters were conducted by full flights or by the elements in turn. This latter approach took into consideration the fact that F-86 fighters under attack liked to split-S and dive away or go into a diving spiral. Consequently, the tail-end pair of MiGs would already be descending while the lead pair attacked, thereby giving it an opportunity to repeat the attack as the F-86 fighters went into their dives. Our pilots were advised to use only vertical maneuvers (zooms, climbing spirals, Immelmanns) in combat against F-86 fighters at all altitudes, due to the MiG's superior climbing ability. It was not recommended to stay and engage in a turning dogfight with the F-86. The most effective ways to attack the F-86 were from behind, from above or below, at top speed from a distance of 500 meters or closer with a low deflection aspect angle[3] of 0/4 to 2/4.

Experience demonstrated that:

1. At altitudes above 9,000 meters, the low effectiveness of the MiG's speed brakes made it almost impossible to follow the adversary in a dive. Because of its greater weight and more solidly built airframe, the F-86 was faster in a sustained dive and could better withstand the stress of pulling out of the dive. Our pilots, on the other hand, had to pay constant attention to whether or not they would have sufficient altitude to pull out of a dive in time.

2. In case of an attack upon our MiG-15 fighters by enemy F-86 fighters from above and behind, the MiG pilot had to be careful not to begin his climb before the F-86 had pulled in behind the MiG at the same altitude. Climbing prematurely would reduce the angle of closure for the attacking F-86, enabling it to close quickly within firing distance.

3. The MiG-15 was superior to the F-86 in speed and vertical maneuvers at altitudes above 11,000 meters.

4. In case of a spin in a MiG-15 while fighting at high altitudes, the pilot had to wait until the MiG had fallen to no more than 6,000 to 7,000 meters in altitude before attempting to pull out of the spin, or else that effort would fail.

5. During dogfights at altitudes of below 4,000 meters, the MiG-15 had restricted room to conduct maneuvers that would cost altitude. Due to this, combat at those altitudes was particularly hazardous and placed great demands on the MiG pilots.

6. Breaking off a fight was done at the group commander's or command post's order at top speed in level flight. After separating from the enemy, the group would smoothly gain altitude, making sure not to let its speed drop below 900 km/hr. It was categorically forbidden to exit the battle in a dive or a climb.

As mentioned earlier, aerial combat in the jet age in Korea was brief. The clashes between our fighters and the enemy planes lasted on average just 10–12 minutes, though in some cases it might continue for 14–15 minutes.

Combats with fighter-bombers had their own characteristics. The F-80, F-84, and the Gloster Meteor jet fighters were used in combat operations in Korea, primarily, for carrying out bombing and ground attacks. In addition, they were used as close escorts for the B-29 bombers.

The combat formation taken up by a MiG-15 group in anticipation of a battle with the fighter-bombers was usually either the 'sharp stagger of flights (pairs)' or the 'column of flights (pairs)'. Such combat formations increased the group's maneuverability and provided for the greatest degree of cooperation among the elements and flights.

Combat with fighter-bombers typically occurred at low altitudes from 4,000 meters down to nearly ground level and involved energetic maneuvers. As mentioned before, the MiG pilot had to be very careful while engaging a target at these low altitudes.

A MiG-15 group was capable of successfully taking on a superior force of enemy fighter-bombers two to three times its own size. Attacks on the fighter-bombers were usually conducted in succession by elements and more rarely by flights.

Again, MiG pilots were advised to use vertical maneuvers against the fighter-bombers, while maintaining a speed of at least 800 km/hr at the top of the climb. It was not recommended to stay and turn with the enemy fighter-bombers, since this would bleed off energy and airspeed, and leave the MiG vulnerable to enemy attack. The most effective attack on the fighter-bomber formations was the initial, well-prepared attack, made from behind the target out of a shallow dive, with a target aspect of 0/4–2/4 [a zero or low deflection shot]. At low altitudes, the possibility of an attack from below was, as a rule, ruled out. If the first attack was unsuccessful, then for a second attack it was necessary to separate from the fighter-bombers, select a new target, and then conduct another attack.

In the optimum case when the enemy fighter-bomber pilot did not see the MiG and try to evade it, pilots were recommended to aim at their target by using the pipper of the automatic gunsight, to open fire at a range of 600 meters or closer, and fire in medium or short bursts. If the target was maneuvering energetically, then the pilot was advised to switch to the fixed gunsight, because the computing power of those early automatic gunsights was too low to calculate the proper lead quickly enough. In order to stay inside or match the turns of a target, our fighter pilots could make momentary use of the speed brakes.

Withdrawing from combat with fighter-bombers that were not covered by F-

86 fighters presented no difficulties. When MiG-15s withdrew from contact with fighter-bombers that had F-86 fighter cover, they were supposed to do so in level flight at top speed, covered by more MiGs at a higher altitude.

The enemy's bombers were the primary strike force. The destruction of enemy bombers thus became the prime objective for our fighter squadrons. Attacks on enemy bombers were carried out simultaneously or one after the other by flights. In most instances, the attack on the enemy bombers was made at top speed, which did not allow the close escort fighters time to react as the MiGs streaked through their formation. The most profitable direction of attack was from the rear at an aspect angle of 0/4–2/4. A head-on attack on the B-29 could also yield good results, but presented some difficulty because of the rapid rate of closure.

It was recommended for the pilots to employ the automatic gunsight when targeting a bomber, placing the pipper on the bomber's vital spots (fuel tanks, engines, and cockpit). Pilots were instructed to fire long bursts from a distance of 800 down to 300 meters. Upon ceasing fire they were to pass directly beneath the B-29 and exit the run out in front of the bomber, before banking away at a 20° to 30° angle to one side or the other. After heading in this direction for one to one and a half minutes, the MiG pilot was to swing back around in the opposite direction and make a second run at the front of the bomber with another low deflection shot at a target aspect of 0/4 to 2/4. When attacking the front of the bomber, the pilots were told to open fire at a range of 1,300 to 1,200 meters and cease firing at a range of 400 meters, after which they were to complete the pass with a side-slip and no change in heading.

Our pilots employed a variety of tactics in the skies over Korea, many of which exploited the MiG's higher operational ceiling and superior climbing ability. Hit and run tactics were the most common, out of the sun if possible. The MiGs would use their superior altitude to make diving passes by elements or flights in turn. After the attack, the MiGs would use the energy gained in the dive to regain altitude quickly. Even if the attack failed, it was difficult for the adversary to counter this maneuver, because the Sabre's engine simply lacked sufficient thrust to match the MiG in climbs. The GCI controller was important to guide the MiGs into position above the Sabre formations.

Knowing that Sabre pilots eagerly pounced upon isolated MiGs or MiG elements, MiG formations took advantage of this tendency by using decoy elements at lower or higher altitudes than the rest of the formation. When threatened, the decoys would climb away from trouble, while the strike flights or squadrons would attack the surprised adversary – through a zooming climb if at lower altitude, or a hit and run from higher altitude. Squadrons often used one of their flights as bait, sending it out in front of the rest of the squadron at a lower or higher altitude to catch the enemy's attention. The remaining flights, staggered in altitude in staircase fashion, would then employ a hit and run attack on the preoccupied Sabres, or climb quickly onto their tails.

A more elaborate tactic involved multiple formations. Two large groups of MiGs would take a southerly heading toward the front lines at 10,000 to 12,000 meters, but on somewhat divergent routes. The interval between these two groups extended far beyond the range of visual sight, so GCI controllers would have to coordinate the actions of the groups. Upon approaching the front lines, the MiGs would descend to an altitude of 4,500 to 6,000 meters and swing back around to the north, following the main supply routes in the hope of meeting enemy fighter-bombers and small groups of Sabres returning to their bases from a mission. At a given time, a third group of MiGs would set out from the Yalu and fly southwards between the closing pincers, looking to destroy any enemy planes trapped between them. On some occasions, this third group played a different tactical role – it provided cover for MiGs in the pincer groups as they returned to base low on fuel.

As a rule, these tactics required analysis of the enemy's tendencies, careful planning and thorough preparation prior to the mission. Proper coordination and timing were critical to the success or failure of these tactics. The flight staff often rehearsed the tactical plan on the ground before a mission. Pilots sortied with an already prepared plan of actions.[4]

Though the speed and operational ceiling of jet fighters in the Korean War had grown by one and a half times over their piston-engine predecessors of the Second World War, one tactical element hadn't changed – their weapons. So pilots still had to maneuver for the advantage and try to get behind an enemy plane, and the ability to spot aircraft was still essential.

Things become crowded at Myaogou

At the beginning of June, Major Pulov's unit of twenty-nine pilots and twenty-eight MiGs was rated as ready for combat operations in squadron-sized formations up to an altitude of 13,000 meters in simple meteorological conditions. On 11 June, the regiment's flight staff flew from the rear airbase at Mukden to the Myaogou airfield. Hero of the Soviet Union Lieutenant Colonel Karasev, commander of the 523rd IAP, became chief of the garrison at Myaogou. Karasev was an experienced veteran of the Second World War, who had earned the title Hero on 24 August 1943; after personally scoring fourteen victories, he had been shot down over the Crimea on 7 April 1944 and spent the rest of the war in a German prisoner of war camp. His regiment had transferred to Myaogou a little earlier, on 28 May.

The military quarters for all three regiments of the division were located about 15–20 kilometers from the airfield in the little town of Tatangou. The personnel, especially the mechanics and technicians, were tightly packed in this location, because of a shortage of housing. For protection from possible enemy air attack, the flight staff of the regiment was dispersed among three buildings by squadron. There were twelve to fifteen men in each room, and the cots were covered with mosquito netting to protect the men from mosquito-borne diseases like encephalitis. A kitchen and eating area was located on the first floor of each building.

Rising in the pre-dawn darkness, the pilots would reluctantly eat their breakfasts, and then leave early for the airfield. They were conveyed to and from the airfield in covered trucks; they couldn't even see the road along which they were driving, and by dawn, were at the airfield and at combat readiness (the ground staff arrived even earlier than the pilots). Tall grass along the road was kept mown for security reasons, while the road itself was patrolled by Chinese troops – guerrilla bands had tried to penetrate in this area.

The hours of sleep for the pilots in summertime were from 22:00 to 04:00, in the wintertime between 22:00 and 05:45. However, the pilots were often roused as early as 02:00 and taken to the airfield, where they would try to catch up on their sleep if they had the chance. The technical staff was roused one to one and a half hours earlier than the pilots. At the airfield, with the aim of creating appropriate rest for the pilots and crewmen, containers from the airplane crates were set up as little huts with awnings between them, and fitted out with cots and plank beds furnished with bedding, where the pilots and mechanics at readiness level No. 3 could rest. Each aviation squadron had a shower facility at the field, where the pilots and ground crews could freshen up after a combat mission or a duty shift on high alert. Showers prevented heat and sun strokes in the summer, as well as skin infections among the personnel.

Very often pilots remained on readiness level No. 1 for prolonged periods, and were required to stay in their cockpits; in the summer, white sunshades placed over the MiG cockpits were used to prevent sun and heat strokes. Ice-filled casks of cold, boiled water were located in each squadron area and at the regiment command post to provide the officers and men with a constant supply of safe drinking water. A room was set up in the regiment command post for post-mission debriefings, where cold boiled water, cold bread kvass, or lemonade was always available, supplied by the commissary.

The flight staff received four meals a day. The first breakfast was offered before leaving for the airfield, the second breakfast and lunch at the airfield, and dinner in the town. The menu was based on the pilots' own preferences: a first course of soup, a second course of pork, omelets, or compotes, with vegetables and fruit on the side. All too often, there was also a rather unappetizing, cheap sausage unpopular with the men that they nicknamed 'red dog's sausage'. There was no special menu for high altitude flights; before a mission, pilots were offered any dish they desired (cold kvass soup, and so forth), both before taking off and upon return from a high-altitude flight. Chinese civilians served in the mess hall, although there were also our own cooks and servants among the number of civilians working for the aviation division.

For better nighttime rest and sleep, at dinner the flight staff received 100 grams of vodka or cognac and a bottle of beer. This had a positive effect, since it relaxed the men and improved their sleep, which simultaneously preserved their strength and combat fitness.

The flight staff underwent daily medical observations, before and after combat missions at the airfield, in the mess hall, and in their barracks. In the evening after flights, the pilots were questioned and in case of necessity, examined in the medical unit. After retreat, the flight staff's rest was monitored, and if necessary, sedatives were distributed. In the morning at the airfield, the pilots were questioned about how they were feeling, and in necessary cases, they underwent an examination at the field's dispensary. Pilots underwent monthly full medical examinations, the results of which were kept in a log. The daily observation at the airfield, in the mess hall, and in the barracks; the examinations and questioning before and after flights; and the monthly medical examinations and consultations with specialists at the hospital all combined to measure the flight staff's level of fatigue. Higher command used this information to determine timely periods of rest for the unit, as well as to determine whether an individual pilot should receive outpatient treatment or hospitalization.

After transferring from the Mukden-East airfield to the airfield at Myaogou, the unit received a new combat mission: to remain ready at the airfield to cover the crossings, bridges and the Suiho Hydro-electrical Station on the Yalu River; the airfields at Antung, Singisiu, and Myaogou; and the supply line and other targets in the northwestern part of Korea down to a line between Pyongyang and Wonsan. At the same time, the regiment had to be ready to repel enemy air attacks on targets in north-east China along the Mukden operational axis. The regiment carried out the given assignment in coordination with the 18th GIAP and 523rd IAP of the same 303rd IAD, and with two aviation regiments of the 324th IAD. The regiment's primary combat duties were to stand watch at the airfield at one of three stages of readiness, to conduct combat missions from a state of readiness in order to repel enemy air strikes, and more rarely, to conduct patrols over key facilities and installations.

The 17th IAP was located at the intersection of the north end of the runway at Myaogou and the taxiway; on the eastern side of the runway, the 18th GIAP was next to the 17th IAP at the other end of the taxiway; and the 523rd IAP was situated at the southern end of the runway. The regiment's command post was located in the vicinity of the airfield's apron, while the division command post was situated about 700–800 meters away near the airfield terminal. The division and regiment headquarters, as well those of the ground support units, were located in a cantonment 6–7 kilometers away from the airfield.

Some time later, a Chinese regiment equipped with MiG-15s was based at the airfield next to the 523rd IAP. For security reasons, our servicemen were forbidden to mention the VK-1 engine, which equipped the newer MiG-15bis, in conversations with the Chinese pilots (at that time, the Chinese had still not been supplied with the MiG-15bis). The Chinese pilots and technicians could see that our jets had superior performance and had certain differences in details of construction, so they were always asking our guys questions, such as: 'Captain, why is that opening on the tail of your plane bigger?' (The diameter of the tailpipe on the MiG-15bis was somewhat larger than that of the MiG-15.) Our technicians had to extricate themselves from the conversation in whatever way they could do it.

Take-offs were made from the direction of the regiment's location on the airfield, independently of the wind's direction. The 17th IAP and the 18th GIAP took off in the direction of Korea Bay, after which they made a 180° turn before reaching the coast. To fly into the airspace over the bay was forbidden: the American Air Force and the American fleet reigned supreme there. The pilots even had to sign a voucher, stating that they had been forewarned about this.

Regiments usually returned to their own airfield, though sometimes one would land at Antung. Reassembly of the groups after a battle was rarely done because aircraft were typically low on fuel at that point. The regiment that was flying at the lowest altitude would land first. It took 2–3 minutes on average to land all the planes of a squadron; a regiment required 9–12 minutes.

After the completion of a combat mission and the return of all the planes, the fighters were immediately readied for another sortie. The ground crews carried out this work in the hardened revetments set up along the runway and taxiways. Each regiment had ten such revetments, where they rearmed and refueled the planes after a mission. At first, the regiment required an hour to an hour and 20 minutes to prepare the planes for another mission, but with constant work and training, this turnaround time was reduced first to 50 minutes, and then to just 35–40 minutes by October.

It required 18–35 minutes to refuel twenty-four to twenty-eight MiGs with the kerosene and 25–30 minutes to refill the oxygen canisters. GAZ-63 and Dodge ³/4-ton trucks towed the jets to the start position for take-offs. Altogether, the 17th IAP had twelve of these vehicles.

The regiments used the following fueling equipment:

- eight ZIS–150 refuelling trucks with two fuel hoses
- one oxygen recharging station
- four kerosene tanks.

As a rule, one plane was set aside for doing the scheduled work on the other aircraft; the mechanics and technicians tried to make maximum use of bad weather and nighttime hours for scheduled maintenance work. Scheduled service was often done during nighttime hours throughout the units.

In rainy weather, cases where the PS-2 starter panels refused to work became more frequent. Therefore, technicians began testing the engines each morning, before the beginning of combat operations for the day.

The Organization of Duties at the Airfield

Duty at the airfield was organized around a duty roster, approved by the formation commander. The regiments put together a chart, which established the squadrons' duty schedule. When a squadron's duty shift began, the duty schedule and readiness level that the flights were to assume was announced, and the list of active duty pilots was specified. During a duty shift, information on the enemy's movements in the air was transmitted by telephone from the regiment command post to the squadrons. If pilots were on the highest level of readiness, they would be receiving information in their cockpits over the GCI controller's radio net. The order for assuming an alert level arrived by telephone from the division command post, and went out to the squadrons also by telephone.

After assuming a readiness level of No. 1 or No. 2, the squadron's adjutant, or on his instructions, the phone operator on duty, would report to the regiment command post the readiness status of the flights and pilots now on alert. The group leader, after establishing solid communications with the flight commanders, would report by radio to the division command post that his group had assumed the assigned readiness level. The operations duty officer repeated this order by telephone to the division command post. A given signal for take–off was repeated from the regiment command post by a series of signal flares. The regiment's operations duty officer, or at his indication a different officer, would note the launch order's time of arrival, and the launch start and completion times for each flight and for the squadron as a whole; this information was then reported back to the division command post. When the aircraft returned from a mission, the arriving planes would be reported, and for verification purposes the identification number on the side of each MiG was recorded as it came in.

After take-off, the vector command from the command post included the target parameters of altitude, course, time to target (in code) and area, as determined and calculated at the command post from the information provided by the radar installations. A typical vector sounded like this: '310, Course 120, 5 minutes, Comet 80, this is Granite.'

Usually, the division's regiments took off on a command from the IAK command post, but were then controlled by the IAD command post, though the division commander had no authority to send up additional forces. Sometimes this practice led to confusion, as, for example, on 5 August 1951, when regiments from different divisions were sent to the same target and each division directed its regiment toward the enemy its own way. The division commander also gave the order to drop the external fuel tanks.

Immediately after landing, the regiment commander would conduct a debriefing of the pilots, while staff officers in attendance took necessary notes and compiled reports. The division commander would analyze typical combat situations. On a day when there had been combat, the division commander conducted a quick debriefing with all the pilots and evaluated their performance. Pilots were expected to report on the types of enemy aircraft encountered on the mission, their recognition markings, combat formations, and tactics. The debriefing would reveal any new type of enemy aircraft and note any new tactics by the enemy.

Anything new noted by the pilots in the aerial combat was reported to the division command post and would be written up in a detailed summary report at the end of a day of combat missions. Efforts were made to identify any unfamiliar aircraft encountered by pilots on the mission, and this information would be passed along to the division command post. Pilots would undergo supplementary classroom sessions to study the available technical and tactical data on each new enemy plane encountered.

Regiment staff prepared the necessary information for the commander's use in making decisions about the next day's operations. At the end of a day of combat operations, the staff gathered information from the chiefs of ground services and the rear supply unit and prepared reports on the status of the personnel, the serviceability of the planes, and the material-technical supplies required for the next day's operations. The regiment commander received oral reports on the information received from the chiefs of the ground services and supply, after which he would determine the force composition and combat formation for carrying out the assigned combat mission.

Preliminary instructions, as a rule, were issued verbally, though in exceptional cases they might be written. The preliminary briefing outlined the mission, for which the pilots had to be ready. Sometimes this included a literal walk-through of the anticipated combat scenario on the ground. Once a mission was under way, the division commander might adjust it in response to the developing situation in the air; once contact was made and an aerial engagement was under way, the division commander would issue combat orders as the combat situation changed.

Staff officers monitored the squadrons and flights for how well the personnel and especially the pilots had performed during the just completed combat mission, identified shortcomings in the operation, and immediately took steps to eliminate those problems and to ensure they were not repeated. Staff officers immediately reported the results of their assessment to the regiment commander.

Launching regiments at readiness level No. 1 in order to reinforce a combat already under way was a complicated process, and they didn't always manage to reach the battle in time. Thus the division commander began to launch two or three regiments at short intervals at the start of a mission, layering them by altitude once they had all taken off. This gave him greater flexibility in conducting the subsequent battle.

After the MiGs returned from a mission, ground crews used all available material and technical resources to turn the planes around for another flight. Squadron adjutants would report to the regiment command post on the expenditure of fuel and lubricants, external fuel tanks, and if there had been shooting, the expenditure of ammunition. A staff officer would summarize this information for the regiment and send the summary to the division command post. As the planes were being turned around for another sortie, the regiment command post would receive regular status reports on progress after every two planes were readied (after two, four, six, eight, etc.).

If there had been an encounter with the enemy, the regiment's operational results would be reported in the following order: the time, place, and altitude of the encounter; what group of planes had been met and what formation they were using; and the combat results. A detailed report on the results of a combat mission was produced only after the analysis of the film footage from the gun cameras. If after a mission some of the planes had been grounded by combat damage or equipment malfunctions, the regiment would shuffle the serviceable MiGs with their pilots and assigned crews between the flights to bring them up to the same strength. This process would occur before the next sortie.

At the end of combat duties for the day, a staff officer would compile a summary combat for the division command post. This officer would attend the debriefings after each of the day's missions and jot down the necessary information for the combat report. In addition, at the end of a duty shift, regiment headquarters would determine the combat effectives for the next day of duty, in terms of both the pilots and the planes. This information would be reported to division headquarters in a summary combat dispatch, which indicated the total number of combat-ready pilots, planes, and crews for the regiment as a whole, and for each squadron in particular.

Basing all three regiments of the division at the same airfield had certain advantages. First, it was possible to bring a regiment back to readiness for a repeat mission more quickly if the entire division hadn't launched, but just one or two of the regiments. This allowed the technical equipment and resources of the idle regiment or regiments to be used for refueling and rearming the planes. Second, it allowed the division commander to meet daily with the regiment commanders and flight staff, which was not possible if the regiments were located at different airfields. Third, it was more convenient to arrange for security of the planes and the personnel of the division's regiments, if the division was not scattered across several airfields.

However, there were also disadvantages to aggregating all the regiments of a division at one base. The crowding of planes on one airfield made it a more attractive target for enemy air attack. The greater number of planes also complicated air traffic control at the base among the division's regiments. This problem was particularly acute when several regiments arrived simultaneously from a combat mission, especially when the MiGs were low on fuel.

The Organization of Ground Control Intercept and Early Detection of the Enemy

A radar service platoon kept the regiment supplied with information from radar installations during combat operations. This platoon had a staff of seventeen individuals and was equipped with one P-3 radar.

When the 17th IAP transferred from the Mukden-East airbase to the airfield at Myaogou in June 1951, its radar service platoon passed to divisional control. Its radar, now part of the division's radar net, was deployed on a small knoll 3 kilometers north of the airfield. It had the purposes of detecting enemy aircraft at longer range, detecting low-flying enemy targets, and controlling the intercept of enemy planes by our fighters. The chief of the 303rd IAD's radar service was Lieutenant Colonel Aksel'rod. Information on enemy planes and our own aircraft was immediately sent to the 303rd IAD's command post, where the general situation in the air was plotted on a table, while the regiment command posts received information on enemy planes. Plotters at the regiment command post recorded the data for the hostile radar targets on displays, but the regiments received no information regarding their own planes.

In the month of July, the radar service platoon was brought up to strength with an additional P-3A radar with its own attached crew. The P-3A radar was also deployed on the knoll 3 kilometers north of the airfield and had the same job as the first radar. The P-3A radar also became part of the division's radar net, served the IAD command post, and was under its operational control. Direction of the radar installation came directly from the command post of the 64th IAK and the command post of the 303rd IAD. One or the other radar installation was always working around the clock. Each installation operated on average for 13–14 hours in a 24-hour period.

The regiment's radar facilities increased the division's capabilities to detect approaching enemy aircraft, and their location atop the knoll facilitated the detection of low-flying radar targets. Targets flying at an altitude of 3,500 to 5,000 meters showed up on the radar at a range of 100–150 kilometers, while targets flying at altitudes of 8,000–12,000 meters became visible at a range of 180–240 kilometers. Operating both day and night, the radar prevented the undetected approach of enemy aircraft.

On 9 August 1951, by order of the division commander, the radar service platoon with its P-3 and P-3A radars moved into North Korea to a location 8 kilometers north-west of the North Korean town of Pakchon. Here the radar stations became part of the 64th IAK's radar net. They had the same basic tasks as they had performed at Myaogou for the division: detecting enemy planes, GCI functions, and notifying anti-aircraft artillery units on the approach of enemy aircraft to defended targets.

For a more complete picture of the situation in the air, two auxiliary control points were organized on the territory of North Korea for our fighter jets, one 7 kilometers north of Pakchon, the other north-west of Pyongyang. The division's system of radar detection included the following:

Two radars and a visual observation post in the vicinity of Fujo-ri (Auxiliary Control Point No. 1)
Two radars and a visual observation post in the area of Pakchon (Auxiliary Control Point No. 2)
Radars around the airfield at Myaogou for detecting low-flying targets
Long-range Lida-type radars of the Chinese Air Force
Short-range radars and visual observation posts at the bases of the IAK.[5]

The corps and division command posts, as well as the Auxiliary Control Points No. 1 and No. 2, directed the fighters in the air through the information from the radar-technical service. The IAK's main command post was located in Fujo-ri, while the reserve command post was back in Antung. The head of the auxiliary control points was Hero of the Soviet Union Major V.G. Seregin, the 303rd IAD's navigator, who had earned the exalted title of Hero back in February 1945 and had finished with sixteen victories against the Germans. He reported on the situation in the air, where and with what forces the enemy was operating, and directed the regimental fighter groups toward these radar targets. The GCI stations, which were located on Korean territory, called all the enemy's fighters and fighter-bombers 'little ones', and the B–29 bombers 'big ones'. So the fighter pilots might hear something like: 'In such and such area up to eighty "little ones" are operating.' All the pilots of the 303rd IAD were quite familiar with the voice of their division navigator, and were very grateful for his precise and timely information on the aerial situation. The division command posts were in control at the airfields during launches and the landings.

To facilitate control over the planes while in the air, the 64th IAK divided its area of coverage into three zones, centered on Antung, Anju, and Pyongyang respectively. Each zone was supported by GCI stations within that zone. Zone No. 1 (Antung) had GCI facilities in the areas of Antung and Sonchon. Zone No. 2 (Anju) had GCI stations in the area of Pakchon. Zone No. 3 (Pyongyang) had its GCI stations in the vicinity of Fujo-ri.

The reference numbers for the call signs of the GCI radar sets consisted of two digits: the first digit indicated the zone number, while the second digit revealed the numerical designation of the GCI radar station within the zone. Each zone itself was divided into four sectors, which were numbered by their position relative to an orientation point according to the hour hand of the clock.

Every defended target in each zone had its own unique reference number. For example, the reference number for the section of the railroad lying between Antung and Charyongwan had the reference 'Zone 11'. The primary area of responsibility, the crossing of the Yalu River near Antung and the airfield complex at Antung, had the reference number 'Zone 1'.

The radar station operators determined a potential target's plane type, number, and flight altitude to within 700 meters by the nature of the echo return on the radar screen. One operator could control up to nine targets on various azimuths. Plotters competently plotted up to nine moving targets simultaneously and helped the operators understand the situation in the air. The controllers used the information from the radar to guide their fighters to intercept the enemy aircraft. Successful conduct of the aerial operation depended on the work of the radar service, especially on the operators and plotters; their information on the enemy air groups was transmitted to the command post, and allowed the aviation commander to figure out the enemy's plans.

Chapter Four

An Auspicious Debut

The First Success of the 17th IAP

Thus, by June 1951 the 17th IAP was ready for combat operations. Before the regiment's return to combat, the Political Department held a meeting. With the aim of raising combat spirit, the squadron commanders conducted a reading and group discussion of Comrade Stalin's speech by radio on 3 July 1941.[1] The pilots began making familiarization flights over the area of combat operations, which counted as combat missions.

The regiment's pilots carried out their first combat sortie from the airfield at Myaogou on 14 June. Before this, they had been tested on their knowledge of the area of combat operations out to a radius of 250 kilometers, the staging zone, and of the GCI procedures.

The situation on the Korean fronts at this time was strained. Fierce ground fighting had been occurring on the eastern sector of the front since mid-May, when the NKPA and CPV forces had launched a major offensive that quickly threatened the capture of Seoul. The American and UN forces reacted with a major counter-offensive at a time when the Communist forces were badly worn down and running low on supplies. Hampered by supply difficulties and the problems of getting reinforcements to the front under almost constant enemy air attacks, the Communist forces had buckled and been driven back beyond the 38th Parallel to a line north-west of Munsan, south of Kumhwa. There, bitter fighting continued until July 9, as the CPV committed major reserves to bring the UN offensive to a halt.

The failure of this operation led the leadership of the PDRK and the PRC to the conclusion that it would be impossible to win the war, and with the agreement of the USSR, truce negotiations between the warring sides began in Kaesong in July 1951. These negotiations continued for a long two years, and were periodically accompanied by major battles on the ground, and importantly, by a fierce struggle in the air.

It was just at this time that the command of the United States' Fifth Air Force started to launch systematic and massed attacks in the depths of North Korean territory, in order to cut off the supply to the front-line units of everything necessary for conducting combat operations: ammunition, food, and reinforcements. The primary targets of the American Air Force became the railroad stations, roads, bridges, and crossings over the numerous rivers and mountain passes. Many of these road and rail bridges were located in the area of Anju and the small towns surrounding it. Another major supply network was the area lying between Antung (PRC) and Sinuiju (PDRK), where there were several strategically important bridges connecting China with North Korea, over which flowed most of the forces and necessary supplies for the CPV and NKPA forces.

Another target for air strikes from the UN air forces was the network of hydro-electrical stations lying on the Yalu River, which supplied electricity to all of north-east China and North Korea. These immense hydro-electrical installations, built by the Japanese in the mountains of North Korea, represented one of the major industrial values in Asia, and one of the largest electrical energy networks in the world. Four major energy systems at Fusen, Choshin, Kyosen, and Suiho, together with many smaller local systems, had been built over the course of twenty years. The four major systems' designed production capacity was approximately 1,650,000 kilowatts.[2] The most important hydro-electrical installation in Korea was the Suiho Hydro-electrical Station, which was situated on the Yalu River about 50 kilometers north of Antung.

Major air battles developed in the sky over these targets, which were constantly subject to attack by the UN air forces and thus required the protection of the 64th IAK. The month of June 1951 brought hot days with it for the pilots of the 303rd IAD and its neighboring 324th IAD – almost every day, aerial battles erupted in the aforementioned areas.

As already mentioned above, the first to enter the fighting were the pilots of the 18th GIAP, who opened the scoring of the 303rd IAD with victories over enemy planes on 1 June. The 523rd IAP flew its first combat mission on 2 June with eight planes. Here's what one of its participants, the assistant commander of the regiment for aerial gunnery service, G.U. Okhai, recalled of the mission in an interview with the authors:

The leader was the regiment commander, A.N. Karasev, and I was his wingman. Karasev was a calm, sober-minded, quiet, hardworking man who respected the personnel serving under him. When we arrived in China, Karasev was appointed commander of our 523rd IAP, while I was chief of the aerial gunnery service and often flew as Karasev's wingman. He led and directed the group skillfully, loved to fly, and courageously took on enemy air groups even when outnumbered. He conducted the post-flight briefings, not overlooking even the smallest details, commenting so that the element or flight might work more effectively in action.

We took off. There was a solid layer of clouds at an altitude of 10,000 meters; we flew at an altitude of 9,000 meters. The command post contacted us by radio: 'Four groups of Sabres are heading right for you,' and when the command post announced that 30–40 kilometers remained until the encounter, the leader gave the order 'Lock' (drop the external fuel tanks) and we began to accelerate from 700 km/hr up to 900–1,000 km/hr. In the region of Anju (this area had the code name 'Sausage'), we met with the enemy, who were also just jettisoning their own drop tanks; the enemy was at a higher altitude, and their tanks might strike our planes.

They were four groups of eight Sabres – a total of thirty-two planes, or four planes to our one. At this point the battle began. We banked our MiGs towards them, and they turned to meet us. Since there were more of them, we performed a vertical maneuver, in which the MiG was better than the Sabre. The battle climbed to an altitude of 10,000 meters, and the sharp change in altitude changed the temperature in the cockpit. As the engagement continued, the wild maneuvering broke our formation down into elements and even single planes. The fighting ended at the command of the leader, and each pilot or element departed the area at his own discretion given his situation at the moment the order went out.

As we were returning to base, some alone, more rarely as a pair that had joined up along the way, we could now feel that we were soaked with sweat. At the debriefing I, as chief of aerial gunnery service, said that in this action, we were being tested by the Americans on our ability to fight. They had really chased us around, but we had passed the test, and everyone had returned to the base undamaged.

On 16 June, the full 17th IAP conducted an overflight of the entire area of combat operations. Division commander General Lobov led the Headquarters section of the 17th IAP and the 1st Squadron; his deputy commander Hero of the Soviet Union Lieutenant Kumanichkin led the 2nd Squadron, while the division navigator Hero of the Soviet Union Major Seregin headed the 3rd Squadron.

There was no encounter with the enemy, but all the same this flight made a deep impression on all the pilots. They were flying at medium altitude (6,000–8,000 meters); it was a clear day, and visibility was excellent. The group's airspeed was high, and on the ground, the damage from recent bombing attacks was not particularly noticeable. Their guns were charged and fully ready. Yet the serene and beautiful view was striking – the green forests, the towns and villages, the rivers and streams. They wondered – was there really a terrible war going on here, one that burned everything in its path, and was spilling so much blood?

On 17 June at 18:17, General Lobov again led a flight of five MiGs from the 17th IAP on a 'free hunt' for enemy planes along the Antung–Pyongyang route at an altitude of 4,000 meters. Senior Lieutenant Nikolai Sutiagin was part of this group. Again, there were no enemy encounters. However, on this day a pilot of the 18th GIAP, Lev Shchukin, shot down an F-86, but he himself was shot down in turn, catapulted from his jet, and wound up in a hospital, where he was out of action until the end of August.

The next day, at 02:36, the division commander conducted an alarm drill in the regiment. The exercise revealed many shortcomings in the response of the personnel to the alarm. If the alarm had been a real one, the regiment would have suffered great losses, and would hardly have been able to perform its combat duties. Yet not everything was so bad in the division. On this day, pilots of the 523rd IAP scored their first victories; between 09:32 and 10:00, they shot down three F-86 fighters in the Chongju–Pakchon area. Lieutenant Colonel Karasev, Captain Ponomarev, and Senior Liutenant Iakovlev were all credited with victories. To this success, it must be added that pilots in another regiment of the division, the 18th GIAP, managed to shoot down another two F-86s.

The 17th IAP experienced its first combat on 19 June against a flight of four F-86s, and in this first action, Nikolai Sutiagin's element shot down two Sabres. Here's how the events unfolded in this first dogfight for the pilots of the 17th IAP.

At 09:34 that morning, ten pilots from the 1st Aviation Squadron, under the overall command of the regiment commander Major G.I. Pulov soared into the sky on an order from the division command post. After assembling, the main group formed into the 'right stagger of flights' formation, with about 500–600 meters of altitude between the two flights of four. Senior Lieutenant Perepelkin's element flew about 1,500 meters above the main group to serve as top cover against unexpected enemy attack.

The group was being vectored toward the enemy by the 'Arfa-1' GCI station, from which soon came the order to assume a heading of 150° to Zone No. 11 (a section of the Antung–Charyongwan railroad). Shortly thereafter, group leader Major Pulov gave the order to drop the wing tanks and accelerate to 900 km/hr, while climbing to an altitude of 7,500 meters. The enemy was somewhere nearby, so the group wanted to gain both speed and altitude before the combat erupted. A minute after dropping the tanks, Pulov's wingman, Senior Lieutenant Miroshnichenko spotted an F-86 element approaching at a lower altitude on a meeting course at high speed; with a chandelle maneuver, it began to move onto the tail of our group, which Miroshnichenko immediately reported to Major Pulov.

Pulov reacted to the threat with a climbing turn to the left toward some clouds, so the squadron arranged itself into a column of flights. At the regiment commander's instruction, Senior Lieutenant Perepelkin's element remained concealed above some clouds, 1,000 meters higher than the main group.

While in the turn Nikolai Sutiagin, who was 150–100 meters below the group, suddenly observed an F-86 element that was trying to swing behind Captain Artemchenko's element. He gave a warning over the radio: 'Two F-86s, behind and to the lower left,' while simultaneously making a sharp, diving turn to the left to set up a diving pass on this Sabre pair. He immediately issued a command to his wingman: 'Cover me, I'm attacking!' At this moment, a second element of F-86s popped out from behind some clouds and attacked Captain Artemchenko, who maneuvered against them. These enemy fighters soon departed for the sea in a dive.

Senior Lieutenant Sutiagin with his wingman Senior Lieutenant Shulev pursued the targeted Sabre element into oblique loops, and in the second oblique loop, Nikolai Sutiagin emerged on the tail of the wingman's Sabre and fired two bursts, the first of which passed in front of the target, the second behind it. The F-86 element's leader and his wingman exited the loop into a 70° dive and began to flee in the direction of the sea. Sutiagin with his wingman continued to pursue the adversary. Deftly using his speed brakes, Nikolai closed to within 100 meters of the target and fired a long burst at the enemy wingman, whose plane burst into flames. After yawing first to the right, then to the left, the Sabre went into an unrecoverable dive and fell to the earth with an explosion in the area of Sonchon.

Vasilii Shulev, following his leader, opened fire on the element leader from a range of 500 meters. While pursuing and firing at the adversary at an altitude of 2,000 meters, a canopy latch failed and a portion of Senior Lieutenant Shulev's cockpit canopy broke off. He immediately terminated the pursuit and exited the combat with a chandelle to the left. Prior to the moment of the canopy's failure, the enemy was in a dive at a leftward pitch. Then Shulev lost sight of him. Senior Lieutenant Shulev did see the falling, burning plane of the F-86 element's wingman, which he stated in his report once back on the ground.

Senior Lieutenant Perepelkin, who was above the clouds at an altitude of 8,500 meters in this area, encountered four F-86 Sabres and evaded them with a climbing spiral to the left. The pursuing enemy planes could not keep up with the MiGs in this climb, and began to lag behind. Having reached an altitude of 13,000 meters, the enemy dived away to the south-west. Perepelkin opted not to pursue.[3]

In this action, Senior Lieutenant Sutiagin expended all his ammunition, while Senior Lieutenant Shulev had only a few shells remaining. The rest of our pilots never had an opportunity to fire.

On the whole, the first dogfight for the pilots of the 17th IAP was quite successful. The group had managed to drive the American fighters out of the defended area without any particular difficulties, while shooting down two of them (the North Korean army found debris from two F-86 Sabres). Thus concluded the first aerial duel in the skies over Korea for the pilots of the 17th IAP; they could be proud of this fight, which they had handled competently and in an organized fashion.

First Lieutenant Robert H. Laler from the 4th Fighter Wing's 336th Fighter Squadron became the first American to be shot down by Nikolai Sutiagin. Laler managed to eject from his burning plane, but was taken prisoner on the ground. Wingman Vasilii Shulev's victim is still unknown, but the Americans acknowledge the loss of two of their F-86A-5 fighters (No. 49-1298 and No. 49-1171) from the 336th Fighter Squadron in this action. A search team returned to the 17th IAP with debris from the wreckage of a downed American Sabre and fragments of the pilot's flight map.

For this successful combat action, N. Sutiagin was written up for the Order of the Red Banner, but he didn't receive it. Incidentally, this was the case as well with many other decorations, for which he was later recommended. It is true, however, that for this, his first successful combat, on 19 June the deputy political commander of the regiment sent a petition to the division's Political Department to remove the Party reprimand from Sutiagin's record. The political apparatus also organized talks by Nikolai Sutiagin and Vasilii Shulev, in which they shared their successful experience against the F-86 Sabre with the rest of the pilots.

At the request of the command, Senior Lieutenant Sutiagin also prepared and delivered a lecture on the theme, 'On the MiG-15's Fire and Maneuver Advantages and the Best Ways to Attack Enemy Fighters and Fighter Bombers'. He presented an analysis of the shortcomings in aerial gunnery displayed thus far and especially the disadvantages of long-range firing. In particular, Sutiagin noted the following problems in the first actions:

Wingmen were leaving their leaders without cover while pursuing crippled enemy aircraft;

The drop tanks were being released prematurely, which reduced the time available for dogfights;

Some pilots were returning with just 25–30 liters of fuel remaining. For example, the engine of Senior Lieutenant Kramarenko's plane had died directly upon landing.

After the two fatal air crashes and the embarrassing performance on its first combat mission from the Mukden airbase in the month of April, the victory of the 1st Aviation Squadron's pilots in their very first combat went far to raise morale and gave a psychological boost to the 17th IAP's entire flight staff. The first combat victories inspired confidence among the pilots in the superiority of the Soviet jet fighters over the enemy's planes, and to a considerable degree foretold their successful combat operations in the future.

The particular value of these first victories lay in the fact that to shoot down a Sabre in a dive was considered a difficult task. Owing to its greater weight, the Sabre was capable of separating from a MiG in a dive. Both the MiG-15 and the F-86 were capable of reaching supersonic speeds in a dive. However, at speeds greater than Mach .86, noticeable buffeting shook the MiG-15, which threw off a pilot's aim, and at speeds of Mach .93, the nose would become heavy and the MiG could depart into a spin.

A Successful String – Three Combats, Three Victories!

Meanwhile, combat operations continued: on 21 June, the division commander General Lobov led fifteen MiGs from the 17th IAP on a 'free hunt', but there were no contacts with the enemy. However, on 22 June, pilots of the 17th IAP conducted three combat missions, and clashed with the enemy on all three. Nikolai Sutiagin participated in two of these missions and became involved in two dogfights, in which he shot down two Sabres. So, in his first three combats, Sutiagin shot down three enemy fighters!

On the morning of 22 June at 08:35, the first regimental launch occurred at an order from the corps command post, in order to repel an attack of enemy planes on the important strategic bridge across the Yalu River. However, just a bit earlier, pilots of the 176th GIAP of the neighboring 324th IAD had received the very same order, and six MiGs from its 3rd Aviation Squadron had launched under the command of Captain Suchkov. Soon Suchkov's group encountered a group of Sabres twice its size. His group split into elements and tangled with the Sabres in combat.

Senior Lieutenant A.A. Plitkin's element, with Senior Lieutenant B.A. Obraztsov flying as wingman, attacked one pair of Sabres, and in the course of maneuvering, the wingman Boris Obraztsov wound up in a more advantageous position relative to the Sabres. Spotting this, Plitkin gave Obraztsov the command: 'Take the lead and attack. I will cover you.' He then took the wingman position himself. Obraztsov skillfully attacked the Sabre element, and from close range shot down the wingman's Sabre.

Unexpectedly, Plitkin's element was jumped from behind by a different pair of Sabres, and Plitkin himself came under attack. Fifty-caliber fire from a

Sabre's machine guns tore into his plane, which went out of control, so at an altitude of 5,000–6,000 meters, Anatolii Plitkin punched out of his stricken plane.

It was at this moment that ten MiGs from the 17th IAP's 1st Aviation Squadron led by Major G.I. Pulov reached the area of combat and went directly into the attack. Arriving over the area of the bridge, Senior Lieutenant Malunov spotted four F-86 fighters, low and to the left, angling toward them. He immediately reported this to the group leader.

Pulov turned his squadron toward the enemy, while also climbing for altitude. The F-86 flight, sweeping past Pulov's lead flight, began to swing around onto the tail of Captain Artemchenko's trailing flight, which was 800–1,000 meters behind and 200–300 meters above Pulov's flight. Artemchenko, while following Pulov in the left turn, caught sight of two F-86s diving on him from above and to his right. He immediately banked sharply right toward the attackers and parried the attack; the Sabre pilots, realizing that the attack had failed, continued their dive at high speed and departed to the south-west.

At this moment, Senior Lieutenant Nikolai Sutiagin with his wingman Senior Lieutenant Vasilii Shulev, located to the left of Captain Artemchenko, spotted a different flight of Sabres that was trying to latch onto their tail. Realizing the threat, Nikolai instantly performing a sharp turn to the left, dropped in behind the trailing F-86 pair and began to pursue them in a 50–60° dive. Closing to a distance of 500–600 meters, Sutiagin fired a long burst at the wingman's Sabre, while his wingman Vasilii Shulev fired a burst at the lead F-86. The wingman's F-86, shuddering from the hits of Nikolai's cannon shells, listed to the left and fell toward the earth. The F-86 leader, catching sight of Shulev's tracers streaking past his plane, pulled his plane into an oblique loop. Nikolai Sutiagin began to pursue this Sabre, and at the high point of the loop drew to within 200 meters of the target and opened fire. Coming out of the loop, he discovered another pair of F-86s on his tail, and immediately yanked his stick into his belly, but the MiG stalled and fell into a spin. Pulling out of the spin, Sutiagin's plane was nevertheless fired upon by another element of Sabres. Apparently this was the other element from the Sabre flight that Nikolai and his wingman had attacked, which they had lost from view when attacking the first pair of Sabres.

Sutiagin hauled his plane out of its dive and went into a zoom climb. Meanwhile, hurrying to his aid, wingman Shulev pounced on the Sabres now pursuing his leader, and fired a burst at the lead F-86. At almost the same moment, Shulev spotted a stream of tracers to his left. Looking back over his left shoulder, he discovered an element of F-86 fighters, their noses twinkling with the fire from the .50 caliber machine guns. Shulev hauled his plane around sharply to the right into the enemy's attack, while radioing to his leader, 'They're attacking; I'm alone!' Then, having lost sight of both his leader and the enemy, he climbed away and headed alone back to the assembly area.

Nikolai also flew back to the assembly area, and was soon on the ground back at the base. In the dogfight, neither Sutiagin nor his wingman Shulev had observed the enemy planes going down. However, the developed S-13 gun camera film footage in the regimental laboratory confirmed the downing of two F-86 planes by Senior Lieutenant Sutiagin. Both victories were also confirmed on the ground by North Korean troops.

In the after-action analysis, it was observed that the Sabre element's surprise attack succeeded only because Senior Lieutenant Shulev was preoccupied with his attack on the leading F-86 of the first element, forgetting about his immediate responsibilities as wingman. Only when the two Sabres of the second element had fired upon him did Shulev warn Senior Lieutenant Sutiagin about them. Sutiagin, after pulling his plane out of the spin was again attacked by this same pair of Sabres, but through a steep climb he had managed to separate from it.

The quantitative results of this side were in the favor of the Soviet pilots. However, the next time, a small number of American fighters managed to tie up the MiGs in combat, thereby giving their fighter–bombers the opportunity to attack their ground targets unmolested.

On 25 June in the middle of the day, the American command tried to attack in the region of Anju with eight B-29 bombers, but the timely approach of eighteen MiGs from the 303rd IAD under the command of Guards Lieutenant Colonel Kumanichkin disrupted their plans. Major Ivanov took off next with a second group of six MiGs to reinforce Kumanichkin's group. However, Ivanov's squadron failed to carry out its assignment, having dropped their external fuel tanks prematurely, and his small group became scattered without encountering the enemy.

For his incompetent actions, Major Ivanov was removed from command of the 2nd Aviation Squadron, and on 5 July he was sent to the city of Anshan, where he was appointed as an advisor to a Chinese aviation regiment. The 523rd IAP's Captain M.S. Ponomarev, a veteran of the Second World War with three victories to his credit against the Germans and who would ultimately score ten more victories over Korea, was appointed to replace Ivanov on 26 June, and took over the position on 17 July. Later Major Ivanov was returned to the roster of the 17th IAP, but he was still considered on assignment elsewhere and remained in Anshan.

At the time of his arrival in the 17th IAP, Captain Ponomarev already had two victories to his credit, which he had scored on 18 and 24 June 1951. He was, by the testimony of those who served alongside him, an exceptionally bold, competent, and determined commander. With his arrival, the 2nd Aviation Squadron heartened up, and its fortunes took a turn for the better.

On this same 25 June, when Major Ivanov's group had failed so badly, the Party held a gathering in the regiment with the agenda 'The Tasks of Communists in the Unit's Combat Operations'. In addition to resolving to create a 'board of honor' to publicize the achievements of the regiment's top-scoring pilots, the Party organization also called upon Sutiagin to conduct discussions with his fellow pilots in the regiment on the subject 'Tactical Methods in Aerial Combat with American Fighters'.[4]

By the 303rd IAD commander's Order No. 43 dated 25 June, a search team of five men was created. Its assignment was to obtain confirmation of downed enemy planes from local North Korean authorities. The team was provided with a GAZ-63 truck and driver and a P-100 radio with a radio operator.

The Regiment's First Combat Loss

On 26 June, the Americans again sent four B-29 bombers to the region of Anju, under the cover of sixteen F-86 Sabres. On this day, the pilots of the 64th IAK had two clashes with the enemy.

Pilots of the 17th IAP were the first to take off to intercept the enemy's planes: at 13:05, eight MiGs of the 1st Squadron lifted off the runway under the command of Captain Artemchenko, and three minutes later, two flights of six MiGs each from the 2nd and 3rd Aviation Squadrons roared off the runway, led by Captains I.P. Mishakin and M.N. Shcherbakov. Once in the air, the division's command post gave the order: 'Everyone head for the area of Anju', and kept the group updated on the situation in the air.

At 13:26 at an altitude of 11,500–12,000 meters, Captain Artemchenko spotted six F-86s passing them on an opposite heading at the same altitude, trying to get behind his flight. He gave the order to Senior Lieutenant Sutiagin: 'Attack the enemy', while Artemchenko himself continued to climb. Nikolai Sutiagin, swinging around to the left, attacked the flight of six F-86s. The enemy sharply reversed heading and began to pass beneath Sutiagin's flight, drawing our fighters into a turning fight. At this time the group leader Captain Artemchenko, while swinging around to his left, caught sight of eight more F-86s Sabres ahead, below and to the left, moving in a column of flights, with about 2 kilometers separating the two flights. Artemchenko immediately turned to intercept this group and attacked. One flight of Sabres evaded the attack with a snap roll and dived away towards the sea, while the second flight maneuvered onto the tail of Captain Artemchenko's flight. His wingman Senior Lieutenant Miroshnichenko radioed a warning about the enemy flight now tailing them. Artemchenko responded with a climbing spiral to the left. By the third turn around the spiral, the enemy aircraft were well below Captain Artemchenko's flight, unable to match the MiGs' rate of climb. Realizing that they could not catch the MiGs and seeing their unfavorable position, the Sabres flipped over and dived away, exiting the battle.

Simultaneously, the flight of six Sabres attacked by Senior Lieutenant Sutiagin found itself in a difficult situation. After reversing course, the Sabres swung into a column of elements. Sutiagin gave an order to Senior Lieutenant Bychkov's element to cover his attack, while he himself moved to attack the second pair of Sabres. At this moment his wingman Senior Lieutenant Shulev discovered a pair of Sabres at a lower altitude behind them and to the left, which he reported to his leader. Nikolai broke off his approach on the pair that he was stalking, and banking around, he attacked the closing element of F-86s from behind and to their right. Closing to within a range of 200–250 meters, he opened fire on the lead Sabre. Vasilii Shulev supported the attack and also opened fire at a range of 300–400 meters.

While chasing the enemy planes, Senior Lieutenant Shulev began to surge past Sutiagin's plane, because he had not deployed his speed brakes, and was forced to break off the attack with a climbing turn to the right. Senior Lieutenant Sutiagin followed him in the turn.

However, the combat didn't finish with this: Captain Mishakin's flight of six MiGs, flying on a southerly heading at an altitude of 12,000 meters, came upon four B-29 bombers in front and below him to his right, covered by up to twenty F-84 and F-86 fighters, moving on an opposite heading at an altitude of 6,000 meters. The enemy bombers were in a combat box formation; the covering fighters were at the same altitude as the bombers, swinging from the left to the right. Captain Mishakin called over the radio: 'I see the enemy bombers', then manuevered with his flight of Polianichko, Fokin and Agranovich to set up for a shallow diving run on the bombers from behind. At the moment when he started his pass on the bombers, Captain Mishakin's flight was attacked from below and to the right by an F-86 element arriving from the direction of the sea. Mishakin and his wingman Polianichko banked sharply left and away from the attack and went into a climbing spiral, after which he lost sight of the enemy group.

Senior Lieutenant Fokin with his wingman Senior Lieutenant Agranovich pressed the attack on the B-29s. Having closed to within a distance of 1,000 meters to the tail-end B-29, Fokin fired two long bursts from behind. At this moment, his wingman Agranovich's MiG streaked past Senior Lieutenant Fokin and broke sharply upwards and away in a chandelle to the left. Upon pulling out of his attacking pass, Fokin was jumped by a pair of Sabres from behind and to the right, which he evaded with a climbing turn to the right, but his wingman Evgenii Agranovich was no longer with him. Agranovich's MiG had pulled up directly in front of a pair of F–84 Thunderjets from the bombers' immediate escort, which riddled his jet with point-blank fire. There was nothing anyone could do for him, and as a result of the attack his MiG–15bis No. 0415340 burst into flames and fell in an area about 17 kilometers south-west of Uiju. Senior Lieutenant Agranovich, who was married and had a four-year-old daughter, was killed.

Captain Morozov's element was attacked by eight F–86 Sabres from below and to the right from the direction of the sea. Morozov turned into the attack of the enemy fighters, which responded by diving away to the right in a retreat toward the sea on the same course as the bombers. Captain Morozov started to pursue them, but at this moment received an order from the corps command post: 'Don't cross the coastline.' Immediately there followed an order from the division command post: 'Everyone is to exit the battle in an organized fashion.' Morozov broke off his pursuit and headed back to his airfield.

Captain Shcherbakov's group of six planes, located in the area of Anju at an altitude of 9,000 meters, also discovered ten F–86 Sabres, flying at lower altitude on a reverse heading in a line abreast formation of two flights, with one element located 400–600 meters higher than the rest of the formation. Shcherbakov went for the enemy in a climbing left turn. Having spotted our MiGs, the Sabre group turned sharply into the attack, resulting in a head-on pass. Captain Shcherbakov pulled out of the pass into a climbing, left-hand spiral. One F–86 flight tried to follow Shcherbakov's group, while the second flight of Sabres departed downwards. The pursuing flight of Sabres could not catch Captain Shcherbakov in the climb, and it eventually rolled over and dived away toward the sea. After this brief clash, Shcherbakov's group also returned to base.

Thus concluded this battle, in which the regiment suffered its first combat loss. After the action, the pilots reported that they had shot down three enemy planes: Senior Lieutenant Sutiagin and Senior Lieutenant Shulev claimed two F–86 Sabres, while Senior Lieutenant Fokin claimed one B–29.

During the post-mission debriefing, it was noted that coordination between Captain Shcherbakov's group and Captain Mishakin's group had not been established before the battle began, as a result of which Mishakin's group had been forced to go up against superior enemy forces.[5] The debriefing also established that Senior Lieutenant Fokin had popped his speed brakes with the toggle switch early in the engagement and had forgotten to retract them, which meant for a prolonged period of time he had been flying and dogfighting with his speed brakes deployed. It would have been more correct, had he needed to bleed off airspeed, to use the button on the pilot's control stick to deploy the speed brakes, and not the toggle switch. With Fokin slowed by his speed brakes,

Senior Lieutenant Agranovich had swept past him and come under the withering fire of enemy fighters.

The Soviet pilots had managed to frustrate the attack of the Superfortresses on Anju, but because of poor guidance from the auxiliary control point (the fighters had been redirected several times from one area to another), the MiGs entered the battle in uncoordinated groups, and failed to inflict great damage on the enemy. Forty-four enemy F-80, F-84, and F-86 fighters and four B-29 bombers participated in this action, against only twenty of our fighters.

According to information from North Korean authorities, two F-86 Sabres fell in the area of Anju, which were credited to the personal scores of Senior Lieutenant Sutiagin and Senior Lieutenant Shulev. Senior Lieutenant Fokin's S-13 gun camera footage preliminarily confirmed the downing of one B-29. Fokin fired at the bomber from a distance of 860 meters with a target aspect of 0/4, and six shell bursts were noted on the B-29 in his gun camera footage. After an analysis of the gun camera film, Senior Lieutenant Fokin was only given credit for damaging the B-29. A little later, confirmation arrived that during this sortie, Senior Lieutenant Agranovich had nevertheless destroyed one F-80, which was trying to attack his element leader.

The death of Evgenii Agranovich strongly shook the regiment staff. It was recognition that this was war, and that not everyone would return from this assignment. As has now become known, Agranovich was shot down by a pair of F-84 Thunderjets, piloted by Captain Harry L. Underwood and First Lieutenant Arthur E. Oligher from the 182nd Squadron of the 136th Fighter Bomber Wing.

The Americans do not confirm the loss of a B-29 on this mission, so most likely, Senior Lieutenant Fokin had only damaged the bomber and it had managed to get back to its base, but was then out of action for some time for repairs. There is confirmation of Evgenii Agranovich's victory, since the Americans acknowledge the loss on this day and time of F-80C No. 49-875 from the 35th Squadron of the 8th Fighter Bomber Wing. Its pilot First Lieutenant Bob A. Lauterbach also failed to return from this battle.

The Americans have not acknowledged the loss of their Sabres in this battle. However, later they announced that on this day, one F-86A (No. 49-1281) from the 4th Fighter Wing's 334th Aviation Squadron had made a crash landing; this plane was being piloted by none other than the commander of this Sabre squadron, Lieutenant Colonel Glenn Eagleston, who escaped with only slight wounds. One can assume that the cause of this crash landing was the damage it had received in the course of a clash with the MiGs on this day, something the Americans still aren't very willing to acknowledge.

There were no losses in the neighboring units in these battles. On this same day, but a little later, between 13:30 and 14:00, pilots of the 1st Aviation

Squadron of the 523rd IAP also had a successful engagement with a group of twelve Sabres, in which Senior Lieutenant G.T. Shatalov downed one Sabre. One can assume that it was either Sutiagin or Shatalov who was the 'culprit' behind Lieutenant Colonel Eagleston's crash landing.

The day after this successful engagement on 26 June, the stain of the Party reprimand on Nikolai Sutiagin's record was removed. This was the first official 'pat on the back' for four victories!

To mark the opening of the regiment's combat score, the regiment commander organized a collective dinner, which the division commander attended. General Lobov wished the pilots of the regiment further successes in their combat work and in enhancing the unit's combat traditions.

A former pilot of the 3rd Aviation Squadron, A.N. Nikolaev, recalls:

> When Nikolai Sutiagin scored his first victories, and he was the first in the regiment to open the combat scoring, one evening after the day's operations, a celebratory dinner for all the regiment's pilots was arranged in the pilots' mess hall. But after all the congratulatory toasts were over, Vasilii Shulev, Sutiagin's wingman and the 1st Aviation Squadron's deputy commander for political affairs, rose and proposed a toast in honor of the fallen pilot Evgenii Agranovich. General Lobov, who was attending the dinner, sharply rejected this proposal, declaring that now was not the time to think about the dead, but instead to think about how to do things in the future, so that we would lose no more men. This episode has been engraved in my memory for the rest of my life.

Immediately after 26 June, the weather turned bad over the territory of North Korea, and for all practical purposes shut down all aerial operations until 6 July, when the weather finally cleared. The pilots of the 17th IAP took off twice to intercept enemy planes on 28 and 30 June, but failed to find the enemy.

Wingtip to Wingtip

Pilots of the 17th IAP didn't conduct their first combat mission in the month of July until 5 July, when at 18:00, a group of four MiG-15s led by Major Pulov took off for a routine sweep of the area of combat operations. They didn't run into any enemy aircraft, but on their way back to base, they were fired upon by their own anti-aircraft artillery. Fortunately, there was no damage.

On 6 July, the 18th GIAP was brought back from Antung to the airfield at Myaogou. The regiment's pilots were given a rest from 6 July to 15 July, as they were kept on a low level of alert, required only to be ready for a sortie within one hour of an alarm. Then the pilots were given another week of rest between 22 and 28 July, when air operations were grounded by more bad weather. Just prior to their return to Myaogou, the pilots of the 18th GIAP had tangled with a group of thirty F-86 Sabres and scored a convincing victory, downing three Sabres without any losses of their own. After this action, the Guards pilots went on their short break, granted to them by the division command, with a clear conscience.

The return of the 18th GIAP to Myaogou also brought a shuffling of assignments within the 17th IAP. On 8 July, Senior Lieutenant Shulev became the wingman to the squadron commander Captain Artemchenko, while Nikolai Sutiagin began to fly with Senior Lieutenant Nikolai Savchenko, who had recently transferred into the 17th IAP from the 18th GIAP.

It was on 8 July 1951 that our allies – pilots of the Chinese and North Korean Joint Air Army – began combat operations, in the form of the 4th Chinese IAD. Since the Chinese pilots had logged relatively few hours in the cockpit of the MiG-15 and had little combat experience, they were still not a serious force in this war, and made easy targets for the American pilots. Therefore, all missions flown by the Chinese pilots were covered by Soviet pilots, who were supposed to protect the Chinese combat formations from Sabre attack.

Pilots of the 523rd IAP were the first to receive the order to provide cover for a mission by pilots of the Chinese 4th IAD. They carried out the task, but in the process they were jumped by sixteen F-86 Sabres and became engaged in an unequal battle. Only a hastily arriving group of twenty-six planes from the 17th IAP quickly forced the Sabres to break off combat. However, before Major Pulov's group arrived, the 523rd IAP group under the command of Hero of the Soviet Union Major N.N. Danilenko had lost two planes and one pilot: the most severe one-day loss for the 523rd IAP in this war.

On the next day, 9 July, it was now the turn for pilots of the 17th IAP to cover missions of the Chinese 4th IAD. At 09:39, ten pilots of the 1st Aviation Squadron led by Major Maslennikov roared down the runway and lifted into the sky with the task of covering the combat operations of eight planes from the Chinese 12th IAP. As the group assembled after take-off and began to climb for altitude, it was vectored to the eight-ship formation of Chinese MiGs. Having linked up with them, Major Maslennikov's group took station above and behind the Chinese group.

Following a heading of 120° on the approach to the area of Anju, Major Maslennikov's group encountered eight F-86 Sabres, approaching from the south at an altitude of 8,000 meters, six F-86s over the coastline north of the mouth of the Sonchon River, and eight more F-86s over the coastline south of the river mouth. Four more specks angling toward them from the direction of the sea indicated another arriving flight of Sabres. As a result, a group of twenty-six Sabres were confronting our group of ten MiGs.

Major Maslennikov's group tied up all the enemy's fighter groups in battle. During the action, Maslennikov spotted two flights of B-29 bombers, which were under attack by the Chinese fighters, heading out over the sea, but didn't see the results of this battle, because he had his hands full at the time against superior numbers of the enemy.

Element leader Captain Artemchenko, while covering a second flight of Chinese fighters, tangled with Sabres over the mouth of the Sonchon River. The combat became a swirling mixture of head-on passes and pursuits with a group of ten to twelve F-86s. During the action, one flight of Sabres banked right and headed towards Anju. Artemchenko went after them and intercepted them with a vertical maneuver. The enemy tried to make it a turning fight. While maneuvering, the enemy began to carry the fight in a south-westerly direction, and then began to accelerate away in a dive in the direction of the sea. Artemchenko with his wingman Senior Lieutenant Miroshnichenko, pursuing the enemy, fired from a range of 1,500 down to 1,200 meters, but he broke off the chase upon reaching the coastline and returned to the vicinity of Anju.

Senior Lieutenant Sutiagin as part of a flight in the area of Anju at an altitude of 9,500 meters came upon a flight of four F-86 Sabres just 800 meters ahead of them and to their right, flying on a parallel course and at the same altitude. The enemy, spotting our fighters, dropped their external fuel tanks and banked sharply to the left, passing beneath the formation of our fighters. Executing a zoom climb followed by a half-roll, Sutiagin began to pursue them and, closing to a distance of 600–800 meters, he opened fire on the tail-end plane in the Sabre formation, using his automatic gunsight. The enemy dived away in the direction of the sea. Ending the pursuit, Sutiagin's flight conducted a chandelle to the left and at an altitude of 8,000 meters ran into another flight of Sabres, moving across its front. The enemy, spotting the MiGs, went into a dive that Sutiagin's flight tried to follow, but because of the extreme range our pilots never fired.[6]

With this, the action came to an end, and the division command post recalled all the pilots of the 17th IAP. They had successfully escorted the pilots of the Chinese 12th IAP, tying up the enemy fighters in battle. The MiG pilots had fired a few short bursts, but the fire was not aimed and was from long range. The pilots didn't see any enemy planes going down, nor did the gun camera footage confirm any victories. Presumably, Senior Lieutenant Miroshnichenko, who finished his tour in Manchuria with six victories to his credit, damaged one F-86 in this action. It was noted by our pilots that the Chinese fighters were carrying out their mission at a low speed (600–650 km/hr) and were flying beyond the coastline.

In the future, the pilots of the 17th IAP conducted no further joint missions with the Chinese and North Korean pilots, but often Chinese units covered our own pilots' withdrawal from combat and return to base. The Chinese pilots had great combat spirit, yet they were plainly lacking in piloting skills and tactical knowledge. At first they paid little attention to coordination in battle. They seemingly flew according to the thought: 'I see a target, I'm attacking, and you go find one for yourself.' This was done without making sure they had any cover first, so they often suffered needless combat losses.

The Chinese pilots also lacked physical endurance. Once they had begun intensive combat operations, the Chinese pilots often lost consciousness during high-G maneuvers in flight. It turned out that the Chinese were feeding their pilots worse than their ground crews, basing this on the observation that 'crewmen work, while pilots … go for a ride!' Later, under pressure from their Soviet allies, they changed their attitude and began feeding their pilots as well as their supporting crews.

After the action on 9 July, the weather again turned bad. The weather cleared briefly on 11 July, but on this day, only pilots of the 324th IAD flew missions into 'MiG Alley', while the pilots of the 303rd IAD remained in reserve. On 12 July, the weather over North Korea worsened again and remained poor: calm settled over 'MiG Alley' right up to the beginning of August. There were no combat sorties by the 17th IAP from 10 July to 28 July inclusive.

However, even in these days of calm, flight operations in the vicinity of the airfields continued in the division, as pilots worked to keep their flying skills sharp and conducted mock dogfights. One of these flights in the 17th IAP almost ended in tragedy: on 13 July in the 2nd Aviation Squadron, Senior Lieutenant Gostiukhin's oxygen mask fell off while performing an oblique loop during a scheduled training flight. Easing off the throttle, he worked to put his mask back on, and lagged behind his leader Senior Lieutenant Komarov. Trying to catch back up with his leader in the dive, he gained too much airspeed and momentarily blacked out as he pulled out at the bottom of the loop. Regaining consciousness at an altitude of 2,000 meters, he attempted to bank around in a turn and discovered that his plane was vibrating heavily, so he ended the sortie and made a landing at his airfield. There it was discovered that the stress of pulling out of the dive had warped both wings on the plane; they had to be replaced. It was good that everything ended well and that the incident didn't cause any victims; however, the regiment commander gave both pilots a reprimand.

In these days of calm, a different misfortune befell the staff of the 303rd IAD: because of the rains, the quality of the drinking water turned bad and many of the division's pilots, who ignored the order to boil drinking water and to wash all raw fruits and vegetables before eating them, began to fall ill. Over the period between 5 July and 20 July, the number of cases of gastro-intestinal illnesses sharply increased in the division's regiments. The 17th IAP had nine cases, and the 18th GIAP had seven cases. The 1st Squadron of the 17th IAP, in which Nikolai Sutiagin served, was particularly hard hit with gastro-intestinal problems. This malady bypassed Sutiagin himself, but for reason of illness, by 13 July pilots Lieutenant Ivan Mikhailovich Alekhin, Lieutenant Vladimir Nikolaevich Makarov, and Senior Lieutenant Aleksei Afanas'evich Ostankov had been dropped from the roster of the 1st Aviation Squadron, and were placed under the command of General Krasovsky (that is to say, they were temporarily placed in reserve aviation regiments).

Then on 17 July, even a flight commander in the 1st Aviation Squadron, Senior Lieutenant S.S. Bychkov, took leave from the regiment for hospital treatment, where he remained until 8 September. In essence, the 1st Squadron lost four pilots at once, of which only Senior Lieutenant Bychkov eventually returned to the regiment after almost a two-month absence. The other three pilots on leave from the regiment in fact never returned to it.

Work on Errors

Taking advantage of the lull in fighting, the regiment command decided to organize a conference on flight tactics with the pilots and command staff of the regiment, in order to summarize the combat experience that the regiment had gained over the period from 17 June 1951 to 20 July 1951. The commander of the regiment himself, Major Pulov, was the first to present a report, which analyzed the initial combats. Nikolai Sutiagin also gave a report at the conference as the top-scoring pilot of the division – by this time he had already downed four Sabres. It is interesting to read his report in full, since in it Nikolai Sutiagin himself provides an objective analysis of his aerial combats, touching on both the positive and negative points.

From the report of aviation squadron deputy commander Senior Lieutenant Sutiagin:

In my presentation, I want to dwell upon the following issues:
1. The search for enemy fighters
2. The aviation squadron's combat formation
3. Aerial combat with enemy fighters and the coordination of elements and flights.

1. Modern fighters demand that one pay special attention to the search for the enemy, since success in aerial combat depends entirely on who is the first to spot the adversary; but at the present time, one must

consider the high combined speed of approach, which complicates the search for the enemy. The search for the enemy begins when the pilot is still on the ground on alert. Sitting at readiness in a cockpit, if his radio is on, the pilot is always monitoring it. Consequently, the pilot while still on the ground is receiving information from the ground vectoring stations about the enemy: where the enemy is headed; his number; and the altitude at which he is flying.

This information already increases the possibility of finding the enemy. From our previous engagements we know that the enemy sees us first. This is not just because our planes, especially in group formation, are easier to spot in the air. Consequently, having spotted us first, the enemy maneuvers into a favorable position for an attack. It is also not coincidental that in our first engagements, we didn't spot the enemy until he had already taken position behind us, and then attacked us at the moment of a turn, knowing that at this moment the vigilance in the group is reduced.

In conclusion: in order to spot the enemy first, it is necessary to assume such combat formations that will enable us to spot the enemy from a greater distance.

2. The correct arrangement of the combat formation and the proper allocation of the pilots' attention is a major assistance in the search for the enemy. The majority of our sorties on combat missions were to the area of Anju, and after assembling, the Aviation Squadron would take a heading down the coastline of 120–140°. In that case what combat formation is it necessary to assume, if we know that the morning sun is always positioned on our right, in the direction of the sea? I believe that the covering flight should fly above and to the left of the main group, on the side away from the sun, since it will be easier for the squadron commander to see the covering flight. On the return heading, the covering flight should be on the right, again opposite the sun.

[...]

Conclusion:

The combat formation of the squadron should be such that it permits coordination between the flights and easy maneuvering of the entire group.

3. Our previous aerial engagements involving the [full] Aviation Regiment demonstrate that elements have fought in isolation from other elements and flights. Accordingly, the matter of cooperation in battles has still not been worked out. But is it possible to maintain

organization in a fight? Yes, it is possible. The engagement of 26 June 1951, which featured organization and some cooperation, demonstrated this. Let me first give a contrary example: our first aerial combat. Ten planes were on the mission. The strike flight was Major Pulov's; the cover flight above and to the right was Captain Artemchenko's. I was flying in the cover flight with my wingman Senior Lieutenant Shulev. While making a left turn in the region of Sonchon, I lagged behind Artemchenko's element by 400–500 meters. In the process of making the 50–60° turn to the left, I noticed left and below an F-86 element moving onto our tail from underneath the lead flight. I gave the order: 'I'm attacking; cover me,' and made a climbing turn to the left, during which I deployed speed brakes and throttled back; at the top of the climb, I pushed over into a half-roll and dived after the F-86 element. By the second loop, we were already on the tail of the F-86s, but above them. From this higher position, I fired two short bursts at the wingman. Both bursts missed: one behind the target, the other in front of it. I decided to close the range. After pulling out of my dive, the F-86 element banked right, and then went into a climbing turn to the left. As a result of these maneuvers, the opponent lost speed, and the distance to the enemy element closed to within 200–300 meters. Noticing this, the enemy planes rolled over and went into a split-S. Deploying my speed brakes to stay inside their arc, we dived in pursuit of the F-86s in the direction of the sea at an angle of 70–75°. Closing to within a range of 150–200 meters, I opened fire at the wingman ... and the F-86 was destroyed.

Conclusion: One pair fought without cover. The strike flight should have gained altitude in the vicinity of the unfolding engagement.

A similar example comes from the second aerial combat, which occurred on 22 June 1951. In the same way, a flight of F-86s began moving onto our tail while our flight was performing a left turn. With the same maneuver, I managed to turn the tables on the enemy and to drop onto the tail of one pair of the F-86s, but in so doing I lost sight of the other pair. Spotting me on their tail, the adversary broke left and went into a dive. Following their dive, I opened fire at a range of 420 meters, and shot down the enemy wingman. At this moment, the second F-86 element jumped my element from behind. My wingman Shulev noticed this, and with an abrupt maneuver, evaded the attack and warned me by radio. But I didn't hear his call to break and began to pursue the leader in front of me, and from a superior position in a loop, opened fire at a range of 280 meters. At this moment I spotted that an F-86 pair had positioned itself on my tail. I sharply broke off my attack and fell into a spin.

Conclusion:

There was no coordination between the elements and flights in this combat, and as a result, a pair of F-86s freely and with impunity wound up on our tail.

The aerial engagement on 26 June 1951 was conducted in a more organized manner; when the enemy was spotted, squadron commander Captain Artemchenko gave me the command: '122, attack!' Before this moment I had still not seen the enemy. But as soon as I received the command, I saw the adversary below me and to my left. When I went into the attack, my airspeed began to increase quickly, and I didn't manage to fix my sights on the enemy. Exiting my pass in a climbing left turn, I spotted four F-84-x in front of me and to my left and began to follow them, but I received an alert from my wingman, 'Enemy plane below and to the left,' upon which I in fact opened fire. Both attacks were covered by Bychkov's flight.

Conclusion:

Coordination between pairs and flights is possible, and the combat on 9 July 1951 confirms this.

While engaged in aerial combat, it is necessary for the leader to pay more attention to his wingman, since the wingman himself is focused on keeping formation with the leader, and making sure the leader's tail is clear. The wingman must systematically keep watch to the rear, especially after an abrupt maneuver. For purposes of better observation, the wingman must also adhere to the rule to always be in an echeloned position relative to the leader to one side or the other, and not to fly strictly behind the leader. During combat, the wingman should periodically inform the leader that his cover is still there; this will mean that his wingman is still in position, and that there is no enemy on his tail.

Conclusion: It is possible to conduct active combat with F-86 planes in oblique loops at medium altitude; using speed brakes, it is possible to pursue an F-86 in a dive.[7]

On the whole the conference played an important role in the analysis of the regiment's initial battles and the generalization of combat experience. Similar conferences for sharing combat experience occurred as well in the other regiments, and then in the division and corps. One of the conclusions of the conference was that combat missions in the strength of only one squadron were inexpedient in view of the adversary's superiority in numbers.

The Cherished Fifth Victory

Later that month, a major engagement occurred on the afternoon of 29 July. The weather over North Korea had improved somewhat on this day, and therefore it stood out as a 'hot' one by the fierceness of the fighting. That morning, the 17th IAP conducted two combat missions to intercept enemy aircraft, but only on the second one at 11:06 did the regimental group of twenty-six pilots under the command of Major Pulov score a result against a group of forty F-86 Sabres, in which the 1st Squadron's Captain S.S. Artemchenko and Senior Lieutenant V.F. Shulev downed one Sabre each.

On the third mission of the day, the entire 17th IAP took off at a call from the division command post to intercept enemy ground attack planes. The mission began at 15:14, when Major Pulov again led twenty-four crews into the sky for the third time that day. The weather was not the most satisfactory for aerial combat, since there were multiple cloud layers at different altitudes, while the relatively clear sky between the layers is a scourge for the pilots; no one knows exactly where and when an enemy plane might pop out of the clouds.

As they gained altitude after take-off, the pilots received the following information from the division command post: 'The enemy is in the area of Unsan, up to twenty fighter-bombers at an altitude of 4,000 meters.' At this time, the 17th IAP's group was over Sinbi-to Island; having received this information, they took a heading of 110°. On the way to the indicated area, Major Pulov spotted six F-84s below and to the left of him, approaching in a stagger of flights formation.

Having evaluated the situation, Major Pulov called out: 'The enemy is below,' and with his own flight moved to attack the lead flight of F-84s, pursuing them until they disappeared in a cloud layer. At this moment, Senior Lieutenant Sutiagin attacked the second flight of F-84s; the enemy, detecting the approaching MiGs, went into a defensive wheel. Using a vertical maneuver, Nikolai Sutiagin closed on one F-84 from behind and fired two bursts at it, and then a third burst at a second F-84, which was just entering into a dive.[8]

At the same moment when Major Pulov's flight launched its attack, another flight of Thunderjets began to track his flight from behind. Senior Lieutenant Malunov, spotting the F-84 flight, attacked them in order to protect his comrades. The enemy, detecting Malunov's maneuver, also adopted a defensive wheel. Having completed one turn around the circle, the enemy planes began to flee to the south on a heading of 180° at a dive angle of 45–50°.

However, a different flight of Thunderjets again selected Major Pulov's flight as a target for their attack and began to maneuver onto its tail, but they were not allowed to reach it. Captain Artemchenko, spotting the danger to

Pulov's flight, attacked this F-84 flight and, having closed to within a range of 600 meters upon the tail-end Thunderjet in the formation, opened fire on it, after which this Thunderjet disappeared into the clouds in an angled dive. Major Pulov's element, exiting from under the attack, spotted a remaining trio of F-84s and, having maneuvered into a position to attack them, initiated a pass, but the F-84s evaded into the clouds.

Captain Shcherbakov's flight, located in the trailing strike group behind Major Pulov's group and 1,500 meters higher, spotted six F-84s below him and to the left. The Thunderjets were moving across their path in a stagger of elements and still carrying their drop tanks. Shcherbakov banked left and dived to attack the targets. The Thunderjets dropped their tanks and went into a leftward spiral, after which, shaking out into a column formation, they began to disappear into a cloud layer. Shcherbakov, pursuing the enemy group, attacked the tail-end F-84 and from a range of 700–600 meters fired a short burst. The attacked plane listed and disappeared into the clouds.

At this time, Captain Ponomarev, located in the cover group at an altitude of 7,000 meters, spotted six more F-84s flying in a stagger of elements below him and to the left. Ponomarev immediately ordered his group to bank sharply to the left, after which they went into a high side pass on the formation of Shooting Stars. The F-84 pilots noticed the MiGs knifing toward them, and banked hard left into a shallow dive on a heading that would take them east of Pyongyang. While pursuing the adversary, one F-84 suddenly reversed course into a head-on attack on Senior Lieutenant Fokin. As the planes closed, the F-84 pilot opened fire first. Fokin opened up with his cannons in return, after which he pulled his MiG into a sharp climb. Just as he started climbing, Georgii Fokin caught a glimpse of an explosion in front of him: it was the Thunderjet that he had attacked.

However, Georgii himself barely escaped destruction at the hands of his victim, since the American Thunderjet pilot had also done some accurate shooting – eight heavy-caliber slugs tore into Fokin's plane. One of them struck the ammunition, which exploded, sending fragments into Fokin's right leg. Another slug severed the aileron control cables. In severe pain, Fokin could not even transmit by radio that he was wounded. He exited the battle and nursed his damaged plane back to the base, where he successfully made a forced belly-landing. The badly wounded pilot was carefully pulled from his cockpit and immediately sent to a hospital.

Georgii Tikhonovich [Fokin] himself describes this battle:

> On 29 July we took off in full squadron strength to intercept F-80 [sic] fighter-bombers. We found them and engaged them. The weather was most unfavorable for aerial combat. The fact was that there were

several layers of clouds, and in those conditions, you could only catch the enemy in the airspace between the cloud layers. You also never knew where an enemy plane might pop out of the clouds. That's exactly what happened: an F-80 dropped out of the clouds in front of me and I immediately hammered him with my cannons until this F-80 exploded in mid-air. I hadn't yet managed to comprehend all that had just happened, when I felt my plane start to roll, and I realized that my plane was damaged. The aileron control cables had been severed. I managed to level the plane out by using the rudder pedals, and with difficulty nursed it back to my airfield. While inbound, I could feel that I had been wounded in the leg. After letting the division command post know about my situation, they allowed me to make a belly-landing with my crippled plane on the ground next to the landing strip, which I then did.

Captain Ponomarev reported observing the exploding 'F-80', but quickly refocused his concentration on pursuing another element of what he reported to be fleeing F-80 Shooting Stars. Closing to within 250–300 meters of the pair of F-84s due to his airspeed advantage out of his plane's dive, he opened fire on the wingman's plane, registering several hits. The attacked F-84 started down in a steep left-hand spiral. Pulling out of his attack, Ponomarev took up a comfortable position for attacking the leader of this element, and after approaching to within 800–700 meters of him, he fired two short bursts. However, he didn't observe the results of his shooting, since the enemy managed to dive into the clouds.

After this, Major Pulov's entire group received the order to return to base. On the ground, they tabulated the results of this action, and through the gun camera footage and the eyewitness reports of pilots, the regiment was credited with four victories, which were assigned to Captains Artemchenko and Ponomarev, and Senior Lieutenants Sutiagin and Fokin – even though confirmation for only three downed planes identified as F-80 Shooting Stars arrived from the North Korean army. This was Nikolai Sutiagin's fifth victory. He had become the first ace in his regiment and in the division!

Nevertheless, Georgii Fokin became the hero of the hour on this day. When the regiment's personnel learned about Senior Lieutenant Fokin's feat, they sent forty get-well cards to the Chienchang hospital, where he was being treated. Fokin's response, in which he wrote that he had only behaved as any other Soviet person would have done, was read out to a formation of the entire regiment. The Political Department dedicated a leaflet to Senior Lieutenant Fokin, with a description of his exploit. The command recommended him for the Order of Lenin. From the hospital, on 12 September Fokin went to convalesce in a sanatorium in the city of Dal'ny. He later returned to the regiment and continued to fight.

As usual, the American side recognized the loss of only one of its F-84E (No. 49-2339) on this day from the 154th Fighter Bomber Squadron (of the 136th Fighter Bomber Wing): its pilot, James Overstreet, was declared missing in action. It is reported that his Thunderjet exploded from its own bombs. Most likely, this coincided precisely with the head-on pass on Senior Lieutenant Fokin's MiG, but the Soviet pilot was luckier. The reported time of the F-84's loss also coincides with the time of this battle.

Then why did our Fokin and Ponomarev refer to F-80 Shooting Stars in their reports? The fact is that our pilots, in the extremely rapid flow of events during air-to-air combat in the jet age, could confuse the types of enemy fighter-bombers attacked by them. This was especially so when several groups of enemy ground attack planes of different types, including naval aviation, were simultaneously working on ground targets in the same area. On this day the Americans also acknowledge the loss of one of their F9F-2B Panthers from the VF-23 Squadron, piloted by Bruce B. Lloyd, who also went missing in action. It is very possible that one of these United States Navy planes, which are similar in the air to the F-80, fell under the attack of one of the 17th IAP's groups. Perhaps the remaining two planes claimed by the 17th IAP in this action were only damaged.

By the evening of 29 July, the weather had again turned bad and remained almost totally unsuitable for flying until the month of September. With the exception of several isolated days of decent weather, the contending air forces were virtually grounded over this period.

On 30 July by order of the regiment commander, the names of several ground crews of the 17th IAP were announced, who were the first to achieve the title 'Distinguished'. They were the crewmen of Senior Lieutenants Sutiagin, Shulev, and Kramarenko from the 1st Aviation Squadron, and of Captain Blagov from the 3rd Aviation Squadron. On 4 September, eight more crews were added to this list.

The following men were members of Nikolai Sutiagin's crew (according to information for 16 May 1951):

Technician – Warrant Officer Innokentii Mikhailovich Kuroptev;
Driver – Sergeant Vasilii Grigor'evich Kichigin;
Armorer – Warrant Officer Nikolai Nikitovich Kaverin.

The technician for Sutiagin's MiG-15bis No. 122, Warrant Officer I.M. Kuroptev, serviced the airplane before more than 150 combat sorties of Captain

Sutiagin, which he completed without a single mechanical or equipment failure. Kuroptev was recognized as the best aircraft technician in the regiment.

During combats, there were practically no failures with his MiG's cannons, with the exception of one instance, when in the middle of a large dogfight on 7 November 1951 involving twenty-four MiG-15s and thirty F-86s, now Captain Sutiagin's cannons began firing spontaneously. So he withdrew from the combat, albeit while remaining in the engagement area until its conclusion. It was later discovered that his trigger button had a defective switch.

In August 1951

During the month of August, N. Sutiagin conducted twelve combat sorties to cover the railroad bridge at Singisiu and the Antung airbase complex, and to repel the ground attack strikes of the enemy aviation. In the process, he became engaged in three aerial combats and shot down two more planes: one American F-80 and one Gloster Meteor from No. 77 Squadron of the Royal Australian Air Force.

Nikolai Sutiagin downed the F-80 Shooting Star on 9 August, when after a short break the regiment returned to active combat operations. On that afternoon, the weather over North Korea had improved somewhat, and pilots of the 17th IAP completed two combat sorties by the end of daylight hours. The American command also decided to take advantage of the improved weather and sent groups of their ground attack aircraft into 'MiG Alley'. Two encounters with the adversary occurred, both of which triggered aerial combat.

First at 15:53, regiment commander Major Pulov led a regimental group of twenty-three crews to repel an enemy air raid. The group encountered a group of eight F-80 fighter-bombers. After a short fight, the enemy group was scattered, during which one Shooting Star was downed. Credit for this victory was given to the commander of the 1st Aviation Squadron, Captain S.S. Artemchenko.

Next at 17:25, ten MiGs from the 1st Aviation Squadron, headed by regiment commander Major Pulov, were scrambled to cover the withdrawal from combat of their brother 18th Guards and 523rd Aviation Regiments. Heading out with six planes in a 'V' formation and the remaining flight of four MiGs echeloned to their right, our planes crossed the Yalu River at an altitude of 5,500 meters north of Antung, at which point they jettisoned their drop tanks.

A message from the division command post crackled over the radio: 'Eight F-80s north of Sinbi–to Island.' After passing over the island, the MiGs swung to the right and flew north along the coastline. Captain Artemchenko soon spotted five F-80s below and to the right, approaching in a shallow stagger formation, and immediately alerted the rest of the group by radio. He himself then banked right toward the enemy, but losing sight of them, he assumed a heading toward the area of Anju.

The remaining group initially followed Artemchenko in the right turn. After swinging around 180°, Senior Lieutenant Miroshnichenko again spotted the five F-80s, which were now flying at the same altitude with the MiGs, off their right wing. Miroshnichenko immediately informed the group leader Major Pulov about his discovery; Pulov, failing to see the enemy, ordered his wingman to take the lead and head toward the targets. Moving ahead of Pulov, Senior Lieutenant Miroshnichenko lined his MiG up on one of the F-80s and, having closed to within a range of 500 meters, he fired a long burst. However, because of their high airspeed resulting from their acceleration into the attacking pass, both Miroshnichenko and Pulov overshot the target and began to exit the attack in a climbing left turn. At this moment, one of the F-80s lifted its nose in order to fire on Major Pulov's MiG. Senior Lieutenant Kramarenko, who was trailing the attacking pair of Miroshnichenko and Pulov, opened fire on the attacking F-80: after one long burst, the target staggered to the right and plummeted toward the ground, while Kramarenko pulled out of his attack in a chandelle to the left.

Senior Lieutenant Sutiagin, who was covering the attack of Major Pulov's flight, spotted a pair of Shooting Stars in a right turn below and to his right, and moved into position to attack them. After circling once to the right, the F-80 element reversed direction and went into a spiral to the left, trying to drag the combat toward the sea. While pursuing the enemy element through the spirals, Nikolai Sutiagin fired three times with all three cannons at one F-80 as the range dropped from 800 meters to 500 meters while remaining locked onto the target's tail, and watched pieces fly from the target. Upon pulling out of this firing pass, an order arrived from the division command post: 'Break off combat, return to base.' Major Pulov repeated the order and headed back to base. Along the way, the entire group reassembled, and the full complement of planes made a landing back at the airfield.

In the ensuing debriefing, the pilots claimed three downed F-80s. Each pilot expended the following ammunition in the combat:

Major Pulov: N-37[mm]=4, NS-23[mm]=8;
Senior Lieutenant Sutiagin: N-37=38, NS-23=100;
Senior Lieutenant Kramarenko: N-37=25, NS-23=64;
Senior Lieutenant Miroshnichenko: N-37=27, NS-23=70;
Senior Lieutenant Malunov: N-37=3, NS-23=10.[9]

After inspection of gun camera footage and evidence obtained by ground forces, only Nikolai Sutiagin received credit for one F-80; the other two claims were not confirmed.

On this day, the Americans acknowledged damage to two of their Shooting Stars, both of which returned to their K-14 airbase at Kimpo. However, one of them (BuNo. 49-677) was forced to make a belly-landing because of the combat damage it had received, and was out of operation for a long time. The other lucky pilot was from the 15th Tactical Reconnaissance Squadron, Captain Joe Daly, who reported that he had been intercepted by four MiG-15s in the area of Sinuiju. The MiGs badly damaged his RF-80A, but Daly managed to nurse it back to his own base with five large holes in it, bearing mute testimony to the destructive power of the MiG's cannons.

On 17 August 1951, the division commander issued a new order, No. 73, 'On the preparation of crews for operations in the role of hunters'. This order proposed the creation of a special unit of four elements in each regiment, comprising the best pilots and their choice of the best planes, for conducting free hunts in the area of combat actions. Deputy commander of the division Lieutenant Colonel A.S. Kumanichkin assumed responsibility for training the hunters, while the division commander himself, G.A. Lobov, assumed leadership of the unit.

The hunters were to operate in twilight hours or whenever worsening weather conditions prevented operations by larger formations. In better weather, they were to operate above or on the flanks of the regiment's formation to target small groups of fighter-bombers or isolated stragglers trying to exit the combat area. They were also to prowl the enemy's ingress and egress routes, seeking vulnerable targets.[10]

Each regiment of the division formed a hunter team. On 20 August, pursuant to the division commander's order, the following pilots were named as hunters in the 17th IAP: Captain Artemchenko, Senior Lieutenants Shulev, Miroshnichenko, Bychkov, Sutiagin, Perepelkin, Malunov, and Kramarenko – all from the roster of the 1st Aviation Squadron. The 1st Squadron was the strongest in the regiment; practically all of its pilots stood out with their combat records and level of political training. Thus, it was not surprising that they were precisely the ones to receive the most difficult assignments.

However, the 'free hunt' concept never really found its place among the 303rd IAD's other operations. Altogether, the 17th IAP's hunters only conducted twenty-two hunt sorties, out of more than 4,000 sorties for the regiment as a whole – that is, only 0.5 per cent of the total.

Meteors' Fiasco

In August, the pilots of the 17th IAP came up against a new opponent for them

– a twin-engine fighter, built in England, the Gloster F8 Meteor (at the time, the Russians knew it as the 'Gloster Meteor IV'). This fighter was being flown by No. 77 Squadron of the Royal Australian Air Force, which prior to the Meteor's arrival had been equipped with the outdated F-51 Mustang. In May, No. 77 Squadron had switched from the piston-engine Mustangs to the jet twin-engine F8 Meteor (the squadron also received one or two two-seater Meteor T7s, the training version of the plane). The Australians hoped that the Meteor would be a match for the MiG-15, but the Soviet aircraft proved to be superior to the British fighter in almost every possible way, and later the Meteors were used mainly as fighter-bombers.

The Australian pilots began combat missions in their new Meteors in August 1951. The task of No. 77 Squadron was to cover ground attack aircraft and protect the bombers of the US Fifth Air Force. The first encounter between pilots of No. 77 Squadron and MiGs of the 64th IAK occurred on 18 August. At 08:00, twenty-four MiG-15s led by Major Pulov took off to repel an enemy air strike in the vicinity of Sonchon.

Flying in a staggered column squadron formation at an altitude of 5,000 meters, our group spotted four Gloster Meteors. Senior Lieutenant Sutiagin was ordered to follow them. As a consequence of the MiGs' high inherent speed, the enemy aircraft quickly receded from our group's view, but then were spotted once again. The Gloster Meteors were flying over the sea on a parallel course to our group.

Reaching the coastline, our group reversed course to the left. While doing so, Major Pulov spotted six F-86 Sabres, flying at an altitude of 600–1,000 meters on a reverse heading in a column of elements, which were entering their own turn, and his attention switched from the Meteors to this new threat. On this occasion, the Australians managed to avoid an encounter with the MiGs. The command came to the conclusion that a previously uncommitted plane of the type Gloster Meteor had made an appearance in the area of combat operations.[11] However, a week later, the pilots of the 17th IAP would have the occasion to test the capabilities of these Gloster Meteors.

On 25 August, the regiment twice took off from an alert level of readiness level No. 1 and readiness level No. 2 to repel raids by enemy bombers with fighter escort in the region of Sonchon and Chongju at an altitude of 6,500–11,000 meters. At 07:58 according to the base control tower, a group of eight B-29 bombers, escorted by up to sixty fighters, had been spotted about 15 kilometers south of Anju, flying nearly due north at an altitude of 6,000–10,000 meters.

Twenty-six MiGs of the regiment under the command of Major Pulov took off at 08:04 to intercept the enemy bombers in the region of Sonchon. The regiment formed into a staggered column of squadrons, with a strike group consisting of pilots of the 1st and 3rd Aviation Regiments, and a cover group, comprising pilots of the 2nd Aviation Regiment.

Flying on a heading of 300°, Major Pulov at 08:37 spotted six Gloster Meteors at a lower altitude, flying in the same direction to the front and right of him. The enemy, having spotted the approaching MiGs, swung left and started to form into a defensive wheel. Pulov, closing to within 200–300 meters, attacked the wingman of the tail-end pair from behind and above at a 30–35° angle, after which he pulled out of the attack in a climbing turn to the right. He then circled around and repeated the attack again in the same sequence. In the course of this dogfight, Major Pulov conducted four attacks, three of which were firing passes.

Senior Lieutenant Sutiagin, who was covering Major Pulov because both of their wingmen had become separated during the maneuvering prior to the attack, pounced on a Gloster Meteor himself. In the very first attack, Sutiagin fired two bursts at the leader of the tail-end pair, one of which found its target, after which he got caught in the turbulent air behind the Meteor and fell into a spin. Pulling his MiG out of its spin, Nikolai found himself in the middle of a flight of Gloster Meteors, which were closing in a circle around him. Jinking sharply to the left and right, Senior Lieutenant Sutiagin accelerated and managed to separate from the Meteors.

As a result of this engagement, two enemy Gloster Meteors were shot down: one was credited to Major Pulov, the other to Nikolai Sutiagin. The gun camera footage of Sutiagin confirmed the downing of the plane. In Major Pulov's gun camera footage, the silhouette of the target plane was washed out.[12]

Here's how Gregorii Ivanovich Pulov himself describes this combat:

I obtained my first victory on 25 August – on that day, I scrambled the entire regiment with twenty-six crews at an order from the division command post, and set out for the designated area.

On this mission we encountered a formation of twin-engine Gloster Meteor fighters, but prior to this a group of our pilots from a different regiment had spotted it, and reported by radio back to the division command post: 'We've encountered a group of Il–28s, what should we do?' From the command post they were informed that there were no Il–28s in the area, and that the unidentified aircraft were enemy. But apparently they had already missed their opportunity to attack, and the Meteors had slipped away. That was when we bumped into them. They were in two six-ship flights.

The Meteor pilots also spotted us and began to form into a defensive wheel, just like our Il–2s used to do back in the Great Patriotic War. I attacked one of the Meteors below me, and striking it with cannon shells from a range of 400 meters, knocked it out of the circle. Very quickly the whole circle fell apart and the Meteors withdrew.

I didn't see whether the Meteor I hit actually fell to the ground, nor did I see the plane burning. But my burst caused the target to start smoking, and then it plunged steeply toward the earth. I was too busy with the battle to watch it further or to follow it down.

In this fight with the Meteors, of the twenty-six MiG pilots that participated in the action, only Major Pulov and Senior Lieutenant Sutiagin fired their cannon. Their wingmen Senior Lieutenant Osipov and Senior Lieutenant Savchenko had failed to cover them. The squadrons led by Captain Shcherbakov and Captain Ponomarev lost sight of the group commander, so a coordinated attack couldn't be mounted.

The combat was evaluated as unsuccessful, with insufficient activity from the MiG pilots, although Pulov and Sutiagin each shot down a plane without any losses to the regiment. The regiment's command staff and pilots thoroughly analyzed this action. Regiment commander Major Pulov demanded better situational awareness and more initiative in combat from his pilots.

It should be noted that Leonid Krylov and Iurii Tersupkaev (Moscow) in their article 'Meteors in Korea' from the journal *Aviation* 1999, No. 1–2, relying on Australian sources, give a somewhat different description of this combat between the MiG-15 and the Meteors. They maintain that in the action on 25 August, the Australians had no losses at all, and that it was only three days later that the Australian squadron suffered its first loss against the MiG-15.

On the afternoon of 25 August, the 1st Aviation Squadron was again scrambled by an alert. At 16:01, radar detected one unidentified aircraft in the region of Changtien, flying down the Yalu River valley at an altitude of 2,500–3,000 meters in the direction of the vital railroad bridge. At 16:12, by order of the division command post, ten MiGs of the 1st Aviation Squadron under the command of Captain Artemchenko were scrambled to intercept the intruder. After taking off, the squadron was vectored to the area of the railroad bridge at an altitude of 3,000 meters. At 16:25 in an area 10 kilometers northeast of the railroad bridge at an altitude of 2,500 meters, the squadron encountered the unidentified plane, which turned out to be a Li-2 variant [a military transport plane with defensive armament modeled closely upon the Douglas DC-3] bearing Soviet markings. Captain Artemchenko and Senior Lieutenant Sutiagin fired three warning bursts of cannon fire. The Li-2 airplane was escorted to the airfield at Siniuju, where it made a landing. After the landing, it was established that this plane (crew commander Davidenko) had been flying the route between Vozdvizhenka and Mukden, had lost its way, and the pilot had headed down the Yalu River to find the city of Antung in order to re-establish his position. So on occasion our fighter pilots had to intercept even their own side's aircraft!

On 26 August, by General Krasovsky's personal decree, Nikolai Sutiagin became the first of the regiment's pilots to be recommended for the title 'Hero of the Soviet Union'. By this date, Sutiagin had conducted more than thirty combat sorties, had been involved in twelve aerial combats, and had shot down seven enemy planes. In his recommendation for awarding the title 'Hero of the Soviet Union' to Sutiagin, regiment commander Major Pulov concluded, 'For outstanding actions while carrying out orders in the struggle with the American–British imperialists, and for demonstrated heroism, fearlessness, and certain ability to defeat the enemy, for the downing of seven enemy airplanes, [SUTIAGIN] is worthy of acquiring the title "Hero of the Soviet Union".'[13]

On 30 August, a Party gathering took place in the regiment under the rubric 'On the example of communists in the battle with American aggressors'. The main speaker was regiment commander Major Pulov. One of the topics of this agenda was the combat of 25 August, when the entire regiment had taken off on a combat mission, but only Major Pulov and Senior Lieutenant Sutiagin had become involved in combat. The remaining pilots, in their own words, had not heard the commands of the group leader.

At the Party gathering, it was observed that certain pilots were spending more time in the hospital than in the unit. Thus, Comrades Gostiukhin, Komarov and Kordanov had fallen ill with gastro–intestinal diseases, had not tolerated the hospital diet, had been discharged prematurely, and were suffering from gastro–intestinal illnesses again.

From Nikolai Sutiagin's presentation at the Party gathering:

> Whenever we can see the enemy, he presents no danger to us. The most important thing in aerial combat is awareness. After each dogfight, it is necessary to analyze it deeply and to take stock of our mistakes. When Comrade Artemchenko initiated an attacking pass on other MiGs, similar incidents were repeated in the 2nd Aviation Squadron. Some pilots are making fun of each other, sometimes tossing needless retorts at each other, like 'Another dogfight – another spin.' To fall into a spin is an unpleasant experience, when an adversary is coming after you. We need to work on the ground as an entire collective to eliminate these mistakes that we are making, and this will give us the possibility to inflict more damage to the enemy.[14]

On 31 August the regiment flew three combat missions, two of them with its full complement of MiGs. Most notable was the third mission of the day, when division commander General Lobov led twenty-six MiGs of the regiment into the sky at 17:02 to intercept enemy fighter-bombers. Lobov headed a six–ship strike group of the 1st Aviation Squadron, which took off first. Senior Lieutenant Sutiagin's flight was in the cover group. The 2nd and 3rd Aviation Squadrons led by Major Pulov took off seven minutes later. In the fight with enemy fighter-bombers, four F–80s were downed without a loss on our part. General Lobov, Major Pulov, Captain Ponomarev and Lieutenant Bozhko were each given credit for downing one enemy plane.

The total combat score of the regiment since the start of combat operations stood at twenty-three planes, fifteen of which were downed by the 1st Squadron (Senior Lieutenant Sutiagin had seven of those planes to his credit). Pilots of the 2nd Aviation Squadron had scored four of the victories, while the 3rd Aviation Squadron and the Headquarters flight had accounted for two victories each.

Chapter Five

The Autumn Marathon

The Combat Intensifies

In the month of September 1951, enemy ground activity was picking up. The commander-in-chief of the US Eighth Army, Lieutenant General Van Fleet, inspected his forces on the central and eastern sectors of the front for their readiness for an offensive. The Americans were engaged in active reconnaissance probes and conducted a number of limited operations to adjust their lines and to seize commanding heights, primarily on the eastern half of the front lines. They had stockpiled necessary supplies of food and ammunition to sustain their forces fighting in the mountainous terrain. Mine-sweeping operations, naval bombardments, and probes by small landing parties along the eastern and western coasts of North Korea also suggested the enemy was preparing an assault landing behind the lines.

On 1 September, the commander of the 17th IAP, Major Pulov, rearranged the primary roles of the squadrons in the regiment's combat formation: he himself began to fly at the head of the 2nd Aviation Squadron, which he made the regiment's lead strike group. The 3rd Squadron, which up to now had been flying primarily as the regiment's cover group, became the regiment's secondary strike group. The 1st Squadron thus became the regiment's cover group. This naturally affected the scoring of the squadrons: in September the 2nd and 3rd Aviation Squadrons led the way in victories, scoring five and four victories respectively. The 1st Aviation Squadron had four of its MiGs taken away from it and reassigned to regimental control, and claimed only three downed enemy planes in September.

The weather began to improve on 2 September, which allowed the division to resume combat sorties. The pilots of the 17th IAP alone conducted three combat missions on this day and twice tangled with enemy fighters. The fiercest fight unfolded during the second mission of the morning. At 09:58, a radar station detected a group of six B–29 bombers, escorted by fighters, flying at an altitude of 7,000–9,000 meters in the area 20 kilometers south of Unsan. At 10:03, MiGs of the 2nd and 3rd Aviation Squadrons soared into the sky with the order to engage and destroy the enemy fighters. Approaching the area of Anju at an altitude of 11,000 meters, Major Pulov at the head of the 2nd Aviation Squadron came upon eight F–86s flying in a left stagger formation in front of and below him, only about 500 meters to the left. Major Pulov ordered Captain Shcherbakov to cover the attack, and for Captain Ponomarev to attack the right-hand flight. With his own flight, Pulov approached the trailing flight of F-86s. The enemy, spotting our MiGs, began to drop their external fuel tanks while simultaneously swinging into a right-hand turn. The left flight of F-86s began to depart beneath the formation of the lead flight. During the turn, the tail-end F-86 lagged behind the rest of the flight. Major Pulov took advantage of this, closed to within 400 meters and opened fire upon it. Multiple cannon hits shredded the Sabre and it plummeted straight into the ground, which Senior Lieutenant Gostiukhin confirmed in his after-action report.

Flying in Pulov's flight, Captain Morozov moved to attack a second pair of F-86-x, still in their right turn. Having approached within range, he fired two long bursts, registering hits on his target, after which he exited the attack with a climbing turn to the right. His wingman Lieutenant Kordanov fired at the second Sabre from a range of 1,000 down to 800 meters, but in the process became separated from his leader. Captain Shcherbakov's group covered the attacks of the 2nd Aviation Squadron pilots. At 10:11, the 1st Aviation Squadron took to the sky with eight MiGs under the command of Captain Artemchenko in order to reinforce the fight. In the region of Chongju, it spotted a group of enemy fighters, which refused to accept battle and departed in a dive. As a result of this action, the excited pilots reported downing three F-86s. Gun camera footage confirmed the victories of Major Pulov and Captain Morozov; however, Lieutenant Kordanov's gun camera footage did not confirm the downing of an airplane, so his claim was disallowed.

Pilots of the 18th GIAP participated in this engagement as well, mixing it up with a large group of Sabres. Many victories in this engagement were announced by the regiment. Yet on the whole, the combat was unsuccessful, since the Guardsmen suffered their heaviest one-day loss for the entire period of its participation in this war: two of the regiment's planes were shot down, and something even more bitter, two of its pilots perished.

On the whole, the division declared nine victories over the Sabres, but in actual fact the score could have been less. According to American sources, only one F-86 went down, and several more received damage.

Stable flying weather finally arrived on 8 September, which led to increased aerial combat activity. On that day, the 17th IAP became involved in another fight that yielded a result. A group of twenty-six MiGs led by Major Pulov was launched at 08:14 to repel a strike by enemy ground attack aircraft in the area of Sukchon. In line with the new arrangement of responsibilities, the 1st Aviation Squadron was the cover group. Clouds covered about two-thirds of the sky, therefore during the pre-mission briefing, Senior Lieutenant

Bychkov's flight was told to stay above the cloud layer.

At 08:29 Major Pulov spotted eight approaching F-86 Sabres in front of him and to his left, flying at the same altitude. Giving an order to Captain Shcherbakov to cover his attack, and to Senior Lieutenant Bychkov's flight to climb above the clouds, Major Pulov himself turned to close with the F-86 group and fired one burst at the tail-end plane in the formation. The shells walked along the left wing of the Sabre, and the F-86 rolled over and dived away toward the sea. Pulling out of his attack, Major Pulov found two more F-86s, flying to his right, which were starting to descend in a southerly direction. Given the extreme range to the target, Pulov didn't fire. His wingman Senior Lieutenant Gostiukhin fired one burst at the lead F-86, but without results.

Captain Morozov, lead of the second element in Major Pulov's flight, closed on a second pair of F-86s, which began a climbing spiral. Morozov, pursuing the F-86s, gained an altitude advantage over them. Then at a 30° dive angle, he slid onto the tail of one F-86, and fired three long bursts while closing to a range of 500 meters. Afterwards, he pulled out of his attack in a chandelle to the left and took a heading back to base. His wingman Lieutenant Kordanov fired at the wingman's F-86 with no visible results.

Captain Ponomarev approached the second flight of F-86s. The leading pair of Sabres went into an oblique loop. Ponomarev followed them. Having carried out one oblique loop, the F-86 element dived away. Captain Ponomarev halted his pursuit because of the high speed, and broke off the attack in a climbing left turn, before taking a course to the north. During this brief scrap, his wingman Senior Lieutenant Ankilov became separated from him.

Captain Mishakin, trailing Captain Ponomarev, attacked a second pair of F-86s, which evaded with a sharp dive in a southerly direction. Mishakin chose not to pursue. Banking away to his left, he spotted two MiG-15s to his right, Major Pulov and Senior Lieutenant Kordanov, and formed up with them.

Captain Shcherbakov, covering the action of the 2nd Aviation Squadron, spotted a solitary Sabre flying below the group's formation. He performed a climbing turn to the right to set up an attack on the Sabre, but the enemy pilot spotted the threat, performed a split-S, and departed toward the sea.

On the return to base, two F-86s were spotted, trying to maneuver onto the tail of Senior Lieutenant Volkov's element. Senior Lieutenant Dokashenko moved to close with them, but the F-86 element, having discovered the MiG-15 stalking them, performed a split-S and retreated in the direction of the sea.

Senior Lieutenant Bychkov, following in the cover squadron, had received the order to climb above the clouds and head toward the area of combat. Only three MiGs emerged together above the cloud layer; in the process of ascending through the cloud, the rest of the flight – Captain Maslennikov and Senior Lieutenants Kramarenko and Shirokov – became separated. Popping into the sunshine above the clouds, Senior Lieutenant Bychkov spotted two eight-plane flights of Sabres in front and above him to the right, flying in a sharp stagger formation with about 1.5–2 kilometers between the groups. Bychkov informed Major Pulov of his discovery, and then climbed undetected to an altitude of 12,000 meters. Making a left turn, he dived in an attack on the rear flight. Approaching to a range of 600 meters, Bychkov took careful aim and opened fire. After the third medium burst, the enemy target burst into flames, tipped onto its left wing and plunged beneath the clouds. Noticing Bychkov's attack, one pair of F-86s in the lead flight of Sabres broke from the formation and maneuvered to attack him. Senior Lieutenant Perepelkin, spotting the danger, warned his leader Bychkov, who evaded the attack by breaking sharply up and away to the right. Finding they had gained an altitude advantage over the adversary, Senior Lieutenant Bychkov led the reduced flight into a second attempt to close upon the enemy element, but the F-86 pair, seeing their unfavorable position, chose to take shelter beneath the clouds.

In this aerial combat, our fighters got the jump on the enemy. Senior Lieutenant Bychkov with three planes engaged sixteen F-86s. However, the mission didn't go smoothly; the after-action briefing revealed the scattering of elements in the flight, the separation of wingmen from their leaders, and the tendency to open fire at extreme ranges. In the post-flight briefing, Senior Lieutenant Bychkov and Captain Morozov each claimed one Sabre, while Major Pulov claimed one Sabre as damaged, but the results of analysis of the gun camera film confirmed only Bychkov's victory. In this action, he shot down First Lieutenant Thompson of the 4th Fighter Wing's 335th Fighter-Interceptor Squadron. Thompson somehow managed to lead his burning, crippled F-86A No. 49-1323 out to sea, where he ejected and was picked up by a search and rescue team.

On the first mission of the day on 11 September, twenty-four MiG-15s under the command of Major Pulov were vectored to intercept a group of twelve B-29 bombers, escorted by a large force of fighters. Three F-84s were shot down in the ensuing battle: two by Captain Ponomarev and one by Senior Lieutenant Volkov. Major Pulov damaged another F-84.

Grigorii Ivanovich Pulov relayed the following to the authors:

Misha Ponomarev was constantly asking my permission to let him have a go at the fighter-bombers, since he 'specialized' against them and always came out on top against them. In one such battle, a pair of F-84s pursued by Ponomarev collided with each other while making a scissors maneuver, and Ponomarev downed another F-84 that day with fire from his MiG's cannons. Arriving back at the airfield, he asked me whether or not the squadron would assign these two victims of the mid-air collision to his score or not? I answered that this was his achievement, and that he would get credit for all three F-84s.

Also on that day of 11 September, deputy division commander Lieutenant Colonel Kumanichkin led a regimental group of twenty-six MiG-15s into battle against eight F-84s in the vicinity of Unsan. Kumanichkin himself shot down one F-84. Captain Ponomarev, who was leading the cover flight, also shot down one F-84. Thus, Ponomarev increased his score by three enemy planes in one day, and became the 17th IAP's second ace. His wingman Lieutenant Bozhko also damaged one F-84, but he himself was shot down while on his way back to the airbase, presumably by the 'friendly fire' of North Korean anti-aircraft artillery. Lieutenant Bozhko successfully ejected and landed in an area 15 kilometers east of Sonchon. He made his way back to the unit on 13 September. The 1st and 3rd Aviation Squadrons failed to find the enemy on this mission.

Veteran of the regiment A.N. Nikolaev recalled:

By the way, there's a story about Bozhko, when he was shot down, that I remember well: on that day our entire division was scrambled into the air. The division commander Kumanichkin himself was leading our regiment. [After so many years, Nikolaev is understandably confused about dates; Kumanichkin did not become the commander of the 303rd IAD until 20 September 1951.] We soon encountered numerous enemy fighters and fighter-bombers. As always, whenever a combat starts, a hubbub fills the airwaves. Then suddenly one could hear in the headset some sort of yell: 'I see someone in a parachute!' And in response, the voice of the division commander Kumanichkin: 'That's my guy! That's my guy!' When we returned home, it turned out that Lieutenant Bozhko hadn't made it back from the mission. In this battle, several enemy planes had been shot down. Soon General Lobov himself arrived for our post-flight debriefing. I remember how vigorously he berated our division commander, asking why he had lost one of his pilots: 'I don't need your crap, jester!' he was shouting at Kumanichkin. Two days later it became known that Bozhko was alive and unharmed, only he had landed without boots, barefooted. His boots had been yanked off his feet when his parachute opened. For a long time after this, we had a laugh over this entire story.

Only someone who has himself participated in an aerial combat – alone, in an element, or at worst in a flight – can describe what it was like in Korea. But I don't think anyone can describe a dogfight that they haven't been around. Yet I'll try to explain how we fought as a flight against the F-84.

Arriving in the designated region, we encountered a large group of F-84s. These planes didn't have swept wings, like our MiGs, but straight wings, and they were very maneuverable in the horizontal plane, that is to say, in turns. And here our four-plane flight was flying above them, while they were maneuvering below us. I had the impression that they were boards, swirling around in a whirlpool at some water-mill. And, as is known, water is always spinning around there. I often watched them at our mill when I was a child.

But now I couldn't stand it, and I blurted out an order over the radio to the flight commander: 'What are you looking at? Attack!' Our commander, as if he'd been lashed by a whip, pounced on these 'boards', that is, on these F-84s. We, of course, started after him. Our speed is high, which is good. The F-84 was slower, but better in horizontal maneuvers. So we often zoomed past them in our attacks and then climbed for altitude again. There was simply no time for lining up the target and firing. Zooming past the next Thunderjet in line, I pull out of my run in a climbing turn. Glancing back, I see the enemy pilot, having raised the nose of his plane, is giving me everything he's got from every machine-gun barrel. The entire nose of his plane is blazing. I think it won't be long before I receive a lead visitor from his guns. I need to be more careful, and not enter the attack in such fervor. We spent a long time flying in and out of this whirling mill of planes, but we were never able to do it any damage. There were really a bit too many of them there. Yet I really wanted to treat one to a good burst from my cannons. Returning, after landing, we had a good laugh and came to the mutual opinion that restraint is necessary, that such attacks like the one we had made just wouldn't do. We had to operate in a different fashion, attack from different angles and unexpectedly. But Khvostantsev remembered this combat for a long time, both my cry 'What are you looking at?' and the way our commander had hurled himself into the attack. I'm sure he even now remembers this episode. You just don't forget such things!

On 14 September, the regiment commander (plainly thinking that Sutiagin had a lot of free time on his hands) ordered Nikolai Sutiagin to conduct an inquiry into the affairs of Senior Lieutenant Aleksei Andreevich Komarov. Among the duties of a military investigator was the collection of evidence and eyewitness statements against the accused in written form, and turning them over to the commander.

Senior Lieutenant Komarov was suspected of feigning illness to avoid making combat sorties, and often went to the doctors, but the doctors always found him to be absolutely healthy. By order of the regiment commander, Komarov was turned over to the Officers' Court of Honor. At the proceedings he confessed his guilt, and gave his word to his comrades that he would make things right. Indeed he kept his word: he soon scored his first victory in the air. In the future he fought successfully; conducting over 100 combat sorties, he was eventually recommended for the Order of the Red Banner.

As for illnesses, in fact many pilots were in real need of medical treatment. In the month of September, the entire flight staff went through a medical check at a dispensary of the Changtien Hospital. According to the conclusion of the medical team, twenty-one of the pilots were declared healthy, and three pilots were considered to be 'practically healthy'. The doctors observed the initial stage of fatigue in four of the pilots, and pronounced fatigue in another. One pilot, Senior Lieutenant Polianichko, was placed under hospital observation. He was directed to the Changtien Military Hospital, where he remained between 5 and 30 October with the diagnosis 'inadequacy of the mitral valve in a phase of persistent compensation and an asthenic condition'. He was then declared ready for unrestricted flying duty, but in need of general treatment in a sanatorium. He spent two weeks at a sanatorium in Kashgar between 3 and 17 November.

Air-raid warnings sounded practically every night – they added to the exhaustion of the pilots, who were also waking up very early each morning to report for duty. Many of the pilots had already begun to ignore these nightly warnings; they simply no longer had the strength to interrupt their sleep and seek shelter, choosing instead to rely on their anti-aircraft gunners and night fighters.

Sixteen MiG-15s of the 2nd and 3rd Aviation Squadrons under the command of Major Pulov became involved in a particularly disorganized dogfight on 20 September. The leader of the cover group, Captain Shcherbakov, found an opportunity to stalk an enemy fighter-bomber group closely, and he began to maneuver onto the tail of eight enemy aircraft. Yet in so doing, he interfered with the attack of our strike group on the same target. Thirty F-86s suddenly joined the fray, and our sixteen MiGs quickly found themselves in a bit of trouble. Major Pulov's wingman Major Vorob'ev became separated from his leader, and Pulov had to fight alone against six F-86 Sabres. Only owing to Major Pulov's composure and skill was he able to escape being shot down: his plane was damaged, receiving a hole in the right wing, but Pulov successfully returned to base.[1] In this same action, Senior Lieutenant Nikolai Dokashenko shot down one F-86. It was the first victory of the future ace.

Major changes came to the command in the 64th IAK on 20 September. General G.A. Lobov was appointed to take command of the corps, while his deputy Lieutenant Colonel A.S. Kumanichkin replaced him as commander of the 303rd IAD. Lieutenant Colonel A.N. Karasev, one of the top aces of the Great Patriotic War, was named deputy commander of the 303rd IAD. Major D.P. Os'kin became commander of the 523rd IAP. Back on 5 September, he had been transferred from the 18th GIAP to take over the position of deputy commander of the 523rd IAP in place of Major N.N. Danilenko, who, in turn, had been sent back to the 18th GIAP in place of Major Os'kin as assistant commander of the regiment for aerial combat tactics and aerial gunnery.

One of the first steps of Kumanichkin in his new command role was Order No. 88 from 20 September 1951, 'On the results of checking the confirmation of downed enemy planes and the analysis of gun camera film', in which he noted that there were a large number of shortcomings in the division's regiments, including in the 17th IAP. In the order, it was determined that 'the primary source in the consideration of credit for a downed enemy plane will be information obtained from the film analysis'. In addition, more than one other pilot had to witness the downing and report it, and there had to be confirmation from local authorities or forces of the NKPA. At the beginning of October, an order issued a standard form for describing an aerial combat throughout the division.

On 23 September, a meeting of the personnel of the division's regiments took place, dedicated to the reading of a congratulatory telegram from the leader of the Chinese people, Mao Zedong. The telegram pointed to the successes of Soviet aviation in the aerial combat over the eight days between 6 and 13 September, in which it claimed the downing of forty-nine hostile planes and the inflicting of damage to eight more in the fighting against the American interventionists in Korea.

Two more major engagements took place in 'MiG Alley' before the end of September. On 26 September pilots of the corps conducted two combat missions, both of which resulted in combat. They were trying to repel a major raid by a group of Thunderjets, covered by large groups of Sabres and with immediate escort by pilots from No. 77 Royal Australian Squadron in their Meteors.

Pilots of the 303rd IAD engaged the covering Sabre fighters, while pilots of the 324th IAD attacked the eight-ship flights of Thunderjets, which were inbound from the sea to bomb crossings and supply routes in the region of Anju. Seeing that the covering fighters had been tied up in battle, and that they now had to face the MiGs alone, the Thunderjet pilots began to reverse course at low altitude and to head back toward the sea. During their retreat, pilots of the 523rd and 196th IAP succeeded in making several attacking passes and downed three of the 'Crosses'. [This was the nickname of the Soviet pilots for the F-84 Thunderjets, because of the configuration of their straight wings and fuselage.] Pilots of the 523rd IAP also shot down one Meteor and one Sabre, while pilots of the 18th GIAP downed one Sabre, without suffering any losses. In the course of the dogfight with the fighters, the pilots of the 17th IAP also downed three planes – two Sabres and one Meteor, two of which (a Sabre and the Meteor) were claimed by Senior Lieutenant Sutiagin in one battle. Here's how it happened.

At 08:42 all three squadrons of the 17th IAP began to roar down the runway and take to the sky in turn – a total of twenty-six MiGs led by regiment commander Major Pulov. Captain Ponomarev's 2nd Aviation Squadron led the way, tasked with tying up the forward Sabre fighter screen in battle. The two other squadrons of the regiment received the assignment to cover the actions of the pilots of the 523rd IAP, which had also taken off to intercept the enemy air raid, and were to attack the enemy's ground attack planes.

In the region of Anju, Captain Ponomarev's group spotted eight F-86 fighters heading toward them and engaged them in battle. Soon, the main forces of the division arrived in the area, in the form of a group of fighters from the 523rd IAP under the cover of the two squadrons (eighteen MiGs) of the 17th IAP. While making a turn, the pilots of the 17th IAP discovered another group of eight F-86 fighters, which Captain Artemchenko's flight immediately engaged; the remaining six MiGs led by Major Pulov continued to carry out their assignment of providing high cover to their comrades from the 523rd Regiment.

Arriving in the area over the mouth of the Sonchon River, Pulov's flight spotted a group of twelve Meteor fighters, which were flying toward Anju at an altitude of 7,000 meters. Major Pulov gave the order to attack the Australians. However, the Meteor pilots spotted the MiGs of Pulov and his wingman Senior Lieutenant Miroshnichenko moving in on them in time and scattered to avoid the attack, but the element of Senior Lieutenant Sutiagin and Captain Osipov, following Pulov's element in the attack, managed to close to within 300–250 meters behind one of the evading Meteors. Sutiagin gave it a long burst from all his cannons, sending it into a steep dive toward the sea. The remaining Meteors quickly reassembled. Pulov tried several more times to break up the formation of Meteors, but this time the Australians maintained their formation and gradually carried the battle out to the sea, where our pilots could not follow. Therefore, Pulov was forced to break off the fight with the Meteors.

While Pulov's flight of four planes had been preoccupied with the Meteors, Sutiagin engaged four F-86 fighters that were coming to their allies' assistance. Soon, with a successful maneuver Nikolai managed to get behind one pair of the Sabres. Closing to a range of 250 meters, Sutiagin fired a long burst, watching pieces fly off the stricken plane as the cannon shells did their work, before the Sabre erupted in flames and fell in the region south-west of Anju. The remaining F-86s dived away in the direction of the sea. After this, Senior Lieutenant Sutiagin took a heading back to his base. Thus in one action Nikolai scored two consecutive victories!

According to information from the command of the No. 77 Royal Australian Air Force Squadron, on this day a new commander of the squadron, G. Steede, was leading the group of Meteors. In this combat with the MiGs, in the very first attack, Sergeant Ernst Armit's Meteor A77-949 was heavily damaged. The pilot, with great difficulty, managed to reach his base at Suwon and land his damaged plane. However, after such extensive damage, the plane had to be written off. Thus, one more Meteor was added to Sutiagin's list of victories. Regarding the downed Sabre, a pilot of the 336th Squadron, First Lieutenant Carl G. Barnett, Jr. who was a wingman in this flight of Sabres, had wound up under the cannons of our ace. Sutiagin had caught him in a turn, when it is difficult to hit a target, but Nikolai had managed it, and soon Sabre No. 49-1113 was left burning on the ground – its pilot Carl Barnett, Jr. was killed.

That afternoon, or more precisely at 14:08, the 17th IAP in a strength of twenty-four MiGs was again scrambled to intercept enemy aircraft. Senior Lieutenant Bashlyklov had to abort the mission soon after take-off due to a malfunctioning speed indicator.

As the 17th IAP group was approaching the area of Taechon, it received information from the division command post that enemy fighters were in the area at an altitude of 4,000–5,000 meters. Receiving this information, Major Pulov took the 1st and 3rd Aviation Squadrons and began to descend, while the 2nd Aviation Squadron remained as high cover at an altitude of 8,000 meters. Seven kilometers east of Taechon, Senior Lieutenant Sutiagin detected eight F-86s in front of him, below and to his right, flying northward in a column of flights formation. Major Pulov's group maintained its current heading until over the city of Taechon, where it conducted a right turn and headed back toward the coastline.

Reaching the vicinity of the mouth of the Sonchon River, Major Pulov spotted eight F-84s only 300–400 meters away, below and to his right, approaching in a left stagger of flights formation. He gave the command: 'I see the enemy, we're attacking!' Pulov's group began to shake out into a column of pairs, while simultaneously swinging around to the left, and began to close on the Thunderjets. The F-84s responded with a left-hand spiral. Major Pulov, followed by the trailing elements behind him, made repeated attacks from behind at a dive angle of 30–40° with a subsequent exit from the run in a chandelle to the right. The F-84s maneuvered frantically to evade the attacking elements, while preventing an easy low deflection shot from behind. Senior Lieutenant Sutiagin with his wingman Senior Lieutenant Perepelkin, and

Senior Lieutenant Shulev with his wingman Senior Lieutenant Savchenko, then carried out one head-on attack at an aspect angle of 1/4–2/4, firing short bursts from a range of 300–250 meters. The F-84 group began to carry the fight toward the sea, while our groups continued to pursue.

Senior Lieutenant Sutiagin next spotted four Thunderjets, flying to the south-east and went after them with Major Pulov's flight covering him from behind. North of Kusong, Sutiagin closed to within 700 meters and fired a long burst at an aspect angle of 1/4, after which he pulled out of the attack in a chandelle to the left and headed toward Anju. In this action, two F-84s were damaged, one by Nikolai Sutiagin, the other by Senior Lieutenant Shulev. The enemy fighter-bomber attack on the target was broken up.

In action the next day (27 September), Major Pulov's group of twenty-six MiG-15s dueled with eighteen F-84s and four F-86s. Major Pulov downed one enemy plane and damaged another. However, Nikolai Sutiagin made a mistake in this dogfight, which almost cost him his life.

Senior Lieutenant Sutiagin's flight was providing cover for Major Pulov's flight. During a turn, Sutiagin's flight entered some clouds and became separated from Pulov's flight. Emerging from the clouds alone, Sutiagin led his flight toward the area of Anju. He received information from the division command post that enemy planes were approaching from the north-east. Soon Sutiagin's flight of four planes encountered eight F-84s on a meeting course. Senior Lieutenant Sutiagin maneuvered to attack the rear element of Thunderjets, but failed to notice that four F-86s had arrived and were now stalking him. Only when he saw tracer rounds streaking past his MiG did Sutiagin realize the predicament he was in. He was forced to break off his attack on the Thunderjets and to maneuver energetically to evade the Sabres, before fleeing back to base.

In the post-mission briefing, the regiment commander offered his critique: the squadron's strike group had been weakened by the separation of Senior Lieutenant Sutiagin's flight, as a result of which Sutiagin himself, having run into a numerically superior enemy group, was unable to inflict any losses on the enemy and had narrowly avoided disaster. Nikolai had to hear out the commander's justified rebuke in his direction. Still, in combat, not everything goes as planned.

Altogether in the month of September, the 17th IAP conducted 604 sorties and destroyed sixteen enemy planes. Nikolai Sutiagin completed twenty-three combat sorties during the month, and had engaged the enemy nine times. For downing two enemy planes in one action, the commander of the 17th IAP Major G. Pulov personally recommended Sutiagin for the Order of Lenin of 27 September 1951, but he never received the honor.

Thus the September engagements in the sky over North Korea had come to a conclusion. The evaluation of results was extremely positive. According to staff documents of the 64th IAK, the pilots of two Soviet aviation divisions had downed ninety-two enemy planes, while losing only five of their own planes and two pilots. This was the most productive month for Soviet pilots since the start of their participation in this war. Pilots of the corps destroyed forty-seven ground attack planes alone in this month (twenty-eight F-84, seventeen F-80 and two F-51), and forty-five enemy fighter planes, of which six were Meteors and the rest were Sabres.

According to American records, over the month of September, MiG-15s appeared 1,177 times in 'MiG Alley' and became engaged in 911 aerial combats, in which fifteen MiG-15s were shot down (F-86s alone conducted 1,119 of these combat sorties and claimed thirteen of these MiGs). The Americans numbered their own loss in these battles at six planes: three F-86 (plus three more Sabres due to non-combat damage), one F-80, one F-84 and one F-51.

According to recent research by our own and foreign scholars, the number of UN losses in the month of September 1951 has increased to twenty-one planes lost in combat with the MiGs (five F-86A, seven F-84, five F-80C, two F-51, one F2N-2 and one Australian Meteor), plus a minimum of an additional seven F-86As and one Meteor that were seriously damaged. Thus, even taking these numbers, the correlation of losses between the opposing sides in the September battles will be 4:1 in favor of the Soviet pilots.

The records of the two sides differ on the number of victories and losses, yet even if we assume that the Soviet records inflate the UN losses by twice, then all the same, the wreckage of forty American planes remained on the ground of North Korea from the fire of the Soviet pilots alone, while a number more were damaged. However, these are only the results of the actions of Soviet pilots of the 64th IAK; in addition, two Chinese fighter aviation divisions, the 3rd and 4th IAD, also flew combat missions over Korea in this period, and they scored up to twenty more victories over the Americans. Thus the official American records on their losses in aerial combat, speaking gently, are unrealistically low, and prompt doubt of their authenticity.

Another Loss and New Replacements

On 1 October, ground forces of the enemy began offensive operations across almost the entire length of the front, with the support of aircraft and ships of the US Navy. At a cost of large losses in men and equipment, the enemy managed in the course of a month to advance from 5 to 20 kilometers on several sectors of the front.

The combat mission of the 17th IAP in October didn't change much. As before, it remained responsible for covering the critical railroad bridge across the Yalu River at Siniuju, the hydro-electrical station at Suiho, as well as protecting the airfield complex in the areas of Kusong, Taechon and Anju from attempts by enemy bombers to render them unserviceable.

October brought further changes to the staffing and roles within the regiment. On 1 October, Major Pulov made the 3rd Aviation Squadron the lead strike group and began to fly with it on combat missions together with his new wingman, Captain Blagov. Because of this change, the 3rd Aviation Squadron finally had its turn as the most productive squadron in the October battles; over the month, it shot down fifteen planes to lead the way. Over the same period, the 1st Aviation Squadron downed seven planes, the 2nd Aviation Squadron three planes, and the regiment's Headquarters flight, five.

Regrettably, the October fighting began with a loss in the regiment: on 2 October, Captain Morozov, a flight commander in the 2nd Aviation Squadron, was killed in action. On this day, at 14:53 a regimental group of twenty-four crews under the command of Major Pulov, who was leading the 3rd Aviation Squadron, was conducting its second combat mission of the day to intercept enemy fighters. Pulov's wingman that mission was supposed to be Senior Lieutenant Miroshnichenko, but for some reason he was late for take-off. Captain Morozov of the 2nd Aviation Squadron took Miroshnichenko's place; Morozov's own wingman Senior Lieutenant Kordanov took off later with Senior Lieutenant Miroshnichenko, but not until after the 18th GIAP had launched, which followed the 17th IAP into the sky.

Flying at an altitude of 7,000 meters, in the region of Taechon Major Pulov spotted thirty F-84s, below and to the left, flying on a meeting course in a column of flights. Pulov issued a command: 'The 2nd and 3rd Aviation Squadrons are to attack the enemy in a column of elements. The 1st Squadron will cover the attack.' Then he himself started on a descending left turn to close with the F-84s. At an altitude of 5,000 meters, while still in the left turn, Major Pulov and his wingman Captain Morozov drew to within a range of 500–600 meters of one F-84 element. Together, Pulov and Morozov opened fire, before sweeping past the target in a right turn. With a subsequent transition into a left turn they began to approach a second element of F-84s. At that moment, they were jumped by a pair of F-86s that caught them by surprise. Captain Morozov, spotting the Sabres behind them at the last moment, shouted a warning over the radio to Major Pulov: 'Break left!' Then Morozov himself, now separated from Major Pulov, began to bank left. The Sabres, closing to within point-blank range, opened fire on Captain Morozov's MiG. Morozov's plane burst into flames, pitched sharply upward to the right, and then went into a steep dive at an angle of 70–80°.

Captain Mishakin with his wingman Senior Lieutenant Komarov, spotting the F–86 element that was attacking Captain Morozov, moved to attack it, but it was already too late. The enemy continued their dive out of the attack and quickly disappeared from view. Captain Mishakin assigned his wingman to the regiment commander and they continued to fight.

Captain Morozov's MiG fell in a location about 24 kilometers north-east of Sonchon. The death of this experienced pilot was caused by the unexpected role he had to play as Pulov's wingman. His inexperience in flying together with his leader clearly affected what happened. Pulov's MiG received one hole in his left wing in this action, but he maintained control of his plane and flew back to his airbase. The regiment carried out its assignment, though indeed at a high price: Ivan Nikolaevich Morozov fell under the attack of Sabre pilots from the 334th Squadron, which claimed three victories over the MiGs on this day.

On this mission the regiment had to take on thirty F–84s and sixteen F–86s; Major Pulov shot down one enemy F–84. However, Grigorii Pulov did not receive credit for this victory, since there was no confirmation from the North Korean authorities. In addition to this, pilots of the 17th IAP on this day also claimed two F–80 fighter-bombers. The pair of Senior Lieutenants Volkov and Nikolaev from the 3rd Aviation Squadron distinguished themselves in this action. Most likely, this duo shot down RF–80A No. 45–8472 from the 67th Tactical Reconnaissance Group's 15th Tactical Reconnaissance Squadron. Its pilot, First Lieutenant Bruce A. Sweney was killed.

In October, the regiment received replacements from the 70th and 180th GIAP in corps reserve: Captain Boris Efimovich Tikhonov went to the 1st Aviation Squadron as a pilot; Captain Nikolai Vasil'evich Masly was assigned as deputy commander for political affairs in the 2nd Aviation Squadron. Masly was joined in the 2nd Aviation Squadron by replacements Senior Lieutenant Aleksandr Georgievich Chernozemov (flight commander), and pilots Senior Lieutenants Nikolai Alekseevich Zelenov and Pavel Petrovich Gostiukhin. Senior Lieutenants Ivan Fedorovich Polishchuk, Rostislav Vasil'evich Khrisanov, and Vladimir Nikolaevich Shestopalov all joined the 3rd Aviation Squadron as pilots. Altogether, eight new pilots joined the regiment. The most experienced of the new pilots was Senior Lieutenant A.G. Chernozemov, a Great Patriotic War veteran who had been decorated with two Orders of the Red Banner. Soon he was appointed deputy squadron commander.

Also in the month of October, the pilots of the American 4th Fighter Wing began to switch over to a new version of the Sabre, the F–86E, which had just begun to arrive in Korea. Then seventy-five more of the F–86E Sabres arrived in Korea to equip the 51st Fighter Wing at the K–13 airbase in Suwon, which was then in the process of converting from the F–80C to the F–86. The planes and personnel for this unit had been brought to Japan aboard the aircraft carriers USS *Cape Esperance* and USS *Sitkoh Bay* at the beginning of November. Thus by December 1951, when the 51st Fighter Wing reached full combat readiness, the complement of F-86 fighters in the skies of Korea had doubled.

The headquarters staff of the 303rd IAD continued to pay strict attention to the confirmation of victory credits. On 5 October, Major Pulov received a reprimand 'for the formalistic composition' of his reports on the aerial combats conducted by the regiment. Yet just that day, Pulov had distinguished himself by shooting down his first F-86.

At 09:51, twenty MiGs of the regiment were scrambled and vectored to the area of Anju to repel an enemy fighter-bomber strike. The 3rd and 1st Aviation Squadrons comprised the strike group of the combat formation, while the 2nd Aviation Squadron flew as the cover group. Gaining altitude while flying at the head of the 3rd Aviation Squadron, at 10:20 at an altitude of 9,000 meters, Major Pulov spotted up to ten F-86s from the enemy fighter barrier, flying in a column of elements about 500 meters higher, to the left and in front of them. Having assessed the situation, Pulov decided to attack the enemy and began to bank left toward this F-86 group. Spotting the approaching MiGs, the first two elements of enemy fighters in the column adopted a right stagger formation and began to bank to the right. Another pair of Sabres in trail began to depart in a descending spiral.

Major Pulov with his wingman Captain Blagov pursued this pair of F-86s in a descending left turn. Closing to a range of 500 meters, Pulov fired one short and two long bursts at the Sabre element's wingman. Yet even as he fired, Major Pulov's element was jumped from above and behind to the left by another F-86 element. Blagov reacted by swinging from the left side position behind Pulov to the right, before turning back to the left to drive away the attacking F-86 element. The Sabres responded with a split-S and dived away in the direction of the sea. While Major Pulov was firing at his target, Captain Blagov had observed shell strikes on the Sabre.

The 1st Aviation Squadron under the command of Senior Lieutenant Sutiagin, arriving in the area of Anju at an altitude of 7,000 meters, began circling to the right. About three-quarters of the way through a full circle, Sutiagin spotted eight F-86s in front of him and about 1,500–2,000 meters above him, which were engaging the 3rd Squadron. Simultaneously, the leader of the second element Senior Lieutenant Bychkov spotted another eight F-86s above, behind and to the left of them. At a command from Senior Lieutenant Sutiagin, the group circled to the left to engage this new threat. The Sabres, declining combat, rolled over and dived away toward the sea. Sutiagin's group, banking to the left to a heading of 110°, continued on this course for two to three minutes, after which it began to make another left turn. Coming out of this turn, the squadron was bounced by a flight of four F-86s from behind. Nikolai Sutiagin immediately ordered an oblique left loop in response. After two or three loops, the Sabres found themselves lagging further and further behind, so gave up the chase and exited the fight. Sutiagin's group returned to base.

The 2nd Squadron under the command of Guards Major Maslennikov remained above the fray as high cover and did not become engaged in this fight. As a result of this action, Major Pulov downed one Sabre and damaged another. However, the regiment failed in its mission: it was unable to break through the Sabre screen to the enemy ground attack planes, having been tied up in battle by a superior force of fighters in the screen. The airplane downed by Major Pulov was confirmed by ground troops, but for some reason the division did not credit him with this victory.

On 6 October at 08:31 Major Pulov again led a group of twenty-two MiG-15s into the sky to repulse an attack by enemy ground attack planes, escorted by fighters. In the ensuing action, Pulov managed to down one F-86. Captain Mishakin and Senior Lieutenant Komarov each shot down another Sabre but two of our MiGs received damage in return: Senior Lieutenant Malunov's plane landed with two bullet holes in the left wing, while Senior Lieutenant Bykov's MiG returned with four bullet holes, also in the left wing.

On this day, Nikolai Sutiagin received a promotion to the next rank of captain. Four and a half months passed before the actual presentation of the promotion. By the same order, Senior Lieutenants Bychkov, Dokashenko and Shestopalov also received promotions.

Autumn introduced its own changes into the lives of our military service personnel. Because of the onset of cold weather, many pilots were put out of action by illnesses. Reports to the command mentioned the need for heating the living quarters and for the distribution of warm footgear. Up to 60 per cent of the pilots had head colds. The doctors concluded that the flight personnel needed a period of rest, especially Pulov, Dokashenko, Miroshnichenko, and Gostiukhin. Many pilots were experiencing vomiting because of inhaling too much oxygen on flights. Eight pilots of the 3rd Aviation Squadron had been flying since the start of combat operations without a break. The pilots Artemchenko, Gostiukhin, Polianichko, Komarov and others were telling others in private conversations that they needed sanatorium treatment to recuperate, not a fifteen-day halt in flight activities. The decision was made to send more pilots on longer R&R. On 7 October, Captain Ponomarev and Lieutenant Kordanov were the first to leave for a sanatorium in the city of Dal'ny.

From the month of October, the burden on the pilots and ground crews increased significantly and reached a maximum in the month of November

(853 combat sorties). If during the first half of the mission to China the regiment had conducted 1,469 sorties until the month of October, then between October 1951 and February 1952, the regiment carried out 2,757 sorties. Pilots were sometimes conducting four combat sorties and two air battles a day; in one month, up to forty combat sorties and eighteen dogfights. The burden on the ground crews grew correspondingly, but they managed to handle the workload. In its orders, the command noted that the engineer-technical service of the regiment was operating well: 75- and 100-hour jobs were being completed in eight to ten hours, and they were replacing engines in just one day. Over a period of one month, the ground crews enabled 520 combat sorties, and replaced sixteen engines in fifteen MiGs.

'For the Model Fufillment ...'

On 10 October 1951, the day long-awaited by all the pilots of the 303rd IAD at last arrived: the official decree came out awarding the title of Hero of the Soviet Union to pilots of the corps, who had especially distinguished themselves in combat, and among them the first Heroes in the 303rd IAD. The following men were awarded this highest honor:

> Major General G.A. Lobov – Commander of the 64th IAK, former commander of the 303rd IAD;
> Captain G.I. Ges' – Squadron commander in the 176th GIAP, a veteran of the Second World War who scored five victories against the Germans, and who was credited with eight more victories over Korea;
> Captain S.M. Kramarenko – Deputy squadron commander in the 176th GIAP, eventually credited with thirteen victories in Korea;
> Senior Lieutenant B.A. Obraztsov (posthumously) – a pilot in the 176th GIAP, who downed a total of four enemy planes before his death;
> Senior Lieutenant E.M. Stel'makh (posthumously) – a senior pilot of the 18th GIAP;
> Major S.P. Subbotin – Navigator of the 176th GIAP, who downed nine enemy planes over Korea;
> Senior Lieutenant F.A. Shebanov – a pilot of the 196th IAP with six victories to his credit (who was killed in action less than two weeks later on 26 October 1951).

Two pilots received this honor posthumously. In the Decree of the Presidium of the USSR Supreme Soviet that awarded the highest honor of the country and in the certificates, which the recipients later received together with the Gold Star Medal and the Order of Lenin, there was the wording: 'For the model fulfillment of a government assignment and the courage and heroism demonstrated in doing so ...'

First on the list of honorees was the former commander of the 303rd IAD, Major General Georgii Ageevich Lobov, who received this title for his skilful leadership of the division's regiments, as well as for the personal heroism that he had demonstrated in the years of the Great Patriotic War, when he personally downed nineteen German planes. Here as well, in Korea, General Lobov repeatedly flew combat missions and participated in aerial combats, shooting down four more enemy planes.

Fulfilling the combat assignments of the command, pilot of the 176th GIAP Senior Lieutenant Obraztsov conducted fifty-six combat sorties and, participating in eighteen aerial combats, he personally downed four enemy planes (one of his victories was over a B–29 bomber on 12 April 1951). During a mission on 11 July 1951, his MiG was jumped by a group of enemy fighters. Entering into an unequal fight, the brave pilot was killed after shooting down two enemy planes. He was decorated with the Orders of Lenin and the Red Banner. On 14 January 1952, his name was entered eternally on the roster of his Guards fighter aviation regiment.

Captain Grigorii Ivanovich Ges', commander of a squadron in the 176th GIAP, had become an ace back in the years of the Great Patriotic War, downing five German planes. He fought successfully in Korea as well. On one mission, he jumped a group of F–51 Mustang fighter-bombers. He opened up from point-blank range and destroyed one enemy plane, but he was unable to avoid debris from the falling plane. As a result, his MiG's horizontal stabilizer became jammed and he lost the ability to make vertical maneuvers. There was little left he could do but to eject from his crippled jet, but Ges' decided to try to save the plane and land it back at his base. He informed the command post about his decision: after some hesitation, the flight controller permitted him to make a crash landing. Demonstrating all his abilities and courage, Captain Ges' managed to bring the plane down safely and to save the plane. For this heroic exploit, the division command presented Grigorii Ivanovich Ges' with the title of Hero. Altogether, Ges' received credit for downing eight enemy planes in Korea.

Deputy squadron commander Sergei Makarovich Kramarenko of the 176th GIAP was also a veteran of the Great Patriotic War. At times he had occasion to fly as the wingman of the famous ace I.N. Kozhedub, but more often he flew with the regiment navigator, Hero of the Soviet Union Major A.S. Kumanichkin, giving his leader the chance to shoot down more than ten enemy planes. Kramarenko himself personally shot down two German planes. He became one of the first aces of the 324th IAD in Korea, after downing six American planes in the first months of fighting. Kramarenko received the title of Hero after reaching a total of eight victories. Altogether, he scored thirteen victories in the skies over Korea.

Major Subbotin had an unusual event in his combat records. Early on the morning of 18 June 1951, two flights of MiG-15s, led by the 176th GIAP's navigator Serafim Subbotin, took off to intercept enemy fighters. On the approach to the city of Sonchon at an altitude of 9,000 meters, our pilots spotted a group of sixteen F-86 Sabres approaching to intercept them. The Americans had twice the number of fighters on their side! Yet Subbotin decided to engage them. Serving as an example to his subordinates, he resolutely attacked the leading American fighter and scored a success: the Sabre exploded in the air. However, it was too soon to celebrate the victory. In the ensuing dogfight Subbotin had to come to the assistance of his wingman. With an energetic maneuver he diverted the attention of the attackers from his comrade, but he himself became a target for the enemy. After one successful Sabre attacking pass on his plane, his engine began to sputter. Serafim threw his plane into a steep dive, trying to separate from the adversary, but unsuccessfully. Deploying his speed brakes, Serafim sharply cut his speed, and in doing so placed his plane again under attack. The American pilot plainly didn't anticipate this maneuver from the Russian pilot, and could not avoid a collision. After ejecting, as Subbotin swung beneath his parachute's canopy, he watched as both fighters, wrapped in flames, fell to the earth.

Serafim had a rough landing. Hemorrhaging in the sclera of his eyes and a strained muscle in his right forearm forced him to stop flying temporarily. After recuperating he again returned to active duty and continued to accumulate victories. Altogether over ten months of the war, Serafim Subbotin downed nine enemy planes.

Senior Lieutenant Fedor Shebanov, as a wingman (!), over a period of just one month (!), downed five enemy planes and became the first jet ace in the 324th IAD. On 20 May 1951, Fedor Shebanov, downing an F-86, scored his sixth victory (and his fifth over a jet). Often, carried away by his fervor in a dogfight, Fedor would commit the cardinal sin of leaving his leader, which was a punishable offense. However, the command forgave him these 'weaknesses', since Fedor Shebanov kept knocking down enemy planes more often than other pilots. Ultimately, however, this manner of dogfighting led to his death – on his next mission, once again fighting in isolation, he came under attack from a superior enemy force and was shot down.

An assembly of the division's units took place at the Myaogou airfield on 13 October, dedicated to the awarding of Hero to a group of pilots of the 303rd IAD: General Lobov, Senior Lieutenant Stel'makh, and Captain Sutiagin. Unfortunately Nikolai Sutiagin himself was not present at the assembly. In the first days of October, Captain Sutiagin had carried out a total of eight missions and become engaged in five combat actions. On 11 October, he and Lieutenant Bozhko had been sent to the sanatorium in Dal'ny. It was there that he learned

Nikolai Sutiagin with his future wife Raisa Baranova, April 1945.

Pilots of the 5th Fighter Aviation Regiment's 2nd Aviation Squadron. N. Sutiagin is seated second from the left. Seated in the middle is squadron commander A. Olenitsa, who would later score five victories himself over Korea.

Nikolai Sutiagin in Manchuria, July 1951, when he would score his fifth victory to become an ace.

Nikolai Sutiagin poses with his first wingman in Korea, V. Shulev, Manchuria, 1951.

Off-duty pilots of the 17th Fighter Aviation Regiment's 3rd Aviation Squadron. From left to right: N.S. Volkov, M.N. Shcherbakov, N.G. Dokashenko, A.V. Bykov, V.M. Khvostantsev (partially obscured), A.N. Nikolaev, and V.A. Blagov, Manchuria, 1951.

Hero of the Soviet Union A.S. Kumanichkin, deputy commander and later the commander of the 303rd Fighter Aviation Division in Manchuria.

Hero of the Soviet Union Capt. N.G. Dokashenko, commander of the 17th Fighter Aviation Regiment's 3rd Aviation Squadron.

Hero of the Soviet Union Maj. M.S. Ponomarev, commander of the 17th Fighter Aviation Regiment's 2nd Aviation Squadron, credited with ten victories in Korea.

A 1945 photograph of S.S. Artemchenko, who would later become the commander of the 17th Fighter Aviation Regiment's 1st Aviation Squadron in Manchuria.

Senior Lieutenant D.A. Samoilov of the 523rd Fighter Aviation Regiment, who was credited with ten victories in Korea.

Maj. Nikolai Sutiagin, after his return from Manchuria, May 1952.

The MiG-15, the Soviet Air Force's primary fighter in Korea.

Another view of the MiG-15, after a return from a training sortie.

Gloster Meteors of the Royal Australian Air Force.

A United States Air Force F-80 Shooting Star, nicknamed 'the Cross' by the Soviet fighter pilots in Korea.

Inspecting the .50 caliber machine guns on an F-86E Sabre.

Readying an F-86F for another sortie.

The armament of the MiG-15 on display: two 23mm cannon on the right and the 37mm cannon on the left.

An RF-80A that managed to make it back home. Note the devastation caused by a shell from a MiG-15's 37mm cannon.

Soviet training diagram for determining the target aspect angle. The caption above the silhouettes reads 'How the aircraft appears', while the numbers on the left and right show the Soviet method of identifying the target aspect angle: 0/4, 1/4, 2/4, 3/4, 4/4.

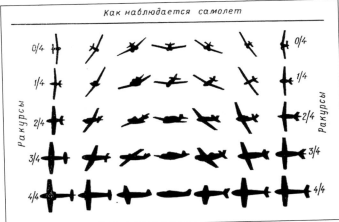

Nikolai Sutiagin stands in front of a parked MiG-21, North Vietnam, 1971.

On his special advisory mission to North Vietnam, Nikolai Sutiagin converses with North Vietnamese pilots through an interpreter, 1970.

Hero of the Soviet Union Major General of Aviation Nikolai Sutiagin in 1978.

of the decree that made him a Hero of the Soviet Union. The brief R&R turned out to be most fortunate: one can become a bit weak on the occasion of receiving such a high honor.

The pilots relaxing in Dal'ny usually visited the city of Port Arthur as well. They took in the sights of the entire city with interest. It was a novelty for them: a typical Russian city. At the time, the Soviet Union still based military units there; Russian women strolled along its streets, and Russian children were running and playing. All these places have been described in detail in Stepanov's well-known book *Port Arthur*, and it was strange for the pilots to see all this in their waking hours. They also visited the Russian military cemetery, where the heroes of the War of 1905 are buried and where the graves of their comrades were being added. Fallen pilots of the 17th IAP were already interred there – Kukhmakov, Morozov, Agranovich.

When Nikolai returned to the regiment, one more bit of news was waiting for him. On 30 October, on the basis of a verbal instruction of General Krasovsky, by order of the commander of the 17th IAP, Sutiagin was made the acting assistant commander of the regiment for aerial gunnery and tactics in the place of Major Vorob'ev, who had been called back to be at the disposal of the Operational Group commander.

The October Engagements with the 'Fortresses'

While Nikolai Sutiagin was resting at the sanatorium in Dal'ny, the 17th IAP took part in the memorable engagements of 22–27 October against B-29 bombers, which in literature on the war have since become known as 'Black Week' and 'Black Tuesday'. They were certainly black days for the US Air Force Bomber Command.

On the eve of this notable period, however, a 'ChP' occurred in the regiment on one of its flights. At 07:41 on 21 October, after returning from a combat mission and while making a routine landing, flight commander Captain Bychkov carelessly handled his plane on the roll-out after landing. After touching down, he was late in applying the brakes, failed to cut his speed quickly enough, and rather than roll off the end of the runway, he chose to swerve off the right side. Bychkov sped across the taxiway and collided with parked MiGs of the 18th GIAP. He put three planes out of action, which according to the assessment of the technicians would require five to eight days of work to repair. Captain Bychkov received a warning about being unfit for service from the division commander, together with a three-month 25 per cent reduction in pay.

Incidentally, in similar cases Chinese pilots received much harsher punishments, right up to a death sentence. In the East, the aircraft were valued much more highly than a human life.[2]

By the way, Captain Bychkov didn't lose heart. He acknowledged his guilt and promised to make amends in battle. Already on the next day, 22 October, he would down two F-84s in one action, and in action on 23 October ('Black Tuesday'), he would shoot down one B-29 and damage another F-84. Altogether Bychkov would have five enemy planes to his credit, three of them from the month of October 1951.

The following events preceded 'Black Week'. Back at the beginning of October, American aerial reconnaissance had detected ongoing construction work on eighteen airfields in North Korea. The three largest of the new airfields at Naamsi, Saamchan and Taechon, which had concrete runways and would be capable of staging jet aircraft, especially stood out. The new airfields, located deep in North Korean territory, would permit the transfer of fresh MiG-15 units to them, which would expand the area of operation of these dangerous fighters and jeopardize the operation of the UN air forces. In this event, the so-called 'MiG Alley' would extend all the way down to the 38th Parallel, and potentially expose the UN ground forces to continuous air attacks. Naturally, this obvious threat could not be ignored by the command of the UN forces, which clearly understood the danger that these new enemy airbases posed.

Thus, the air force command of the UN forces quickly decided to conduct an urgent military operation to destroy the new airbases, in order to forestall the transfer of air units to them from their Manchurian bases. They selected B-29 bombers to be the primary strike force in this operation; these bombers could carry several tons of powerful bombs and were capable of putting all the runways of these airbases completely out of commission, as well as other airfield facilities and installations.

At first, it was decided to operate the B-29 groups at night in order to avoid MiG opposition. However, two trial B-29 attacks on the Saamchan airbase, undertaken on the nights of 13 and 14 October, demonstrated that these night-time raids had little effect and that the Superfortress crews would not be able to knock out the airfields. It was then decided to launch a powerful daytime strike on these bases, using every possible air force unit equipped with jet fighters to protect the bombers. All serviceable F-86s, as well as F-84 and F-80 units and even the British Gloster Meteors of No. 77 Royal Australian Squadron were employed to cover the B-29 bombers.

The first trial daytime attack took place on 18 October, but it proved to be unsuccessful: because of a lack of coordination among the ground services, the B-29 bombers failed to rendezvous with the escort fighters and therefore opted against flying toward a strongly protected target without cover; instead, they attacked secondary targets. The same thing happened on 21 October, and again the B–29 bombers had to bomb alternative targets.

Only on Monday, 22 October, did twelve bombers from the 19th Bombardment Group rendezvous with their escort, which according to various estimates consisted of sixty to 100 fighters; that is, each bomber on this mission was covered by five to eight fighters. Taechon was the selected target for this attack. It is still difficult to determine the precise number of fighters activated for this mission, for the reason that one portion of the fighters provided stayed with the bombers to provide immediate cover, while another portion operated as ground attack planes to carry out a diversionary blow against railroads in the Sukchon–Anju–Sunchon region.

To repel this major enemy air raid, all combat-ready crews of the 303rd IAD were scrambled: fifty-four MiG-15bis fighters. Starting at 14:03, fighters of all three regiments of the division began to launch from the airfield at Myaogou in sequence: twenty pilots of the 17th IAP under the command of Major Pulov; twenty pilots of the 523rd IAP led by Captain Okhai; and fourteen pilots of the 18th GIAP led by Lieutenant Colonel Smorchkov.

The 17th IAP and the 523rd IAP were the first to make contact with the enemy: in the region of Uiju and Sukchon they encountered several groups of F–80 and F–84 fighter-bombers and engaged them in combat. Thus only pilots of the 18th GIAP managed to reach the group of B–29 bombers. Despite the superior numbers of escort fighters, they decided to have a go at the bomber formation. Part of the regimental group went for the bombers, while the remaining MiGs took on the bombers' direct escort, which consisted of F–84 Thunderjets. As a result of this action, pilots of the 18th GIAP led by Lieutenant Colonel Smorchkov succeeded in downing three B–29s and four F–84s from the fighter escort. The MiGs of Senior Lieutenants Shavsha and Konev received combat damage in this action. Simultaneously, pilots of the 17th IAP and 523rd IAP scattered several groups of enemy fighter-bombers. In the process, they downed five F–84s without any losses of their own.

Nevertheless, the 17th IAP made mistakes on this mission. Captain Artemchenko's cover group became separated from the strike group and failed to provide cover for it. On his own initiative Artemchenko then made the decision to pursue a group of enemy aircraft, which he unsuccessfully followed to Pyongyang. In doing so, the group's formation became stretched out and several pilots straggled behind their leaders.

Meanwhile, the strike group of eight MiGs, led by Major Pulov, detected a group of sixteen F–84s at an altitude of 2,000–4,000 meters, which were flying in two groups of eight aircraft. Pulov led his group in an attack on the Thunderjets. In the course of this attack, Senior Lieutenant Aleksandr Bykov downed one Thunderjet, their formation was broken up, and they began to flee in ones and twos toward the safety of the sea.

During this attack, the cockpit canopy on the plane of Major Pulov's wingman, Captain Viktor Blagov, fogged up during the steep dive upon the targets and he was forced to exit the battle. Pulov was now alone without a wingman, so he too had to leave the battle.

As the scattered Thunderjets were racing toward the sea, Captain Artemchenko's group arrived from its detour to Pyongyang and also began a low-altitude chase after the Thunderjets. During this pursuit, Captain Sergei Bychkov was particularly successful: he managed to attack two Thunderjets in succession and added both to his personal score.

However, the initial successes of this battle almost ended in great losses for the pilots of the 17th IAP. Their pursuit of the retreating F-84s was interrupted when a group of Sabres arrived on the scene, plainly responding to calls for help from the Thunderjet pilots. Now the tables were turned, and the pilots of the 17th IAP found themselves in a very difficult position, with their own combat formations now scattered, and with many pilots operating totally on their own. Among them was Captain Bychkov, whose wingman had lagged behind him in the chase. Captain Shcherbakov had also exited the battle prematurely, and his wingman Bykov had to take on four F-86s alone, one of which he managed to damage.

From the recollections of a pilot in the 3rd Aviation Squadron, A.N. Nikolaev:

> Captain Shcherbakov, putting it gently, showed excessive caution in combat, although he had solid flight experience in the MiG-15. When he was named to command the 3rd Aviation Squadron, we had high hopes for him, but he didn't justify them. He deliberately avoided getting involved in battle. At first we trusted him and waited for him to do something. But then our belief in him gradually faded away, and our flight began to operate at its own discretion. His wingman was the deputy squadron commander for political affairs, Senior Lieutenant A.V. Bykov. Naturally, he couldn't show any special initiative as Shcherbakov's wingman, although he was an experienced and fine pilot.

The Soviet pilots sought to extricate themselves from their precarious situation as quickly as possible. While exiting from the battle, Major Pulov linked up with Senior Lieutenant Shirokov, who had lost his own leader and was now alone, and they both headed back to base. As they were approaching the Yalu River, they were suddenly jumped by a pair of F-86s, which first struck Major Pulov's plane, leaving twelve bullet holes in his wing, fuselage, and engine area. Then the same pair of Sabres turned their attention to

Shirokov's MiG as well, which received sixteen bullet holes in its wing, fuselage, engine area, rudder, and horizontal stabilizer. Senior Lieutenant Shirokov received a slight wound to the right shoulder.

Grigorii Ivanovich Pulov himself tells the story of this battle in the following way:

> In the action I damaged one fighter-bomber at low altitude, but in the course of the battle I found myself paired up with a new wingman, Shirokov. While we were returning back to base as a pair, the flight of Captain Blagov linked up with us. There were scattered clouds above us, and we were flying below the clouds. Suddenly, a Sabre popped out of these clouds unnoticed by anyone, and approaching my plane from below, shot up my plane from an aspect angle of 0/4. Immediately my wingman shouted at me over the radio with the late warning: 'Break left!' I made a sharp turn to the left and went into a dive. Plainly thinking that my plane had been fatally damaged, the Sabres (there were about eight of them) engaged my wingman Sasha Shirokov.
>
> Eight blades of my plane's turbine had been shot out and the engine lost a lot of power, but despite this I squeezed everything I could from it, the airbase was nearby, and I managed to nurse it home and land. There were a dozen holes in my plane, and they turned it over for major repairs, while I received a new plane.
>
> Shirokov's plane was also damaged in this same action, and he himself was lightly wounded in the face by shattered fragments of his cockpit canopy's glazing. The Sabres, apparently, also considered him as fatally damaged and left him alone. Therefore Sasha decided against bailing out and successfully landed the plane at his airfield. Our technicians soon restored his MiG to working order.

On the whole, although the regiment's mission concluded with no losses on our side and with several victories over the opponent, it should not be considered a success. At the fault of Captain Artemchenko, the regimental group had become split up and it went into combat in an uncoordinated fashion, which led to the scattering of the entire group into separately acting pairs. The leader of the regimental group, Major Pulov, who lost control over his groups on this mission, also carries some of the blame for this as well.

Incidentally, before moving on with our narrative, it is interesting to share with you some of the other observations about fellow pilots in the 17th IAP told by A.N. Nikolaev to the authors. It is useful to understand that these were all men with their own personalities and characteristics, some of which were reflected in their way of fighting:

My leader Nikolai Volkov quite often fired his guns in combat, but he suffered from one flaw – he opened fire from long range. We were constantly quarrelling over this, sometimes approaching the use of swear words. If he hadn't been in such a rush, likely he would have had as many victories as the flight commander Captain Dokashenko. We flew well together as a team, and it was very rare when one of us arrived at a point without the other.

There was also a pilot in the 1st Aviation Squadron, Boris Tikhonov. He arrived in the regiment as a replacement. He very often fired his guns, but as I recall, his results were less than modest. Our commander liked to joke: 'Tishka blackened the whole sky with his shells!'

Back in the USSR, Vladimir Khvostantsev had been a senior pilot, that is to say, the leader of an element. When we were preparing to travel to China, they proposed that he act as Dokashenko's wingman, as a regular pilot – and he agreed! This decision unquestionably did him credit! He was a wonderful, sincere man. As they say, we got along like soul mates. He was also exceptionally able as a pilot. He returned from China as the deputy commander of a squadron.

On 23 October, Captain Ponomarev with Lieutenants Kordanov and Bozhko returned from the spa, and without any 'warm-up' almost immediately plunged back into the fighting on 25–26 October. However, the main events of 'Black Week' unfolded on the day of their return, 23 October.

The full picture of the events of 'Black Tuesday' has already been presented in the work of L. Krylov and Iu. Tepsurkaev, *Chernaia nedelia Bombard-irovochnogo komandovaniia* [The Black Week of Bomber Command], published in 1999. Here is an extended excerpt from this article:

If the encounter between the MiGs and the B-29s on Monday had been something of a coincidence, then on Tuesday the crews of the Superfortresses anticipated a well-planned and hot reception. All the veterans recall the combat on **23 October 1951** [emphasis in original], and authors around the world refer to it. We are paying particular attention to this day, since it became a real turning point in the story of the war – **Black Tuesday** [emphasis in original]. From a description of the fighting:

'In the period 0810–0830, our radar stations detected eight groups of enemy planes, each consisting of eight to thirty-two aircraft, for a total of up to 200 fighters of the types F-86, F-84, F-80 and Gloster Meteor IV at an altitude of 6,500–8,000 meters; two bomber groups of ten to twelve B–29s each were also detected, which between 0835–0904 carried out a concentrated bombing on the Naamsi airbase from an altitude of 7,000 meters (the bombs fell 2 kilometers south of the base, which received no damage). Meanwhile, fighter-bombers attacked targets in the areas of Anju, Pakchon, and Taechon from an altitude of 4,000 meters down to nearly ground level.

'The fighter-bombers and bombers were protected by a fighter screen consisting of forty F–86s, patrolling in Kusong–Sonchon area at an altitude of 8,000 to 10,000 meters, and a direct escort consisting of up to eighty fighters at altitudes between 6,000 and 9,000 meters. Altogether, up to 200 fighters and fighter-bombers and twenty-two bombers took part in this mission. The enemy was aiming to disrupt the flow of supplies to the Korean and Chinese forces and to put the airbases at Naamsi and Taechon out of action, and to inflict a concentrated strike on bridges, crossings, railroads, and the airbases currently under construction. Having evaluated the situation, the commander of the 64th IAK decided to use two divisions of the corps to counter the concentrated attack of enemy bombers and fighter-bombers, introducing them into the battle sequentially.

'Accordingly, the 303rd IAD with the 17th IAP, 18th GIAP and 523rd IAP (fifty-eight MiG-15s) comprised the first echelon and was assigned to attack the primary group of enemy bombers and fighter-bombers. The 324th IAD's 176th GIAP and 196th IAP (twenty-six MiGs) comprised the corps' second echelon and were responsible for reinforcing the battle and covering the 303rd IAD's exit from battle. The 351st IAP was held back as the corps commander's reserve.

'... At 0812–0816, units of the corps went to readiness level No. 1. At 0824–0833, at an order from the command post of the IAK, the entire 303rd IAD, consisting of the 17th IAP (twenty MiG-15s) under the command of Major Maslennikov, the 18th GIAP (twenty MiG-15s) under the command of Lieutenant Colonel Smorchkov, and the 523rd IAP (eighteen MiG-15s) under the command of Major Os'kin soared into the sky.

'At 0840–0845, on an order from the command post of the IAK, the 324th IAD's 176th GIAP (fourteen MiG-15s) under the command of Colonel Vishniakov and the 196th (twelve MiG-15s) under the command of Major Mitusov were scrambled ...

'The regiments of the 303rd and 324th IAD assembled in the air by means of a turn of 90° and 180° along the north bank of the Yalu River. After ascending to an altitude of 5,000–6,000 meters, the units were vectored to the Anju–Taechon region. Our fighters were receiving directions from the corps command post, their respective IAD commanders, and Auxiliary Control Post No. 2. The command's primary attention while vectoring the units was on directing the MiGs to the bomber groups.

'The combat formation of the 303rd IAD consisted of a strike group and a cover group, flying in a column of regiments spaced within visual range of each other. The 523rd IAP and the 18th GIAP comprised the strike group, while the 17th IAP flew as the cover group. Lieutenant Colonel Smorchkov was leading the divisional group.

'The combat formation of the 324th IAD also consisted of a strike group and a cover group, flying in a column of regiments with 6–7 kilometers between the regiments. The 196th IAP served as the strike group, while the 176th GIAP flew as cover. Colonel Vishniakov was placed in command of the 324th IAD's divisional group.

'At 0940, the 176th GIAP, flying at an altitude of 8,000 meters at the head of the strike group, encountered up to forty F-86s of the enemy fighter screen, flying in a variety of combat formations: a staggered column of eights, an echelon of eights, and flights in a stagger of pairs.

'At the same time, group commander Lieutenant Colonel Smorchkov spotted eight B-29s in front of him and to the left, flying in a line abreast formation to the south, with an interval of 40–50 meters between the planes. The bombers were under the immediate escort of up to thirty F-84s, in groups of six to eight planes located to the right, the left, and 600 to 800 meters above and behind the bomber formation.

'Having assessed the situation, the group commander ordered the 1st and 3rd Aviation Squadrons (fourteen MiGs) to engage the F-86 fighters, and the 2nd Aviation Squadron (six MiG-15s) to attack the bombers. Our fighters joined battle according to these orders. As a result of the combat, according to the pilots' reports and the gun camera footage, two B-29 bombers and two F-84s of the immediate escort were downed.

'At 0943, the 523rd IAP (eighteen MiG-15s) under the command of Major Os'kin, flying at an altitude of 9,000 meters as part of the strike group behind the 18th GIAP, noticed eight F-86s at an altitude of 7,000 meters 20 to 40 kilometers south-west of Taechon, flying across the strike group's heading. Os'kin opted to follow them, and having completed a 90° right-hand turn with his flight, Os'kin spotted nine B-29s and up to forty F-84s, F-86s and Gloster Meteors, in front and to the left of him at an altitude of 5,000 meters.

'The B-29 combat formation consisted of a lead flight of three bombers in a compact wedge formation, while the trailing six bombers were about 4,000 to 5,000 meters behind and to the right of the lead formation, in a line abreast formation. These six bombers became the target of our fighters' attack. The enemy's close escort fighters were deployed as follows: eight Gloster Meteors were flying about 2,000–3,000 meters in front of the bombers, about 1,000 to 2,000 meters to the right of them, and about 600–800 meters above them; and F-84s in groups of four to eight fighters each were arranged to the left, right and behind the B-29s at a distance of 1,000–2,000 meters. Two groups of eight F-86s each in a combat formation of an echelon of flights were patrolling at an altitude of 8,000 meters to the right and behind the B-29s, about 10–15 kilometers away. At the leader's signal, the regiment attacked the enemy bombers and fighters.

'As a result of the aerial combat, according to the pilots' reports and an analysis of the gun camera footage, five B-29s and one F-84 were shot down. The MiGs did not come away unscathed: Senior Lieutenant Khurtin, who was jumped by four F-86s in a region 15–20 kilometers north-west of Antung while returning to his base, was shot down.'[3]

It is apparent from this article that on this day, the pilots of the division's 523rd IAP and 18th GIAP, who were being covered by the 324th IAD, particularly distinguished themselves. In the 18th GIAP, both Lieutenant Colonel Smorchkov and Captain Kornienko claimed one Superfortress each, while Senior Lieutenant Shchukin downed one of the Thunderjets in a head-on attack.

Senior Lieutenant Lev Kirillovich Shchukin himself recalled to the authors:

They were trying to intimidate us. They were perhaps thinking that we would be frightened by their numbers and would flee, but instead we met them head-on. Such an attack is like driving an automobile without brakes! I had two hostile planes directly in front of me. I nudged my plane slightly to one side to bring one of them into my sights, and opened up on him from a range of 150 meters. He immediately exploded into an enormous fireball. I had no chance to avoid it and flew directly through the center of the explosion, instinctively shutting my eyes. When I opened my eyes again, all I could see behind me was the dark cloud of smoke from the F-84's explosion and the cascading fragments of the plane.

In the 523rd IAP, Major Os'kin claimed two Superfortresses. There were no survivors from the crews of these planes – twelve and thirteen men respectively. Captain Bakhaev and Senior Lieutenants D'iachenko and Shevarev each claimed an additional B-29.

Senior Lieutenant Dmitrii Aleksandrovich Samoilov, who was Major D.P. Os'kin's wingman on this mission, relates:

> Flying toward the region where enemy planes had been detected, our regiment was attacked by two groups of enemy fighters. We were forced into a difficult battle with them. My commander evaded the attack with a vertical maneuver and quickly turned the table on his attackers. Just as it seemed that he was going to open fire, I caught sight of nine B-29s and immediately radioed him that 'big ones' (that's what we called the B-29s) were to the right and below us. Os'kin broke off his attack on the fighters and moved to attack the B-29s, transmitting the command: 'Everyone attack the big ones!'
>
> Os'kin made his first attack head-on and left one B-29 in flames after a barrage from all three of his cannons. As the commander was maneuvering for another attack, a pair of F-84s from the direct escort moved to intercept him. I fired a long burst across their fronts and forced the Thunderjets into an evasive maneuver, while my commander attacked another B-29 from behind and sent it burning out of the formation. By this time, our fuel was running low, and the command arrived to exit the battle. Our regiment shot down several enemy fighters and bombers in this action, while we ourselves had no losses – only one pilot received a bullet hole in his jet from the fire of the B-29 gunners.

On 23 October, the 17th IAP together with the 18th GIAP and the 523rd IAP had actively engaged the enemy again. Thirteen of the regiment's twenty-three pilots fired their cannons, a high proportion that rarely occurred in battle. The regiment claimed three B-29s and one F-84: Captain Bychkov and Senior Lieutenants Nikolaev and Bykov each received credit for a Superfortress, while Senior Lieutenant Shulev downed the single Thunderjet.

However, one of the regiment's jets was damaged: Captain Nikolaev's MiG-15 received a bullet hole in his lower fuselage. He was forced to exit the battle, but successfully landed his damaged plane back at his airbase.

Here's now Aleksei Nikolaevich Nikolaev himself describes the details of the 23 October engagement:

> I especially recall the battle with the B-29 bombers in the month of October 1951. On that particular morning there was a heavy layer of

clouds over the airfield, but despite this, the command post of the division placed us at readiness level No. 1. Soon thereafter, the command 'Launch' rang out through our headsets. Both our division and Kozhedub's 324th IAD took off.

Emerging above the clouds, we soon encountered enemy fighters. Somehow, my leader Volkov and I wound up beneath the main action with the enemy's fighters. Below and to the right, I caught sight of a group of British Gloster Meteors and reported this to my element leader. They were an enticing target, since the Meteors were slower and less maneuverable than our MiGs. But Volkov replied, 'We're going after the "big ones".' It was only then that I spotted the 'big ones' – these were the B-29s, the well-known Superfortresses, which had at a previous time dropped the atomic bombs on Japan. They were flying in two flights of four bombers each, in a box formation.

My leader dived to attack them, but as often happened Volkov opened fire too soon and pulled out of his attack in a chandelle to the left before even reaching the bomber formation. I decided to press the attack, since there were no enemy fighters visible nearby. At about 400 meters range, I opened fire at the left engine of a B-29. My MiG's cannons began to chatter, and I streaked over the bombers before pulling out of my attack in a climbing left turn. I gained altitude and took a careful look around. I didn't see any threats, other than the B-29 bomber formation. The bomber I had attacked was blazing and lagging behind the rest of the formation. I selected another target and made another attack. As I was passing over the B-29 formation, I heard and felt a powerful blow against my plane. The thought flashed through my head: 'They've hit me, the swine!' But my plane faithfully responded to my stick and there were no flames as I climbed out of the combat area to head home. Some enemy fighters raced to intercept me, but I quickly separated from them. The radio channels were full of chatter. I successfully reached my base, but I had to lower my landing gear by hand. Having taxied back to my place on the parking apron, I clambered out of my cockpit and learned from the technicians that my plane's hydraulic system had been damaged, and fragments had penetrated the ammunition magazines. But fortunately, everything turned out OK. This particular combat became so deeply engraved in my memory that it seems like it was just yesterday.

I also recall that three days after this engagement, the regiment commander Pulov dropped by our quarters early one morning. His voice woke me up – 'Nikolaev, get up, a gunner has sent you a letter!' I told him that I didn't know any gunner. In response, he handed me a sheet of paper, upon which had been sketched the scheme of attack on a B-29 group by a solitary MiG-15, and below it was some writing in the English language. Pulov had made a translation of the letter and turned it over to me to memorize.

As later became clear, this letter had actually been written by a captured gunner from the B-29 that Nikolaev had shot down. Sometime between 22 and 25 October, while on assignment to search for the remains of downed enemy aircraft in the area of Chongju, the chief of the regiment's chemical service Captain E.V. Grigor'ev bumped into two North Korean soldiers, who were escorting a captured radio operator from a B-29. Taking charge of the prisoner from the soldiers, he brought him to the police in Sonchon in his vehicle, where through an English-speaking Chinese interpreter, he interrogated the prisoner. The next day, the prisoner was delivered to Singisiu in a convoy.

Upon returning to the regiment, Captain Grigor'ev was placed under three days of arrest for his unauthorized initiative, since communication with prisoners was categorically forbidden to our military personnel. In addition, the regiment chief of staff Major Danilov received a reprimand for the actions of his subordinates.

However, let us return to the events in the air. In the combat on 23 October, Senior Lieutenant Shulev was forced to accept an unequal battle with four F-84s of the B-29s' close escort. During the combat, his engine stopped. Restarting an engine in the air is always a tricky matter. Shulev, taking advantage of a double layer of clouds, exited the battle, managed to get his engine going again, and then returned to combat. He shot down one F-84 and conducted two attacks on the B-29s.

Although the pilots of the 64th IAK claimed the destruction of ten B-29s and another four F-84s on this day, according to American records, only three bombers were downed, while another five B-29s and one F-84 were seriously damaged and later written off. Even so, these were quite painful losses for the American command.

The Americans claimed to have downed seven MiGs in this action: two were supposedly the victims of Sabre pilots from the 336th Squadron, another four were claimed by Superfortress gunners from the 307th Bombardment Group's 371st Bombardment Squadron, and one more by Thunderjet pilots from the 136th Fighter Bomber Wing's 154th Squadron. Marine pilot Lieutenant Walter Schirra – the future American astronaut – scored one victory in an F-84.

However, according to the records of the 64th IAK, on this day only one Soviet MiG-15 was lost: its pilot, Senior Lieutenant V.M. Khurtin of the 523rd IAP, was killed. If you recall, he had been shot down while returning to his base, when his plane was running low on fuel.

The 17th IAP was less successful in the subsequent fighting of 24–27 October, recording only three 'kills' over this period (Dokashenko, Pulov and Khvostantsev received credit for these victories). One of our MiGs was shot down (Kordanov's) and another one was damaged (Perepelkin's). The fatigue of our pilots and the inexperience of the new replacement pilots in the regiment were beginning to tell on performance. Likely, the fact that Lieutenant Kordanov had just returned from a sanatorium and hadn't managed to reacquire his touch on the controls was also partially to blame. Moreover, on this mission, he took off as a pair with someone who was not his usual leader.

During these days, Captain N.G. Dokashenko scored one more victory, with Vladimir Mikhailovich Khvostantsev flying as his wingman. Early on the morning of 25 October, nineteen MiGs of the regiment led by Major B.V. Maslennikov took off to intercept enemy aircraft. Our pilots on this mission encountered a group of twenty F-80 fighter-bombers under the cover of Sabres and took them on in battle. Vladimir Khvostantsev continues the story:

> Our flight, as usual, tangled with the Sabres. As a result of maneuvering during the dogfight, Dokashenko and I found ourselves beneath the action. Then the GCI informed us that piston-engine fighter-bombers were working over targets under some clouds beneath us. Well, Dokashenko immediately dived below the clouds on some target he had spotted. In the difficult flying weather, all my attention was focused on staying with Dokashenko. Then I also saw these four planes, but they were moving at an aspect angle of 4/4 – a full-deflection shot. I nevertheless gave them a burst while keeping with my leader. He was also firing and quite accurately too – one of the enemy planes burst into flames.
>
> Back at base, we spent a long time examining the gun camera film, trying from the footage and our observations to determine the type of enemy plane Dokashenko had downed. There were a lot of different opinions, some maintaining it was a Corsair, but we wound up deciding it had been a Hellcat. Other than our pair, no one from our group took part in this combat with the piston-engine fighter-bombers.

Thus on the regiment's list of victories there appeared the first, and as later turned out, the only piston-engine plane of the US Marine Corps. In actual fact, Nikolai Grigor'evich Dokashenko had knocked down F4U-4 Corsair No. 81576 in this action, which was being flown by L.W. Dorsey of the VF-713 Fighter Squadron. He bailed out of his stricken plane over the sea, and was successfully picked up by an American ship.

On one mission on 26 October, Major Pravotorov, the 303rd IAD's inspector of piloting technique, took part. His wingman was Lieutenant Kordanov of the 2nd Aviation Squadron, who was shot down, and ejected at an altitude of 3,500 meters. After returning to the unit he was sent to a hospital, then to a sanatorium, and he took no further part in the war.

The events of this engagement on October 26 unfolded in the following manner. Sometime in the middle of the third duty shift, a radar station tallied a large group of about fifty enemy aircraft in the area of Chinnampo. Responding to the alarm, twenty-two MiGs of the 17th IAP led by Major Pulov were scrambled from the airfield at 14:36 to intercept this group of enemy planes. After climbing to 5,000 meters in altitude, the regiment formed into a staggered column of flights and flew to the area of Anju. Flying at an altitude of 7,000 meters in the region of Anju, Major Pulov noticed to the left and below four F-80s, heading west. Pulov conducted a descending left turn, and then swung back to the right to close on the F-80s. At a range of 500 meters he opened fire on the trailing element of F-80s from a position behind and to the left of them. Exiting from the attack, Pulov banked to his right and repeated the attack on the wingman of this F-80 pair, after which the target began to burn and started going down. The remaining Shooting Stars evaded to the sea, at which point Pulov could not follow them further. So Major Pulov's flight headed back to base.

While that action unfolded, the 1st Aviation Squadron under the command of Captain Artemchenko spotted six F-80s, which turned to attack his flight: Captain Bychkov and his wingman disrupted their attack, and the Shooting Stars immediately broke off and departed for the coastline. The pilots of the 1st Aviation Squadron subsequently discovered a pair of F-86s and six F-80s and sought to attack them, but the enemy, avoiding combat, immediately headed for the coast. At this point, the pilots of the 1st Aviation Squadron also received the order from the division command post to return to base.

Pilots of the 2nd Aviation Squadron's second flight, which was being led by Major Pravotorov, wound up in a more difficult situation. The 2nd Squadron was in the cover group in the area south of Anju. While reversing course to the right at an altitude of 9,000 meters, Major Pravotorov's flight fell behind the lead flight and descended beneath some clouds below them. Emerging from the clouds at an altitude of 1,000 meters, Pravotorov failed to spot any enemy, and making a 180° turn to the left, began to climb back through the clouds. While doing so, the second element of Captain Mishakin fell behind and was slow to reach the clouds. Just then, a pair of F-86s popped out of the clouds and attacked Mishakin. His wingman Senior Lieutenant Gostiukhin bailed his leader out of the precarious situation by firing at the Sabre pair that was going after his leader, but registered no hits. However, the Sabres immediately left Mishakin alone and departed in a dive. Gostiukhin, suddenly finding himself isolated, was then attacked by four F-80s, but through a sharp maneuver he evaded the attack and exited beneath them. Subsequently, Gostiukhin climbed back through the clouds and conducted a quick search for his leader. Failing to spot Mishakin's MiG, he linked up with Captain Blagov's element and returned to base with them. There he learned that Captain Mishakin had climbed sharply through the cloud layer in response to the Sabres' attack; emerging from the clouds and seeing no one around him, he had headed alone back to base.

Meanwhile, Major Pravotorov and his wingman Lieutenant Kordanov had continued to climb through the clouds. Once above the clouds, they began to reverse course. At an altitude of 4,500 to 5,000 meters, Lieutenant Kordanov was surprised from behind by a pair of Sabres that latched onto his tail. The lead F-86 opened up on Kordanov's plane at a range of 100 to 150 meters and riddled his fuselage, cockpit area and engine with bullets. There was an explosion in Kordanov's cockpit; erupting flames burned Kordanov's face and set fire to the left side of his trousers. Kordanov decided to eject. His parachute opened and he made a safe landing about 15 kilometers south-west of Sukchon. Major Pravotorov, in light of the unexpectedness of the nearly point-blank attack on Kordanov, had been unable to do anything to prevent it. After seeing Kordanov eject from his burning MiG, Pravotorov sought shelter in the clouds and took a course back to base.[4] In this combat, Major Pravotorov's element had been jumped by pilots of the 4th Fighter Wing's 336th Squadron. The victory over Kordanov was scored by First Lieutenant Claude C. Mitson.

Every such incident was thoroughly analyzed in order to prevent similar mistakes in the future. In the given case, it was determined that the leader Major Pravotorov had made an incorrect decision to climb through the clouds above him, since the maneuver had cost him speed by the time he emerged from the clouds. The enemy Sabres, exploiting their superior speed, were able to pounce on the MiGs and flame Senior Lieutenant Kordanov's plane from close range.

On 27 October, around 09:00 twenty MiGs of the 17th IAP led by Major Maslennikov were launched to intercept another enemy formation. They encountered a group of thirty-six F-84 fighter-bombers that had already spotted the MiGs and were heading toward the sea. Therefore the regiment had time to conduct only one attack, in which the pilot Khvostantsev was the most fortunate of all.

Here's how Vladimir Mikhailovich Khvostantsev of the 3rd Aviation Squadron himself tells about his victory in this engagement:

I remember how I shot down my only F-84 Thunderjet fighter-bomber. I downed it in a head-on pass from a range of 450 meters. We barely avoided colliding with each other. Of course, during such a high-speed attack, I couldn't see whether my shots had hit the adversary or not, and when we returned to base, I didn't even mention a possible victory. But during the post-flight briefing, it became apparent that one F-84 had gone down, and no one other than me had fired on an F-84. Moreover, my gun camera footage confirmed my victory, and North Korean troops later found wreckage of the jet.

One Soviet MiG received combat damage on this day. The MiG-15bis piloted by Senior Lieutenant Perepelkin received a bullet through the engine's turbine.

The next day, it was Captain N.G. Dokashenko, a flight commander in the 3rd Aviation Squadron, who particularly distinguished himself. In one dogfight, he downed three F-86 fighters, which he added to his existing three victories. On this mission, Major Pulov was leading twenty MiG-15s. The group ran into fourteen Sabres and tangled in a swirling dogfight with them. There were no losses on our side. (Only one other pilot, the commander of the 196th IAP Colonel E.G. Pepeliaev, succeeded in downing three F-86s in one battle, on 6 October 1951. However, one of his victories was not credited to him personally, but instead went to the shared credit of the 176th GIAP.)

On 28 October, Major Pulov again received a reprimand for the poor handling of the battles on 24 October 1951 and 26 October 1951, when Lieutenant Kordanov was shot down. Among the shortcomings, it was noted that even Major Pulov's own MiG had been damaged three times in the fighting.

As of 29 October, there were thirty-nine pilots on the roster of the 17th IAP, of which thirty were capable of conducting a combat mission. One pilot, Senior Lieutenant Polianichko, was in the hospital; one pilot, Captain Sutiagin, was away on R&R; five pilots were still undergoing combat training; and two pilots, Major Vorob'ev and Senior Lieutenant Ankilov, had been suspended from flight operations.

The regiment had a complement of thirty-one MiGs, of which three were under repair until 1 November, and two lacked functioning hydraulic controls for the flaps. The Yak-11 plane's fuel gauge was not working.

The bad news kept coming for Major Pulov: on 30 October, the division commander formally warned him about being unfit for his position due to shortcomings in the conduct of the action on 27 October 1951 and to the regiment's 'reduced combat activity'. These accusations, at the very least, seem strange – after all, in October the regiment had downed more enemy planes than in any other month: twenty-eight. The regiment completed 592 combat and 163 training sorties, at a time when many experienced pilots were temporarily absent, and the recently arrived replacements were just beginning to see active duty! As is evident, the commander of the 17th IAP was receiving undeserved reprimands much more often than merited decorations.

Confirming Victories and Reviewing Film Footage

The month of October was the most productive for the entire period of the 17th IAP's combat operations. Pilots of the regiment had downed twenty-eight enemy planes and damaged several more. At the same time, it had lost only two of its planes, and one of its pilots – Captain Morozov – had been killed.

However, everything didn't go as smoothly with the determination of our pilots' victories. Often, some of the pilots' victory claims failed to receive confirmation in the form of material evidence from the wreckage of enemy planes, but were credited to the pilots of the division only after careful review of the gun camera footage. Confirmations from ground forces and search groups often arrived late, because of the inaccessibility of crash sites in the rough terrain and difficult weather conditions.

Obviously, of course, some of those enemy aircraft that had been registered as 'kills' may only have been damaged, and some may have entirely avoided being hit by the MiG's cannons. Such a situation with the reckoning of victories has existed since the dawn of air combat in the First World War and with the pilots of every air force; this was how it was during the Second World War, just as it was in the air war over Korea. Every participant in this war 'sinned' with similar claims of 'victories', both our pilots and the Korean and Chinese pilots of the Joint Air Army, as well as the pilots of the UN air forces. True, in contrast to the American command, our command of the 64th IAK recognized a formal category of so-called 'disputed victories', which in the majority of cases were never even credited to a pilot's score, or were subsequently removed from their totals as unconfirmed. Below are some documentary examples of how the command of the Soviet air divisions and corps struggled with this issue.

In the commander of the 303rd IAD's Order No. 0122 from 3 November 1951 'On the results of assessing the registration of downed enemy planes and the analysis of film', it was observed that questions were continuing to occur in all the division's regiments over the confirmation of victories, particularly in Belostotsky's 18th GIAP and Pulov's 17th IAP. Pilots had received tentative credit for claims that had not been confirmed by the results of film analysis. Seven pilots of the 17th IAP had a combined ten such unconfirmed victory credits:

1. Major Pulov – two F-84s and one F-86;
2. Senior Lieutenant Nikolaev – one F-86;
3. Senior Lieutenant Komarov – one F-86;
4. Guards Major Maslennikov – two F-86s;
5. Senior Lieutenant Shulev – one F-86;
6. Captain Shcherbakov – one F-86;
7. Captain Blagov – one F-84.

Nine pilots of the 18th GIAP had a combined thirteen such unconfirmed tallies:

1. Captain Sokhan' – one F-84;
2. Senior Lieutenant Kapitonov – one F-84;
3. Lieutenant Colonel Smorchkov – two F-86s;
4. Captain Shalev – one F-84;
5. Captain Maznev – two F-84s;
6. Senior Lieutenant Shavsha – one F-84;
7. Captain Gerasimenko – one F-80 and one F-86;
8. Major Os'kin – two F-84s;
9. Lieutenant Colonel Belostotsky – one F-84.

Nine pilots of the 523rd IAP had a total of nine such unconfirmed victories:

1. Senior Lieutenant Shal'nov – one F-86;
2. Senior Lieutenant Rybalko – one F-86;
3. Senior Lieutenant Samoilov – one F-84;
4. Senior Lieutenant D'iachenko – one B-29 (later confirmed);
5. Captain Popov – one F-84 (later confirmed);
6. Senior Lieutenant Iakovlev – one F-84;
7. Senior Lieutenant Moskvichev – one F-86;
8. Senior Lieutenant Churkin – one Gloster Meteor;
9. Major Os'kin – one B-29 (later confirmed).

By this order, 'improperly' credited victories were dropped from the records. Regiment commanders Lieutenant Colonel Belostotsky and Major Pulov both received reprimands and warnings.[5]

Corps headquarters assumed supervision over the veracity of the records in the divisions. Between 9 and 20 November, it conducted a review of the records in all the regiments and checked on the presence of confirming documents for downed enemy planes.

This review established that:

1. A portion of the planes were being registered as downed without sufficient justification and confirmation, especially in the 303rd IAD. There had been little collection of pieces from the wreckage of downed enemy planes, especially in the 324th IAD.
2. The pilots, often lacking any possibility to watch as enemy planes exited from the combat, were often claiming damaged planes as downed planes, which were later assigned to their personal score without sufficient review and confirmation from other sources.

The corps commander ordered:

1. In the future, only division commanders would determine credit for downed enemy planes, using more precise criteria for awarding victories.
2. A reprimand to the commander of the 303rd IAD Lieutenant Colonel Kumanichkin, and to the chief of staff of the 324th IAD Lieutenant Colonel Malevanyi.
3. To notify the commanders and chiefs of staffs of the divisions that in the future such cases of tallying unconfirmed victories would be viewed as hogwash.[6]

Back in Action: In a New Role

Nikolai Sutiagin returned to the regiment at the end of October, when the bitterest October battles had already concluded. He was now flying in his new role as assistant commander of the regiment and with the title Hero of the Soviet Union. Indeed, he justified this esteemed title with honor, actively participating in the regiment's combat work and adding to his personal combat score. On 1 November, the regiment commander Major Pulov departed for the sanatorium in Dal'ny. Several more pilots accompanied him. The 1st Squadron again became the regiment's strike group, and the new combat roles of the regiment's squadrons never changed again prior to the end of combat operations. Until Major Pulov's return, his deputy Major Boris Maslennikov carried out the duties as acting regiment commander. Meanwhile the pilots frequently had to conduct three to four sorties a day. Senior Lieutenant Perepelkin became Captain Sutiagin's wingman.

Over the first two days of November, the pilots of the 64th IAK downed seven of the enemy's F-84E planes in aerial combats. Their losses in these battles consisted of only one plane, though its young pilot Senior Lieutenant Anatolii Ivanovich Shuliatev of the 18th GIAP was killed in it. Shuliatev had only arrived in this Guards regiment as a replacement in October. In a dogfight on 2 November, Shuliatev became separated from his leader and he was intercepted by a pair from the 4th Fighter Wing consisting of Lieutenant Colonel George L. Jones and First Lieutenant Richard A. Pincosky, who shot up Shuliatev's MiG from point-blank range.

The pilots of the 303rd IAD managed on the following day, 3 November, to down only one Sabre, and it was the 'Menace to Sabres' Captain Nikolai Sutiagin of the 17th IAP who was responsible. At 13:45, radar stations detected two large groups of enemy planes in the region of Pyongyang and Chinnampo. Four minutes later, Major B.V. Maslennikov led twenty MiGs of the 17th IAP into the sky at a signal from the division command post. After climbing to an altitude of 5,000 meters, the unit was vectored to the area of Anju in a staggered column of squadrons, assigned to cover the activity of the 523rd IAP. The 1st and 3rd Aviation Squadrons comprised the regiment's strike group, while the 2nd Aviation Squadron flew as top cover for the regiment's combat formation. About 700–800 meters separated each group.

The overall group, flying in the region of Anju at an altitude of 9,000 meters, was redirected by the division command post to an area 20–25 kilometers north of Sonchon and given the order to engage enemy F-86 fighters that were approaching from the south from the direction of the sea. Nearing the coastline, our group conducted a climbing right turn to an altitude of 9,500 meters. As it straightened out on its new heading, the group received fresh information from the division command post: 'The enemy is below you on a meeting course.' Failing to see the enemy, group commander Major Maslennikov decided to reverse heading to the right in order to fly along the enemy's current heading. Arriving over Anju at an altitude of 7,000 meters, Maslennikov finally noticed sixteen F-86s to his right at the same altitude, in the process of a right-hand turn: he decided to attack the enemy and climbed for altitude as he turned toward them. The adversary, spotting the MiGs moving into an attack position above them, banked sharply to the left and departed toward the sea in a shallow dive.

At this moment the leader of the second flight Captain Artemchenko observed eight additional F-86s to his left, approaching from the region of Pakchon on an intercepting course; he immediately informed the group commander. Maslennikov ordered a left-hand turn to close with the enemy. The enemy responded with a descending left-hand spiral. Maslennikov and the 1st Aviation Squadron attempted to pursue the enemy, but failed to catch the diving Sabres.

At this time, a pair of Sabres suddenly materialized and started to make an attacking pass on Maslennikov's group, but Nikolai Sutiagin, flying behind Captain Artemchenko's lead element, spotted them in time and moved with his wingman Senior Lieutenant Perepelkin to disrupt this attack. After an energetic climbing left turn, Sutiagin rolled back onto the tail of this pair of F-86s, which he began to chase. The Sabres responded with a shallow loop. In the second loop Nikolai, having closed to within 700 meters of the F-86 element leader, opened fire. The enemy plane smoothly rolled over to the right and plummeted toward the earth in a right-hand tilt. The F-86 wingman performed a split-S to the left and dived away in the direction of the sea.

At this moment, Nikolai Sutiagin spotted four more F-86s arcing towards him from the right and above by about 500 meters. Hauling his MiG around in a climbing left turn, Captain Sutiagin emerged on the tail of the wingman in the second element of Sabres and opened fire at a range of 700–800 meters. The adversary, noticing the shells streaking past his plane, immediately rolled over into a steep, descending spiral to the left. Sutiagin didn't bother to pursue the enemy and headed back to base.

Next the approaching pilots of the 2nd and 3rd Aviation Squadrons entered the action, and sparred for a few minutes with several more flights of Sabres. In the course of this engagement, only Captain Dokashenko twice fired at two Sabres, but because of the long range he didn't score any hits. Soon all the Sabres were driven out to the sea and the pilots of the 17th IAP safely returned to their base. The pilots of the 17th IAP had successfully carried out their mission of tying up the advanced screen of Sabres so that the 523rd IAP could operate without interference. Taking advantage of this, a group of MiGs from the 523rd IAP successfully intercepted a group of Gloster Meteors in the region of Sukchon and downed two of them.

Major engagements developed on 4 November as well. The Americans undertook two massive raids in the area of Anju, with formations of F-80 and F-84 fighter-bombers working over supply routes at low altitude. Both divisions of the 64th IAK were launched to intercept them, and the 303rd IAD and 324th IAD became involved in heavy combat. During these two large clashes, pilots of the 64th IAK downed eight American planes. The pilots of the 303rd IAD took on the escorting Sabres, while the pilots of the 324th IAD went after the fighter-bombers.

On the first morning mission to the area of Anju, twenty-two MiGs of the 17th IAP were flying in support of the 523rd IAP, which was simultaneously operating in this same area. Pilots of the 523rd IAP had been the first to encounter a group of Sabres. This was a hard fight, and although pilots of the 523rd IAP claimed two victories, they themselves suffered the loss of one MiG, and several more received damage. The 523rd IAP lost another MiG-15 in combat later the same day; in combination with the MiG lost that morning this marked the heaviest one-day losses for the regiment during its entire assignment to Manchuria.

Flying to the relief of the 523rd that morning, pilots of the 17th IAP encountered eighteen F-86 fighters in the region of Anju. In the ensuing dogfight with this group, the regiment scored a victory, destroying one Sabre, which was downed by Senior Lieutenant Shulev. This was the 400th victory claimed by the 64th IAK since the start of the war. The regiment had no losses or damage to its planes. Around noon there was another mission to intercept an enemy formation, but the MiG pilots did not encounter any enemy.

That afternoon at 14:15, radar stations south of Pyongyang detected another large group of approximately eighty enemy planes, which were heading into the interior of North Korean territory. Pilots of the 17th IAP's 1st Squadron began taking off from readiness level No. 1 at 14:26, and at 14:29 the remaining active-duty pilots began to launch. Twenty MiG-15s of the 17th IAP assembled in the air under the overall command of deputy regiment commander Major B. Maslennikov and headed for the area of Sukchon. As usual, pilots of the 1st and 3rd Aviation Squadron comprised the strike group of the regiment, while a flight from the 2nd Aviation Squadron flew as high cover.

Following directions from the division command post, Major Maslennikov led the group to the vicinity of Anju, where it initiated a right-hand turn in order to sweep the skies for the presence of enemy aircraft. During the 180° turn, Nikolai Sutiagin, flying as the leader of the second element in Major Maslennikov's flight, spotted a large group of F-86 fighters some distance away, above and to the right of them, and immediately informed the group commander. However, at this moment, a call came in over the radio from Captain Mazilov, a pilot of the 523rd IAP: 'I'm in a tussle south of Anju and request assistance.' Group commander Major Maslennikov headed towards the indicated area in a shallow dive, but in a right-hand turn at 7,000 meters, the group was unexpectedly jumped from behind and to the right by a group of up to thirty F-86 Sabres.

Two flights of the 1st Aviation Squadron under the command of group commander Major Maslennikov broke into a sharp, climbing turn to the left to evade the attack. The trailing flight of Captain Artemchenko (consisting of the pairs Artemchenko-Shulev and Miroshnichenko-Savchenko), which had come under attack first, went into a series of oblique loops to the left in an effort to shake off six Sabres that were positioned behind his flight. In the third loop, Artemchenko's flight managed to gain a superior position above the opponent; seeing this, the adversary conducted a split-S maneuver and dived away toward the sea.

Coming out from under the attack in a climbing left turn, Captain Sutiagin's element was attacked from the right and above by four F-86s. Nikolai Sutiagin sharply turned right into the attack, then with a subsequent turn to the left he gained position behind the enemy and began to pursue. One pair of Sabres, seeing the MiGs behind them, conducted a split-S and separated downwards, but the second element went into a climbing turn to the right with a subsequent transition into an oblique loop; Nikolai Sutiagin chose to follow their maneuver. On the third oblique loop, Sutiagin closed to within 600–700 meters of the enemy, and opened fire on the lead Sabre. An accurate volley from all three of the MiG's cannons converged on the doomed Sabre.

Coming out of the loop, the Sabre wingman went into a steep 60° climb, and then reversed into a head-on run at Nikolai Sutiagin. Sutiagin didn't lose his cool, and as the range rapidly closed to less than 300 meters, he opened fire at the Sabre, after which Sutiagin exited the battle at an altitude of 3,000 meters.

At this moment, Captain Sutiagin's wingman Senior Lieutenant Perepelkin was attacked from above and behind to the right by six F-86s. Perepelkin tried to evade the attack in a climbing turn to the right, but failed to shake the enemy off his tail. When Senior Lieutenant Shulev spotted the precarious position of his comrade, he moved to attack the pursuing Sabres from above and behind; noticing the MiG now behind them, the Sabres went into a split-S maneuver and departed to the south. Vasilii Shulev linked up with Senior Lieutenant Perepelkin, and they headed back to base.

The pilots of the 3rd Aviation Squadron, located in the second echelon of the strike group under the command of Captain Shcherbakov and flying on the 1st Aviation Squadron's left, while in a right turn at an altitude of 7,000 meters in the area of Anju, noticed eight F-86s approaching in a column of flights to the left and below them by 500 meters. At the command of Captain Shcherbakov, the squadron's flights went into a left turn to get behind the F-86s. The adversary countered with a climbing left-hand spiral, after which the formation split into two groups. One flight of four continued to climb, while the second group went into a dive; Captain Shcherbakov's flight went after the second group. The enemy, noticing the pursuit, steepened their dive and began to spiral to the left. Scherbakov's flight broke off the pursuit with a right-hand turn and exited the battle.

Meanwhile, Captain Dokashenko's flight went after the climbing flight of F-86s, which after turning to the left, nosed over into a dive. Pursuing the enemy, Dokashenko's flight was attacked by a pair of Sabres from behind and to the left, which were firing from a range of 1,000 to 1,200 meters. Noticing the attack of the Sabres, Captain Dokashenko initiated a climbing left turn. The enemy tried to pursue Dokashenko's flight through the turn, but falling behind, they gave up the chase and headed toward the sea in a dive.

The second flight of the 2nd Aviation Squadron's cover group under the command of Captain Ponomarev didn't see the strike group's tangle with the Sabres, but pursuant to group commander Major Maslennikov's orders, maintained high cover over the area of the battle at an altitude of 8,000–9,000 meters. At an order from the division command post, the flight headed back to base.[8]

Despite the unfavorable tactical situations, the regiment had fought in an organized manner, and the pilots had shown a lot of initiative. After a successful mission, the entire group of the 17th IAP returned intact to Myaogou with a victory: Captain Nikolai Sutiagin had downed another Sabre!

For his successful actions in these battles, Nikolai Sutiagin was recommended for promotion to the next rank of major. The recommendation, signed on 5 November 1951 by the temporary acting commander of the 17th IAP Guards Major Maslennikov, cited Sutiagin's fortitude, bravery and heroism, and his tactical skill, which he used to impose his will on the adversary. The recommendation noted that by this point, Sutiagin had flown seventy-seven combat missions, downed eight enemy aircraft and damaged four more, and had become a Hero of the Soviet Union.[9]

The almost daily combat sorties and dogfights were taking a very heavy toll on the pilots' stamina. The medics were noticing that the short-term R&Rs were ensuring no more than a month of intense combat work before pilot fatigue began to tell again. Many pilots, including Bykov, Komarov and Ponomarev were experiencing reduced appetite and frequent vomiting due to their many hours in the air and overexposure to the on-board oxygen.

Not all the pilots could endure the physical and nervous strain. Senior Lieutenant Vasilii Fedorovich Ankilov, the deputy commander of the 2nd Aviation Squadron for political affairs (and a veteran of the Great Patriotic War, who had been decorated with two Orders of the Red Banner and two Orders of the Patriotic War, which testifies to his personal courage) began to complain to doctors from the start of combat operations. On each combat sortie, he became separated from his leader and arrived back at base without participating in battle. After seventeen sorties, he declared that he could no longer fly because his nerves had collapsed and that he no longer had confidence in himself. He was sent to the Changtien Hospital for a medical check-up, after which the medics suspended him from flight operations. On 5 November, Senior Lieutenant Ankilov left for a different unit. On 8 November, Captain Nikolai Vasil'evich Masly was named as deputy commander of the 2nd Aviation Squadron for political affairs to replace the departed Ankilov.

On 5 and 6 November, there were no sorties. The division held a celebratory assembly, dedicated to the anniversary of the October Revolution. The gathering was memorable for its participants as well as because of the following episode, as told by a pilot of the 523rd IAP, D.A. Samoilov:

From one of the search team's trips, some men of the 1st Aviation Squadron returned to the regiment with a monkey. Somehow an enemy fighter had been brought down, which made a landing on North Korean territory and its pilot was taken prisoner by North Korean troops. Our search group discovered a little monkey in the plane's cockpit behind the pilot's headrest; they returned to our base with it along with some pieces of the downed plane.

The monkey was a small one, like a little marmoset, so we called it 'Martyn' [the Russian word for 'marmoset' is 'martyshka']. Martyn lived on the base around one of the airplane crates that had been furnished inside with plank beds for the pilots' rest. At first they kept him on a tether, but then he began to walk around freely with the pilots and ground personnel. Each person considered it his duty to bring him fruits or some other kind of treat from the mess hall. Martyn became one of the amusements of the flight staff. He had his friends, but also considered some of the men indifferently; others he viewed as 'hostiles' … He permitted friends to pet him or scratch him behind the ear, and he loved to sit beside them and pick motes from their trousers, or take apple seeds from their open palms. He paid no attention to others, and they didn't bother him. Martyn was aggressive with respect to the 'hostiles' – he might bite or scratch them.

Martyn accompanied us to the mess hall, scaring the servants – in general, he kept us entertained. When we left, we heard that an epidemic went around the animals in the area, and Martyn fell sick and died.

Once, some soldiers brought Martyn into the town. On this day, the entire flight staff had gathered in the club on the occasion of the 8 November holiday. The division commander Colonel Kumanichkin stepped out onto the stage, walked up to a table, behind which the presidium would sit, and was about to open the festivities, when at that moment Martyn clambered up onto the rostrum. Kumanichkin tried to chase him away, but Martyn adopted a threatening pose. Kumanichkin shouted at the commander of the 1st Aviation Squadron, Major Trefilov: 'Trefilov, get your Martyn out of here!' But Trefilov himself was afraid of the monkey. There was laughter in the hall. Then a soldier ran out onto the stage – Martyn's owner – in order to get him on a leash, but Martyn clambered up a cable behind the curtains. The soldier backed away – and Martyn returned to the rostrum. This scene was repeated several times, before someone finally managed to lure Martyn down and get a leash on him, after which the assembly finally started.

On 7 November, the regiment again dueled against the Americans, who by all appearances didn't consider the day to be a holiday. The scrap between twenty-four MiGs and twenty F-86s ended peacefully for the pilots of the 17th IAP, or more accurately, without results.

The next day, 8 November, the regiment flew three combat missions, two with its full complement of planes. The pilots of the regiment became involved in two dogfights.

On the first mission of the day, the regiment was covering the actions of the 18th GIAP pilots. At 09:27, the 17th IAP's squadrons tangled with thirty Sabres in the region of Anju. The combat ended without results. Only six pilots of the regiment managed to fire on an enemy plane.

According to the reports of Captain Artemchenko, Senior Lieutenant Bykov, and Captain Sutiagin, they had initially confused the F-86s with MiG-15s (the nose of the Sabres' fuselages had been painted red, like our MiG-15s). Moreover, according to Captain Shcherbakov's report, the upper part of the rudder had also been painted red. The adversary that confronted the pilots of the 17th IAP in this action had been pilots of the United States Air Force 4th Fighter Wing's 334th Squadron.

In the second action at 15:03, the regiment in the same strength again clashed with thirty F-86s. This combat ended more successfully for our pilots: the group leader Major Maslennikov managed to down one Sabre. In the following days, there were several more combat sorties, but no encounters with the enemy.

That month of November, a mission plan with a list of the pilots' last names went missing in the regiment, and it was only found almost three weeks later. This incident did not reflect well on the regiment.

Several other occasions during the month of November put the pilots of the 17th IAP in a more flattering light. On 10 November, the flight personnel lined up in formation to hear a Decree of the Presidium of the USSR Supreme Soviet on the awarding of Orders to men in the flight staff, and learned about promotions in the regiment. Captain Artemchenko, Captain Maslennikov, Captain Ponomarev, Captain Shcherbakov, Senior Lieutenant Osipov, Lieutenant Kordanov and Lieutenant Shirokov all received promotions.

In November the command and Party organization of the regiment also organized an evening to honor Captain Sutiagin's receipt of the title Hero of the Soviet Union. In addition, on 22 November, the units of the 303rd IAD assembled to honor the awarding of the title Hero of the Soviet Union on 13 November 1951 to another group of distinguished pilots of the regiment: Stepan Bakhaev, Dmitrii Os'kin, Grigorii Okhai, Mikhail Ponomarev, Dmitrii Samoilov, Aleksandr Smorchkov and Lev Shchukin.

Fighting in 'MiG Alley' continued unabated and grew in intensity, although the autumn weather often intervened, and combat days alternated with compulsory lulls due to bad flying conditions. Between 8 November and the end of the month, the pilots of the 17th IAP conducted thirty-three combat missions, but only eight of these resulted in contact with the enemy. In these eight aerial combats, the regiment scored only seven victories: two F-84s and five F-86s. The regiment had no losses of its own, but three planes received combat damage, which were quickly put back into service by the regiment's technical staff. One pilot of the regiment received a light wound to the hand.

From the outset of combat operations, either Major Pulov or his deputy Major Maslennikov had led the regimental formations into the sky, but at the end of November, Captain Sutiagin began to receive the assignment to lead the regiment into battle. Nikolai Sutiagin conducted his first sortie as the leader of a twelve-ship formation on 24 November, but they did not encounter any enemy aircraft.

On 26 November, the pilots of the 64th IAK drove off several raids by small groups of fighter-bombers, shooting down one F-86 and one F-84. On this day, pilots of the 17th IAP were launched three times: at 08:04, 11:28 and 15:00. The regiment became involved in only one fight, in which Captain Nikolai Sutiagin scored the only victory.

Around 11:00 on 26 November, corps radar stations detected several small groups of enemy aircraft in the area of Pyongyang. At 11:28, a regimental group of twenty-two MiGs led by Major Pulov took off from readiness level No. 1 to intercept the enemy. As usual, the regiment's formation consisted of a strike group made up of fourteen pilots of the 1st and 3rd Squadrons of the regiment, while eight pilots from the 2nd Squadron trailed the strike group to provide cover for it. The 1st Aviation Squadron took off with a first flight consisting of the pairs Pulov-Osipov and Sutiagin-Shirokov, and a second flight consisting of the pairs Artemchenko-Kramarenko and Bychkov-Tikhonov.

Major Pulov's group climbed to an altitude of 8,500 meters before being vectored to the Sukchon area in order to reinforce the 523rd IAP, which was already involved in a dogfight. In the area of Anju, Major Pulov noticed up to sixteen enemy F-86 Sabres flying over the Unsan–Sukchon region. Pulov led his MiGs toward the enemy, which was higher in altitude by 800 to 1,000 meters. The enemy immediately responded by swinging left to close with Major Pulov's group. Pulov gave Major Shcherbakov an order to take on the left-hand group of eight Sabres in the area of Unsan, while he himself moved to attack the second group of eight Sabres, which at that time was coming in from the sea in the area of Sukchon. Major Ponarev's group was given the command to cover the actions of the strike group.

Passing the enemy flying on an opposite heading now below him and to the left, Pulov began to swing around to the left in pursuit of the Sabre flight, which was departing in a diving left-hand turn back toward the sea. At the moment of beginning the turn, Nikolai Sutiagin spotted another flight of Sabres above them and to their right, which were in a left turn with the intention of taking position on the tail of Major Pulov's lead element. Sutiagin conducted a climbing left turn to intercept the rapidly approaching enemy, but the adversary quickly flashed past in front and below him at a large angle of deflection. Nikolai banked to the right, and then with an energetic left-hand turn started after the Sabres, which had begun to pursue Pulov's element. In the left turn, Sutiagin gained a position behind the Sabres and closed on them. From a decreasing range of 440 meters down to 200 meters, he fired on the wingman in the second pair of Sabres. The Sabre listed to the right and plunged toward the earth at an angle of 70–80 degrees. Captain Sutiagin's wingman Senior Lieutenant Shirokov fired at the lead Sabre from a range of 1,000 to 800 meters. The three remaining Sabres, finally noticing the fire from our fighters, went into a split-S and dived away toward the sea. Nikolai Sutiagin's element pulled out of the attack into a right-hand chandelle.

The pilots of the 3rd and 2nd Aviation Squadrons also ran into flights and elements of Sabres, but the enemy, avoiding combat, immediately headed for the sanctuary of the coastline. Only one pair of Sabres attempted an attack on Major Ponomarev's eight MiGs of the cover group, but our pilots spotted this threat in time and quickly turned to meet the Sabres head-on. From a range of 700–800 meters, Ponomarev opened fire on the lead Sabre, after which this pair swerved sharply away and descended toward the coastline – they were not pursued. The entire regimental group returned to base without any losses or damage.[10]

Missions on 26 November were plagued with mechanical and other problems. Due to an error by a technician, who had failed to fully close the hatch of the camera gun after inspecting it, the hatch tore off in the air, forcing pilots Chernozemov and Zelenov to abort the mission. On this same mission, eight more planes returned early because they were unable to retract their landing gear. The senior engineer of the 303rd IAD, Colonel Nesterov, who came to investigate this case, concluded that the day's frigid temperature was primarily responsible, but that the pilots (Shestopalov, Masly, Tikhonov, Bozhko with their leaders) had also been very late in raising their landing gear after launching and were already at a high airspeed when they attempted to retract the wheels.

The division's senior engineer also had criticism for Nikolai Sutiagin. One of his ground crew, Junior Technician-Lieutenant Bereznev, had failed to close the engine hatch on Sutiagin's MiG before releasing it for flight operations. Captain Sutiagin then failed to check the plane before the mission and had not followed proper procedures when he accepted the plane from the technician. In the air, naturally, the hatch cover was ripped off the aircraft, jeopardizing the planes in the formation behind him.

On 29 November, fighting in 'MiG Alley' continued with its previous intensity. Early that morning, radar stations of the corps detected two large groups of enemy planes in the area of Pyongyang. At a signal from the division command post, pilots of the 17th IAP began taking off at 06:44. Twenty MiGs of the regiment roared into the sky and assembled under the overall command of the assistant commander of the regiment for aerial combat tactics and aerial gunnery, Captain Nikolai Sutiagin: this was the second time for Sutiagin to lead a regimental group on a combat mission. They received their order in the air: move to engage enemy fighters in the region of Sukchon, with a subsequent vector to repulse a ground attack strike by UN aircraft.

The strike group of two groups of six MiG-15s each from the 1st and 3rd Aviation Squadrons led the way, while 1,000 meters behind them and 800 meters above them flew the cover force of eight MiGs from the 2nd Aviation Squadron. The 1st Aviation Squadron was flying in a six-ship formation, consisting of the pairs Sutiagin-Shirokov, Artemchenko-Kramarenko, and Bychkov-Tikhonov.

Captain Sutiagin's group received an order to intercept some low-flying targets in the area of Sukchon. Arriving over Anju at an altitude of 6,000 meters, Nikolai Sutiagin's group conducted a right-hand turn toward the town of Sukchon. No enemy planes were found in this area, so our group headed toward Pyongyang, where they carried out a 180° turn to the left.

Coming out of the turn, the group was vectored toward the area of Unsan and north-east of the city of Anju. Approaching the city of Unsan, Captain Bychkov spotted an approaching group of F-84 and F-80 planes in front of them, below and to the right, and informed group commander Captain Sutiagin of his discovery. Nikolai Sutiagin, who only then saw the enemy, banked to the right to set up for an attack and gave the command: 'Major Artemchenko and Major Shcherbakov are to engage the F-84 and F-80 planes, and to attack in a column of pairs. Major Ponomarev's group will cover the combat area.'

Sutiagin selected a flight of F-84s as the target for his attack and began to approach the enemy from behind and above in a descending left turn. The enemy, spotting the MiGs closing in on them, abruptly broke left into a tight turn, causing Sutiagin's element to streak past at a high deflection angle. Sutiagin pulled up into a steep climb and then pitched over to his left, where he saw a pair of F-84s in front of him, to the left and below him at an altitude of 800–1,000 meters, moving on a parallel course in a left-hand turn. Perfectly set up for a firing pass, Nikolai dropped in behind this pair of Thunderjets, and closing to within a range of 250–200 meters to the trailing F-84, lined it up within his sights and opened fire. The Thunderjet abruptly flipped over and fell in a wild spin toward the earth. Its fate was sealed. Captain Sutiagin's element pulled out of the attack in a steep climb with a subsequent turn to the left.

Major Artemchenko's element and Captain Bychkov's element, which had been trailing Captain Sutiagin's pair, encountered four approaching F-84s to the right of them. Artemchenko turned to meet them and flashed past the enemy in a head-on run, before pulling up and circling around to the left to make another pass. The pugnacious enemy had also banked around to accept another head-on pass. At this point, the order came from the division command post to exit from the battle and return to base, so Artemchenko 'blinked first' and broke off the attack.

The pilots of the 3rd Squadron under the command of Major Shcherbakov, flying in column behind the 1st Squadron, also ran head-on into the enemy and swung around for another attack, but they lost the enemy in the sun. Receiving an order from group commander Captain Sutiagin to exit the battle, Major Shcherbakov returned with his squadron to base.

The 2nd Aviation Squadron led by Major Ponomarev, flying as high cover at an altitude of 7,000 meters in the region of Unsan, detected four F-84s 2,000 meters below them and to their right. Ponomarev made a descending right-hand turn with his group and emerged behind the enemy. During the turn, Captain Mishakin and his flight chose an incorrect dive angle. Mishakin's flight accelerated past Ponomarev's lead flight, streaked past the enemy target at high speed, then pulled out of the dive well below the enemy formation into a climbing left turn. Seeing that they were low on fuel, Mishakin headed back to base with his flight.

Ponomarev, calculating the angles more correctly, led his flight into position behind the enemy and began to close the range to 700–800 meters. Seeing the approaching MiGs behind them, the adversary broke abruptly to the left, and at this moment Major Ponomarev and Captain Masly opened fire from a range of 800 meters, with a subsequent exit from the attack into a chandelle to the left. Then they broke off the combat at a command from the division command post and headed back to base.

The regiment had carried out its assignment to break up the enemy ground attack, but because of the delays in vectoring them to a contact with the enemy, they had only enough fuel remaining to conduct one attacking pass.[11]

Later that day at 13:30, Major Pulov led a regimental group of twenty MiG-15s on a mission to repel an enemy fighter-bomber strike, with the order to reinforce the actions of the 523rd IAP's pilots. The 1st Aviation Squadron with Pulov at its head flew in column behind the 523rd IAP, thereby creating the MiG 'train' so familiar to American pilots, while the 2nd and 3rd Aviation Squadrons were to cover the actions of the strike group. Approaching the region of Taeju, the cover group was engaged by F-86s.

The 3rd Aviation Squadron under the command of Major Shcherbakov, flying at an altitude of 8,000 meters, encountered up to ten F-86s, 500 meters above them and rapidly approaching on a meeting course. After passing over our fighters, the Sabres clawed around to the right and tried to get on the tail of our group. Captain Blagov's element broke up this attack and in the subsequent dogfight downed two Sabres, both of which were credited to the leader Captain Blagov.

The 2nd Aviation Squadron under the command of Major Ponomarev also discovered eight F-86s, which were about 1,000–1,500 meters above them and closing. Yet the enemy pilots evidently failed to see the MiGs, as they simply flew on past and continued on a heading toward the coastline.

As previously mentioned, the 17th IAP's 1st Aviation Squadron was flying with the strike group behind the leading 523rd IAP. Arriving in the area of Anju at an altitude of 5,000 meters, the group conducted a right-hand turn. Having reversed course, Captain Sutiagin, flying as the leader of the second element in Pulov's flight, noticed a pair of Sabres in front of them, to the right and above, which was in the process of winging over to attack the tail formation of the 523rd IAP. Nikolai Sutiagin energetically banked to the right in order to intercept the enemy and began to close. Seeing they'd been discovered, the Sabre element chose to break off their attack in a dive to the left. At this moment, Sutiagin suddenly saw tracers streaking past his MiG. Craning his head around, he saw six Sabres behind and above him, firing from a range of 400 meters. Nikolai abruptly broke right and clawed for altitude towards the sun. As a result of the Sabres' fire, a bullet struck the left side of his wingman Senior Lieutenant Shirokov's cockpit canopy, sending bullet fragments into Shirokov's right hand. His plane was not the only MiG to be damaged in this fight. The MiG-15 flown by Senior Lieutenant Shestopalov received a bullet hole through the rudder.

Major Pulov, noticing that Sutiagin had banked away to the right in his move to intercept the Sabres, turned to follow him, but at this moment received a warning from Major Artemchenko about a large group of twenty-four F-86s, above, to the left and in front of them, which was in the process of diving on them. Pulov responded with a climbing left turn to meet the enemy. The adversary, seeing Pulov's aggressive counter, broke off the attack into an oblique loop to the left, but realizing that they were being followed, opted to go into a steep dive toward the sea.

In the course of this flurry of action, Major Artemchenko had seen the six F-86s that were attacking and firing on Captain Sutiagin's element and moved to intercept them. Closing to a range of 1,200–1,000 meters of the enemy, Artemchenko opened fire on these Sabres, trying to divert their attention from Sutiagin's pair. The Sabre pilots saw Artemchenko and chose to break off their attack and head for the coast. Major Pulov's and Captain Bychkov's elements pursued the enemy to the coastline and fired at two of the F-86s. Lieutenant Bashlykov, Pulov's wingman, managed to hit one of the F-86s. Later, confirmation of an F-86 crash in the area arrived from ground forces, and this F-86 was credited to Lieutenant Bashlykov.

Having received the order to exit the battle, the entire group returned to base. The regiment had fulfilled its assignment, engaging in a difficult combat with forty-two Sabres. All twenty planes of the regiment, including Lieutenant Shirokov's, landed safely back at base.

Here's how Pulov himself describes his wingman's victory:

> In one of the dogfights, a Sabre attacked my plane, but my wingman Vasia Bashlykov gave me timely warning, and I evaded the Sabre attack through a steep, climbing left-hand turn. In the process of pulling out of its attack, this Sabre luckily popped out right in front of Bashlykov; he only had to adjust the nose of his MiG slightly to fire on the Sabre at point-blank range. Vasilii fired at such close range (30 to 40 meters) that he could see the face of the American pilot in a yellow helmet; his teeth were clenched. Upon arrival back at the base and after checking the gun camera film, it was apparent that Bashlykov had shattered the Sabre's wing with his cannon fire.

On 30 November, the 17th IAP conducted three combat missions to intercept enemy fighters. On the first mission at 09:22, a group of eighteen MiGs led by Captain Sutiagin became involved in a dogfight with sixteen F-86s. The action ended without results. Captain Tikhonov's MiG-15 received a bullet hole in its right wing during the dogfight, but managed to get back to base.

Altogether in the month of November, the regiment conducted 1,019 sorties, of which 853 were combat and 116 were training, and downed ten enemy planes. Captain Nikolai Sutiagin flew a total of thirty-nine combat sorties, engaged in fifteen fights, and shot down four enemy aircraft – three F-86s and one F-84, bringing his total personal score to thirteen planes. He was recommended for the Order of the Red Banner (which, as you might guess, he once again failed to receive).

Senior Lieutenant Vasilii Shulev received a recommendation for the title of Hero. By this time, he had downed five enemy planes and had helped his leaders, Artemchenko and Sutiagin, to shoot down seven more. Deputy commander of the 1st Aviation Squadron for political affairs Vasilii Fedorovich Shulev was one of the regiment's best pilots. He first served as Sutiagin's wingman, then Artemchenko's, and then he himself became a leader. His wingman was Captain Osipov. Promoted to captain in December 1951, Shulev would later serve a second tour of duty in Manchuria in 1953 with the 37th IAD as the 236th IAP's deputy commander for political affairs. Altogether Shulev was credited with seven enemy planes (though according to the regiment's own records, he shot down ten, of which one was ultimately declared as only 'damaged', one never received verification from ground forces, and one was never credited to him).

The 'Menace' in December

In December, Captain Sutiagin conducted nineteen combat sorties, eighteen of which were at the head of the regimental group, engaged in ten aerial combats, and downed four more enemy planes, two F-86s and two F-84s, raising his personal total score to seventeen planes. The UN air forces were continuing active operations against bridges, airfields, railroads, troop concentrations and equipment, conducting two to five large raids daily in groups of sixty to 130 aircraft.

The day of 3 December was a particularly memorable one for Nikolai Sutiagin. The day's events began when corps' radar sets at 12:45 first detected incoming enemy formations. The enemy consisted of four groups of aircraft, with up to fifteen to twenty planes in each group, which were approaching 'MiG Alley' from the south of Pyongyang on headings of 240–350°.

Already by 12:58, twenty MiGs led by Major Pulov were launching from the airfield at Myaogou. Once in the air, the regiment was directed to fly to the vicinity of Sonchon at an altitude of 8,000 meters, and prevent enemy attempts to penetrate the assigned area. Eight pilots of the 1st Aviation Squadron and four pilots of the 3rd Aviation Squadron comprised the strike group. About 1,000 meters behind the strike group and 800 meters above it, eight MiGs of the 2nd Aviation Squadron were flying as the cover group.

Even as they were crossing the Yalu River on a heading of 110° Captain Sutiagin, flying in Pulov's flight behind the lead element, noticed a group of up to sixteen F-86s ahead of them and to the right, at the same altitude and higher, and promptly informed the group commander of this. The enemy was flying from right to left in a climb. Pulov gave the order to jettison the drop tanks and began to turn to the left to get behind the enemy, but at that moment the command post issued erroneous information: 'They're our own; you are to patrol the area of Sonchon.' Pursuant to the order, the group commander began to turn to the right toward the indicated area, which simultaneously presented his group's tail to the enemy. Fortunately, Pulov realized just in time that these 'bogeys' were not our own, and took measures to lead his group out from under the attack.

As the group turned to meet the enemy, Nikolai Sutiagin noticed eight F–86s approaching to the left and below them, which were flying in the direction of the Gisiu airfield. Sutiagin informed the group leader about this, and then went after the enemy in a descending left turn. The Sabres, spotting the approach of Sutiagin's element, began to carry out an oblique loop to the left. Captain Sutiagin followed the maneuver and in the second loop, having closed to a range of 600–700 meters, opened fire on the tail-end Sabre, which evaded with a steep dive to the left. At this moment Nikolai caught sight of a second flight of four Sabres, which were diving on his pair from behind and above to the left. Sutiagin ordered his wingman Senior Lieutenant Khrisanov to break left. Banking sharply around to the left, they turned to meet their attackers. As they were making the turn, however, Khrisanov's MiG stalled and started to depart into a spin. He quickly managed to regain control of his MiG, but at the command of his leader, Khrisanov withdrew from the fight.

Meanwhile, group commander Major Pulov had decided to continue to Sonchon as ordered and was making a turn toward the area they were to cover. At this moment, eight Sabres jumped Captain Bychkov's trailing element from above, behind and to the right, before continuing their high-speed dive and departing in the direction of the sea.

Having arrived over Sonchon, Major Pulov began to circle over the assigned area. He soon spotted four enemy F–86s, apparently unaware of the MiGs, passing beneath them from the right. Pulov fell in behind the Sabres with a descending left turn and began to pursue the enemy, which was heading toward the sea. Unable to catch the enemy before they reached the coastline, Pulov broke off the chase in a left turn and headed for the area of Gisiu. There, at an altitude of 7,000 meters he noticed a pair of Sabres heading toward them in the direction of the sea. However, Pulov's intention to attack them was thwarted by an order from the division command post to exit the battle. Pulov was forced to leave the enemy alone and head back to base.

The crews of the 3rd Aviation Squadron under the command of Captain Blagov were flying in column formation behind the 1st Aviation Squadron. When Pulov made his swing toward Sonchon, Blagov noticed a pair of Sabres above and to his right, which passed beneath his flight and dropped onto the tail of Senior Lieutenant Tikhonov from the 1st Squadron. Captain Blagov rolled to his left and began to pursue the enemy. Closing the range quickly, he opened fire from a range of 600–700 meters on the wingman's F–86, giving him two bursts from his cannons. Then as Captain Blagov's MiG streaked past the wingman's Sabre, it got caught in the turbulence behind the leader's Sabre and went into an involuntary roll. As Blagov worked to regain control of his aircraft, he lost sight of the enemy. Senior Lieutenant Bykov's flight covered the attack of Captain Blagov's element.

The crews of the 2nd Aviation Squadron under the command of Major Ponomarev were flying in the cover group at an altitude of 9,000 meters, behind and above the 3rd Aviation Squadron. Arriving over Gisiu, Ponomarev observed a pair of Sabres below him and to his right, moving in a right-hand turn. Major Ponomarev and his flight went after the enemy in a descending right turn, but at this moment received a warning: 'We're being attacked from above and behind to the right!' Ponomarev immediately broke off the attack in a climbing right turn. A pair of Sabres streaked past at a steep angle downwards, where they became lost from view against the backdrop of the terrain.

Coming out of the attack, the leader of the second element in Ponomarev's flight, Senior Lieutenant Chernozemov, spotted yet another pair of Sabres to the left and 1,500 meters below, which he immediately attacked together with his wingman. However, having closed to within 1,200 to 1,500 meters of them, he caught sight of six F-86s in a staggered column of elements slipping onto their tail from the right, above and behind them. Chernozemov radioed his wingman Senior Lieutenant Zelenov: 'Roll right!' The enemy quickly closed to within 500–600 meters and opened fire. Chernozemov slewed his plane to the left, and then turned back sharply to the right toward their attackers. The Sabres responded by banking away to the left. However, the enemy fire had damaged Zelenov's plane, which forced Senior Lieutenant Chernozemov's element to exit the battle.

During the sharp turn to evade the initial Sabre attack, Major Ponomarev's wingman Captain Masly became separated and exited the battle. Ponomarev, coming out of the turn, also withdrew from the combat area, where Captain Sutiagin formed up on him as his wingman after becoming separated from his own wingman Senior Lieutenant Khrisanov. Together, they headed back into the battle area, but as they approached the Yalu River, they were called back by the division command post and returned to base.

The dogfight had lasted for ten to twelve minutes. During the action, Captain Sutiagin had downed one F-86 at an aspect angle of 3/4 from a range of 650 meters, while Captain Blagov had also shot down another F-86 from a range of 550 meters at an aspect angle of 1/4. The regiment had carried out its assignment.

True, on the ground during the post-flight debriefing, it was noted that the combat had been disorganized due to poor direction from the ground. Perceiving the enemy formation as one of its own, the GCI controller had relayed instructions for the group to proceed to the area of Sonchon, thereby placing the group under enemy attack.[12]

After lunch, pilots of the regiment sortied on a second combat mission, and this time the leader was Captain Sutiagin. After the corps' radar stations again detected a large group of approximately sixty enemy planes south of Pyongyang, the signal arrived from the division command post, and regimental groups of the 303rd IAD began to roar down the runway and lift into the sky.

Pilots of the 17th IAP began to take off from the airstrip at Myaogou at 14:52. Altogether, Nikolai Sutiagin led eighteen MiGs on the mission. The regiment's combat formation and squadron assignments remained as they had been on the earlier mission; the strike group consisted of six MiGs from the 1st Aviation Squadron and four MiGs from the 3rd Aviation Squadron, while eight MiGs from the 2nd Aviation Squadron were flying as high cover above and a little behind the strike group. After climbing to 5,000 meters, the regiment in a column of squadrons was vectored to the Sukchon–Uiju area with the order to repel an enemy fighter-bomber strike.

Sutiagin's group was instructed to engage the enemy fighter-bombers in the region of Unsan. Arriving in the area at an altitude of 8,000 meters, Captain Sutiagin noticed a group of up to thirty-six F-84s behind and below them, flying north-east along the Sonchon River at an altitude of 3,000–4,000 meters. The 17th IAP reversed heading to the left while shedding altitude and then set up for an attack on the enemy. Nikolai Sutiagin issued the command: 'The 1st and 3rd Squadrons will attack the enemy. The 2nd Squadron will cover the combat.' Having descended to an altitude of 5,000 meters, the adversary was still below them and to the right. Nikolai Sutiagin with his flight banked to the right and began a run on the leading group of eight Thunderjets, which were flying in a left stagger of flights. Having closed to a range of 700–800 meters, the enemy began to break to the right, which Sutiagin followed. The range dropped … 500 meters … 400 meters … 300 meters … and Nikolai opened fire on the lead plane of the second element, which burst into flames and plunged into the hills below with an explosion. Captain Sutiagin pulled out of the attack in a chandelle to the left, and then conducted a second attack on the other pair of F-84s, firing another burst at the wingman's F-84 from a range of 400–300 meters. His own wingman, Senior Lieutenant Khrisanov, also opened up on the leader's F-84. As he pulled out of this attack, Nikolai Sutiagin saw tracers seemingly filling the airspace around him. Turning around in his seat, he saw up to eight F-84s behind them, firing on his element. Jinking erratically to throw off the aim of his pursuers, Captain Sutiagin opened the throttle and accelerated to 1,000 km/hr, leaving the Thunderjets receding behind him. His wingman Khrisanov evaded the attack by breaking sharply up and away to the left, and then exited the battle.

After the turn to the right toward the enemy, Captain Bychkov's pair, flying behind Captain Sutiagin's element, noticed a pair of F-84s in front of them and to the left. Captain Bychkov went after them, and after closing to within 800 meters, he opened fire. Coming out of the attack into a climbing left turn,

Bychkov circled around and spotted a flight of Thunderjets in a right-hand turn in front of them, and decided to attack them. While approaching the target, Captain Bychkov's wingman Senior Lieutenant Tikhonov suddenly radioed a warning: 'Four F-84s are approaching from the right and above.' Bychkov broke off his attack and went into a chandelle to the left.

The final element in Sutiagin's six-ship flight was Captain Artemchenko's. Captain Artemchenko had followed Sutiagin through the turn to the right, but then moved to attack a different pair of F-84s, which spotted his attack and banked sharply to the left to evade it. Artemchenko pulled out of his attack into a climbing turn to the right, noticed in front and below him four more F-84s, and attacked them. As one F-84 began to fill up his gunsight, Artemchenko was just about to open fire when his wingman warned him over the radio that eight F-84s were attacking from the left and above. Artemchenko broke off his attack and exited the battle in a climbing turn to the right.

The 3rd Aviation Squadron under the command of Captain Blagov was flying behind the 1st Aviation Squadron as the second strike group. During the initial dive upon the enemy, Captain Blagov suddenly felt a sharp pain in his ears and pulled out of the dive.

Senior Lieutenant Bykov's trailing element continued the dive and after following through with a turn to the right, he noticed eight F-84s in front of him, which were firing at MiG-15s in front of them. Bykov began to fire short, long-range bursts, trying to force the enemy formation to break off its attack. The American pilots, noticing Bykov's tracers, abruptly broke right. Bykov watched as one Thunderjet, attacked by other MiGs, erupted in flames and plunged into the hills below. Having driven off the attacking Thunderjets, Bykov pulled up and into a climbing left turn.

Major Ponomarev's 2nd Aviation Squadron, assigned to cover the strike groups, remained in the battle area at an altitude of 7,000 meters, but took no part in the dogfight, since it never received an order to join in. Soon the order arrived from the division command post to exit the battle, and the entire regimental group returned to base without any losses. The fight with the enemy fighters had lasted for seven to eight minutes. As a result of the action, Captain Sutiagin had downed one F-84 at a target aspect angle of 1/4 from a range of less than 400 meters.[13]

The regiment conducted two missions on 6 December. On the first mission at 10:42, Captain Sutiagin, leading a group of twenty MiGs, became engaged with sixteen F-86s. Major Artemchenko downed one Sabre. The regiment suffered no losses in this combat, although Senior Lieutenant Zelenov's MiG limped back to base with five bullet holes in the right wing and engine area.

All five regiments of the 64th IAK took part in major clashes on 11 December. In the first battle, the pilots of the 17th IAP tangled with eighteen F-86s, which resulted in one downed Sabre, credited to the commander of the 3rd Aviation Squadron, Captain Dokashenko. Again, the regiment escaped with no losses. In this clash, the 17th IAP served as the strike group of the division, and Captain Sutiagin was leading the regiment, so it fell to him to direct the actions of the full division in the air. The combat did not go entirely successfully, although there were no losses on our side.

On this sortie, Nikolai Sutiagin was leading the full complement of serviceable MiGs from all three squadrons of the regiment. Twenty-four MiGs started taking off at 10:33 and assembled into a column of squadrons after climbing to 6,000 meters in altitude. The regimental group was then vectored to the Anju–Sukchon area with the order to intercept and destroy enemy fighter-bombers.

Pilots from the 1st and 3rd Aviation Squadrons comprised the strike group of the regiment; the MiGs of the 3rd Squadron were flying behind those of the 1st Squadron at a distance of 700–800 meters. The 2nd Aviation Squadron's MiGs remained as the cover group for the entire regiment, and trailed the 3rd Squadron at a distance of 1,000 meters and about 800 meters higher.

Heading toward the Anju–Sukchon region, at an altitude of 8,000 meters in the area of Pakchon, Major Artemchenko directed Captain Sutiagin's attention to eight F-86s forward and about 500 meters above them, approaching at an angle from the right. The Sabres were in a descending left turn. Nikolai Sutiagin issued the command: 'Commander of the cover group Lieutenant Colonel Smorchkov [18th GIAP] is to take on the F-86s on the left.' Sutiagin watched as the first Sabre flight passed him to the left and attempted to swing around onto the tail of Major Ponomarev's squadron at the back of the regimental column. Captain Sutiagin gave the command: 'We are engaging the F-86s', and with a climbing left turn he went after the trailing flight of Sabres.

The adversary, seeing that he was being pursued, went into an oblique left loop. Nikolai followed the Sabres through the loop, closed to within 500 meters of the enemy, and opened fire on the tail-end Sabre. At this moment, Sutiagin noticed six to eight Sabres in front of him and to his left, diving toward him at a 45–50° angle: he halted his pursuit of the Sabre flight and climbed abruptly to counter the Sabre attack. When the range to one of these Sabres dropped to 440 meters, Sutiagin opened fire. The Sabres flashed past beneath him at a steep angle, and Nikolai Sutiagin, finding he was alone, continued his climbing left turn and linked up with Senior Lieutenant Khvostantsev's flight.

Senior Lieutenant Malunov with his element followed behind Captain Sutiagin's pair and at the moment when Sutiagin had opened fire, Malunov spotted two F-86s closing in on Sutiagin's element from behind. Senior Lieutenant Malunov and his wingman Senior Lieutenant Tikhonov opened fire from a range of 1,000 meters to ward off Sutiagin's pursuers. The Sabre pair, noticing the tracers, went into a split-S maneuver to the left and dived steeply in the direction of the sea. Malunov, while firing at the Sabres, lost sight of Captain Sutiagin, and after conducting a shallow left-hand turn in the battle area, headed back to base at a command from the division command post.

Major Artemchenko's flight trailed Captain Sutiagin's flight, and at the start of the second oblique loop, lost him from view. Leveling out, Artemchenko circled to the left in the area of Anju at an altitude of 6,000 meters: failing to spot any enemy targets, he also turned back toward base at the command of the division command post and the group commander.

Captain Blagov's 3rd Aviation Squadron, following in column behind the 1st Aviation Squadron, went into a gradual climbing turn to the left as the dogfight erupted in order to cover the 1st Aviation Squadron's actions. Also failing to spot any enemy, Blagov and his squadron passed over the area of Anju, where it received the command to head back to base.

The 2nd Aviation Squadron under the command of Major Ponomarev as high cover followed in column behind the 3rd Aviation Squadron at an altitude of 9,000 meters. In the area of Pakchon Ponomarev noticed eight F-86s to his left and 300–400 meters below him, approaching in a left turn with the evident aim of getting behind his group. Ponomarev countered with a climbing left turn that spoiled the enemy attack. Pilots from the 1st Aviation Squadron then got in behind these eight Sabres; the enemy, noticing this, responded with a diving left turn. Ponomarev also decided to pursue the enemy, but at this moment he was jumped from the left by a different group of eight Sabres. Major Ponomarev evaded this attack with a climbing left turn.

This maneuver caused Ponomarev's group to become scattered into separate pairs and flights, which began operating independently. Major Ponomarev's element, after completing the climbing turn, noticed a single Sabre to the left and below, chasing and firing at a MiG-15. Ponomarev energetically banked to his left and dived in the direction of the enemy, and from a range of 1,000–1,200 meters fired a burst across the front of the Sabre. The enemy, spotting the tracers, immediately broke off his attack with a split-S maneuver and dived away, while the MiG-15 scrambled for altitude.

This flurry of action between our fighters and those of the enemy lasted eight to ten minutes, ending with no results. Moreover, the regiment had failed to carry out its assignment of breaking up the enemy ground attack strike, because it had become tied up in a dogfight by eighteen F-86s. The 18th GIAP, flying in the cover group, had not enabled the 17th IAP to perform its mission.[14]

The second mission of the day, which began at 14:27 when Major Pulov led twenty-two MiG-15s of the regiment to repel another ground attack strike, went more smoothly, and pilots of the 17th IAP scored successes: in a combat with ten F-86s, Captain Dokashenko and Senior Lieutenant Khvostantsev each received credit for a victory. There were no sorties on the following two days.

On 14 December, first Captain Sutiagin, and then Major Pulov, led the regiment to intercept enemy fighters, and two aerial combats resulted. On the first early morning mission, Nikolai led a regiment-sized group consisting of twenty-four MiGs. The regiment's mission was to engage the forward screen of Sabres in the region of Anju and tie them up in battle, thereby allowing the strike group of fighters from the 324th IAD to attack the approaching groups of enemy fighter-bombers.

On this sortie, Nikolai Sutiagin fully rehabilitated himself after the disorganized mission of 11 December, and directed the combat in such a way that the full complement of thirty-two F-86s were pinned down in battle by the pilots of the 17th IAP, and never had chance to come to the assistance of their other groups.

While en route to Anju, Sutiagin decided to climb to 9,000 meters, where the MiGs would leave no contrails to betray their approach. Near Anju, he noticed a group of eight F-86s ahead of them and to the right, about 600–700 meters above, but at this moment Major Ponomarev relayed by radio that a dogfight had erupted behind them and to their left. Sutiagin ordered the regiment to reverse course to the left. Coming out of the turn, Nikolai observed an ongoing fight in front of him, and led the entire group toward it.

Approaching the combat area in an area north of Taeju, Nikolai Sutiagin spotted to the left and 1,000 meters below them a flight of Sabres, angling toward their flight path in a left turn. He immediately gave the command: 'We're going on the attack', swung his MiG to the right, and then in a descending left turn lined up to attack the Sabres. Having closed to a range of 1,000–1,200 meters behind the enemy flight, Sutiagin suddenly heard Captain Bychkov relay a warning that Sabres had appeared behind them. Nikolai immediately responded with a climbing left turn to move out from under the attack of these Sabres. Swinging around in a wide turn, he noticed four F-86s to the left and below him that were moving from left to right on an intersecting course. Letting them pass below him, Sutiagin dropped in behind them with a descending right turn. Pursuing this flight of Sabres, Nikolai caught sight of two other F-86s that were moving to attack his element from the left and behind. Captain Sutiagin broke off his pursuit of the enemy flight and evaded an attack from this F-86 pair with a climbing left turn. At that moment, the instruction arrived from the division command post to exit the battle, and Sutiagin, having relayed this command to the entire group, returned to base.

Senior Lieutenant Malunov's element, while following Captain Sutiagin in the climbing left turn to evade the attacking Sabre element, spotted four more F-86s in front, below and to the right of him. Malunov decided to go after the left-hand element, and having closed to within 800–1,000 meters, opened fire.

At this moment a second pair of Sabres dropped in behind Malunov's tail, and he was forced to break off his attack in a climbing spiral to the left. Having received the command to withdraw from the battle, he headed back to base.

During this flurry of action, the flight of Major Artemchenko, seeing that a flight of Sabres was stalking Captain Sutiagin's flight to attack it, banked sharply to the left in order to thwart the Americans' intentions. The Sabre pilots, spotting they were under attack, evaded in a descending right-hand spiral. Artemchenko's flight refused to leave them alone and continued to pursue the Sabres. Soon, however, they were attacked by a different flight of Sabres from behind and above to their right, forcing Artemchenko to break off the chase and evade in a climbing right turn. At the order of the division command post, Major Artemchenko's flight exited the battle and headed back to base.

Eight pilots from the 3rd Aviation Squadron under the command of Captain Blagov were flying in column behind the 1st Aviation Squadron at an altitude of 9,500 to 10,000 meters. After circling around to the left, Senior Lieutenant Khvostantsev had noticed a solitary F-86, which was stalking Captain Blagov's element from below and behind. Khvostantsev, flying in trail behind Captain Blagov's pair, approached unseen to within 700 meters of this Sabre and gave a single short burst, but the Sabre continued to stalk Blagov's MiG. Khvostantsev then closed to within 450 meters of this Sabre and resumed fire. The Sabre flipped onto its back and went into an uncontrolled plummet toward the earth.

Captain Blagov's element began a turn to the right, and at this moment Senior Lieutenant Khvostantsev observed another pair of F-86s to the left and in front of him, approaching on a meeting course. Khvostantsev moved to engage this F-86 element. The Sabres responded with a left-hand turn, but Khvostantsev stayed with them and drew within 300 meters of the wingman's Sabre before firing a burst. Closing the range further, he fired another burst at a target aspect angle of 1/4 from 220 meters, after which his target's right wing began to blaze. The lead F-86 conducted a split-S maneuver to the left and dived away toward the sea. Senior Lieutenant Khvostantsev's pair exited the battle in a climbing right turn and headed back to base.

The MiGs of the 2nd Aviation Squadron under the command of Major Ponomarev were in the cover group and followed in column behind the 3rd Aviation Squadron. After the 180° turn in the region of Taeju, Ponomarev noticed a flight of Sabres in front and to the left, 800–1,000 meters below them, approaching at an angle. Ponomarev let the Sabres pass beneath them, and then banked around to the right to go after them. While pursuing the enemy flight, Ponomarev received a warning from Captain Mishakin: 'Four F-86s behind us.' Ponomarev immediately ceased the pursuit and went into a climbing right-hand turn. Indeed, a flight of Sabres was pursuing Ponomarev from behind, but having followed him through 270° of the turn, the enemy gave up the chase and headed toward the sea. After the climbing turn, the group broke up into separate flights, which operated independently.

Three-quarters of the way through the turn, Captain Mishakin's flight lost sight of the lead flight and headed toward the region of Pakchon. In a circle over Pakchon, Mishakin noticed four F-86s below him, approaching at an angle. Turning to the right to meet the enemy, Captain Mishakin began to close with them in a head-on attack, but the enemy refused the challenge and opted to dive away beneath Mishakin's flight. At this moment the command arrived from the group commander to exit the battle, and the flight returned to its base.[15]

This clash between our fighters and the enemy fighters lasted for ten minutes. As a result of the dogfight, two enemy F-86 fighters were downed by Senior Lieutenant Khvostantsev. Fellow pilots Polishchuk and Blagov both observed the final plunge of both aircraft, and Khvostantsev's gun camera footage provided additional confirmation. However, later he received credit in this dogfight for only one downed Sabre. Khvostantsev didn't dispute this decision – a victory is a victory, and our pilots didn't pursue victories for solely personal scores! Vladimir Mikhailovich Khvostantsev himself later recalled the combat in this way:

> The most memorable day for me was 14 December! It was an early morning sortie; we encountered a group of F-86s and engaged them. I see four Sabres firing on a pair of our MiGs. At a zero deflection angle, I fired a burst to try and force them to break off their attack; as it happened, I fortunately happened to hit one (well, of course, I had taken aim) – and one F-86 began to smoke. I then and there lined him back up in my sights and finished him off, and then immediately fired at a second Sabre, which erupted in flames. The two remaining Sabres departed, and I received sincere gratitude back on the ground from the pilots of the pair of MiGs I had rescued – Captain Blagov and his wingman.

In the month of December, the pilots of the 64th IAK were involved in almost daily combat, chiefly against Sabres, the number of which had doubled with the re-equipment of the 51st Fighter Wing with these modern American fighter-interceptors. If in the month of November only one squadron of the 51st Fighter Wing had entered combat – the 25th Fighter Squadron, which in fact had scored no victories in this month – then by the end of December a second squadron of this Wing, the 16th Fighter Squadron, had become operational as well. The pilots of the 25th Squadron, which had received some experienced pilots from the 4th Fighter Wing in the month of November, proved to be more successful. In December 1951, pilots of the 25th Fighter Squadron announced their initial victories in the skies of Korea, the first of which was gained on 2 December by First Lieutenant Paul E. Roach, one of the veteran pilots brought in from the 4th Fighter Wing. Altogether in December, pilots of the 51st Fighter Wing claimed five MiG-15s, four of which were credited to pilots of the 25th Fighter Squadron. However, on 15 December, even the pilots of the 25th Squadron had to experience their first loss in the war, and it was the 'Menace to Sabres', Nikolai Sutiagin, who was responsible.

On the first morning mission of that day, the 17th IAP was given the order to lead the division's strike group and to engage the forward screen of F-86 fighters in the region of Anju. Between 09:55 and 10:00 that morning, radar had detected up to forty enemy fighters and fighter bombers 70 kilometers south of Pyongyang at an altitude of 8,000 to 10,000 meters, flying due north in groups of eight to sixteen planes each. Immediately, a regimental group of twenty MiGs from the 17th IAP under the command of Captain Sutiagin was launched in response.

The regiment assembled into its usual formation, with the 1st and 3rd Aviation Squadrons forming the strike group of fourteen MiGs, and six MiGs of the 2nd Aviation Squadron flying a little above and behind as the cover group. After reaching an altitude of 5,000 meters, the regiment was vectored in a column of squadrons to the area of Sukchon with the assignment to cover the operations of the 18th GIAP's pilots. Captain Sutiagin's group was to engage the enemy F-86s in the area of Anju.

The group arrived in the vicinity of Anju at an altitude of 10,000 meters, and Captain Sutiagin immediately noticed eight F-86s in front and 400–500 meters above him, flying across their flight path from right to left. Nikolai issued the command to engage the enemy, and banked left to go after the Sabres. The Sabre pilots also spotted our group, reversed course and headed toward the sea. Over the coastline, one Sabre flight began to circle in the 'safe zone' just offshore, while the other conducted a right-hand turn to the north-east.

Captain Sutiagin with his wingman Senior Lieutenant Perepelkin banked right to pursue the second flight of Sabres, flying to the north-east, but temporarily lost sight of them during the turn. Having circled around completely, Nikolai again spotted the four F-86s, which were now being pursued by an element of MiGs. Seeing that the MiG-15s were too far behind the adversary (at a distance of 1,000–1,200 meters), and that he held a 500–600 meter altitude advantage over the Sabres, Sutiagin decided to jump them and initiated a sharp turn to the right. The Sabre pilots, seeing they were now threatened by additional MiGs, went into an oblique loop to the right. Nikolai pursued and slowly closed to within 600–700 meters of them. The Americans noticed this and pulled out of their loop into a sharply banking turn to the right. Sutiagin stayed with them, and cutting inside their arc, closed to within 270 meters of the tail-end Sabre in the American formation and opened fire. The Sabre abruptly tumbled into an uncontrolled plunge toward the earth. It had been a difficult shot, requiring a lot of lead, but Sutiagin's shooting skills were second to none. Losing sight of the rest of the Sabre formation, Captain Sutiagin conducted a gently climbing right-hand turn and returned to base at the order of the division command post.

Major Artemchenko's flight, which in addition to his wingman Kramarenko included the pair of Bychkov and Osipov, was following Sutiagin's element. At the moment when Sutiagin's pair went into the attack, Major Artemchenko caught sight of eight F-86s in front and to the left of them at the same altitude, which were moving onto the tail of Sutiagin's element. He swung sharply to the left to intercept this threat. The adversary, seeing Artemchenko's maneuver, countered with a climbing left turn with the aim of dropping in behind his flight, but at this point Major Artemchenko received the command to exit the battle and return to base, so he and his flight departed without having engaged the enemy.

The 3rd Aviation Squadron under the command of Captain Blagov was following in column behind the 1st Aviation Squadron. In the area of Anju, Blagov spotted twelve approaching Sabres in the distance to his left: he informed the group commander about this and turned sharply with his flight in order to meet the oncoming enemy. However, during the turn, Blagov lost sight of the enemy against the backdrop of the terrain, and lacking radio contact with the group commander, conducted a gently ascending left-hand turn over the area of Anju, before receiving the command to return to base.

Captain Dokashenko's flight had continued to follow behind the 1st Aviation Squadron, and having completed a 180° turn to the left, Dokashenko noticed a solitary pair of F-86s about 800 to 1,000 meters below, off to his left and in front of him, which was in a left-hand turn. He decided to attack them, banked to his left, and began to approach the adversary, but when he had closed to a distance of 400–500 meters, the F-86 wingman spotted our MiGs, broke sharply into a high-speed turn to the left and departed downwards. The lead F-86 began to make a more gradual, descending turn to the left. Dokashenko pursued, and having drawn within a range of 600 meters, he opened fire, but missed his target. After this, Captain Dokashenko's flight conducted a chandelle to the left and exited the battle.

The 2nd Aviation Squadron led by Major Ponomarev was following above and behind Dokashenko's 3rd Squadron as the cover group. During the combat, Ponomarev's six MiGs remained at an altitude of 10,000–11,000 meters and did not get involved in the action.

This combat with the enemy fighters lasted for five to seven minutes and resulted in the downing of one F-86 by Captain Sutiagin, which was observed by both Sutiagin and his wingman Senior Lieutenant Perepelkin. Two pilots had fired on enemy planes. The total expenditure of ammunition consisted of twenty-one 37mm shells and fifty-two 23mm shells. The regiment had carried out its assignment of tying up the enemy's fighter planes, and had downed one F-86 in the process.[16] The new F-86E (No. 50-0665) of the 51st Fighter Wing's 25th Fighter Squadron had been seriously damaged by Sutiagin's fire. Its pilot, Wheeler, had been forced to eject from his badly crippled plane.

Nikolai Sutiagin could hardly be accused of shunning battle, but nevertheless, as the group leader for the combat on 17 December, he was unable to avoid such a rebuke. In the 303rd IAD division commander's Order No. 0149 from 19 December 1951, 'On the insufficient initiative of group leaders while conducting aerial combat', it was noted that 'on 17 December 1951, group leader Captain Sutiagin flew together with the group of Colonel Vishniakov (from Kozhedub's 324th IAD). Colonel Vishniakov's group entered into battle, but Sutiagin's group didn't see the enemy and never became involved.'[17]

Such things happen often in war, when in the vast expanses of the sky one fails to spot the enemy aircraft, which are usually doing everything they can to remain unnoticed for as long as possible. Usually, the ground control officers prompted the pilots on the enemy's location, but this time, that didn't happen. The division command decided to place the blame on the group leader Captain Sutiagin, evidently as some sort of example. However, no one from the command had the courage to rebuke Nikolai Sutiagin in person for avoiding battle with the enemy. Nikolai himself dispelled any such notions on his next sortie, which occurred the very next day, on 18 December.

That morning, between 11:15 and 11:20, ground radar stations had detected two large enemy groups totaling more than fifty planes. From readiness level No. 1, eighteen pilots of the regiment took off under the command of Captain Sutiagin as the division's strike group in order to repel a ground attack strike by enemy aviation in the Taeju–Anju region. The launch began at 11:24, and as usual, the strike group of fourteen MiGs from the 1st and 3rd Aviation Squadrons took the lead, while the flight of Captain Mishakin from the 2nd Aviation Squadron flew as high cover.

After climbing to an altitude of 5,000 meters, the regiment in a column of squadrons was vectored to Anju. Flying in lead of the division's formation, at an altitude of 8,500–9,000 meters in the area of Taeju, the 17th IAP's 2nd and 3rd Aviation Squadrons were jumped by enemy F-86 fighters and became engaged in combat.

The 1st Aviation Squadron of six MiGs (Sutiagin-Perepelkin, Malunov-

Tikhonov, Artemchenko-Kramarenko), led by group commander Captain Sutiagin, continued on to the area of Anju, where it conducted a descending right turn. Having reversed course, at an altitude of 6,500 meters Sutiagin noticed six approaching F-86s at a higher altitude to the right and in front of him, which were flying in a column of elements and descending in a right turn with the aim of swinging in behind our group. Nikolai issued the command, 'Bank right', and all six MiGs went into a climbing right turn. Sutiagin's element was flying on the left side of the formation, and at the moment of the right turn, became the tail-end pair. Having completed a 90° turn to the right, Sutiagin observed a pair of Sabres in front of him, high and to his left, which were moving to attack Senior Lieutenant Malunov's element. Nikolai sharply rolled his MiG out of its right-hand bank and into a left turn to intercept the Sabres, and opened fire on the lead Sabre at a moderate deflection angle. The Sabre pilots spotted his attack and broke sharply to the right in order to escape the fire of this persistent MiG.

Proceeding in his left turn, Nikolai noticed another flight of Sabres to his left and 500–600 meters below him, which were in the process of making an oblique loop to the right. Nikolai allowed the Sabres to pass below him, and then went after them with an energetic turn to the right. From a range of 600–700 meters, he opened fire on the wingman of the second element. Observing no shell strikes on the target, Nikolai closed the range to 400–450 meters and opened fire again. The Sabre tipped over to its right and began an uncontrolled dive. At this moment, Sutiagin's wingman Perepelkin radioed him: 'Two Sabres are attacking you from behind!' Nikolai Sutiagin instantly reacted to the warning and made a climbing turn toward the right in the direction of the sun with a sideslip and began to pull away from the enemy. Having separated from the enemy, Nikolai swung around to the right a full 180°, where he spotted six MiGs above him and to the left. At his command, they descended into the combat area and covered the exit from battle.

The elements of Major Artemchenko and Senior Lieutenant Malunov continued in their right turn, and then went into an oblique loop to the right to shake off their pursuers. Having looped twice, Artemchenko emerged on the tail of two F-86s. The enemy spotted the attacking MiGs behind them and banked sharply left into a spiral. Artemchenko began to pursue the Sabres, but on the second evolution of the spiral, his element was attacked by five Sabres from the left and behind. Artemchenko evaded with a climbing left turn and separated from the enemy. Senior Lieutenant Malunov while in the second loop noticed a pair of Sabres was firing on his wingman, so he started to lead his element out from under the attack with a climbing turn to the right. During the turn, several MiGs approached him, which caused the enemy to break off the attack. At an order from the group commander, the 1st Aviation Squadron exited the combat and headed back to base.

The 3rd Aviation Squadron under the command of Captain Blagov (his wingman was Senior Lieutenant Shestopalov) was attacked in the area of Taeju by eight F-86s from above and behind to the right. Blagov and his flight turned sharply to the right into the enemy attack, but lost them because his cockpit canopy fogged up. At the moment of the right turn, the leader of the second element Senior Lieutenant Khvostantsev with his wingman Senior Lieutenant Polishchuk noticed a pair of F-86s to the left, which were trying to attack Blagov's element. Vladimir Khvostantsev swung to the left toward the enemy, but the adversary spotted his maneuver and conducted a sharp right turn to pass beneath Khvostantsev's element. At that moment Khvostantsev saw yet another flight of Sabres in front and to the left on a parallel course. He shifted his flight path to get behind the enemy flight and started to close on it, managing to draw within 1,000–1,200 meters, but at that point his element was jumped by a different flight of Sabres from above and behind to the right. Senior Lieutenant Khvostantsev noticed this attack in time and countered it with a climbing right turn.

The flight of Captain Dokashenko (consisting of the pairs Dokashenko–Khrisanov and Volkov–Nikolaev), under the attack from the eight F-86s, evaded it with a climbing left turn. An element of F-86s clung to the tail of the trailing Senior Lieutenant Volkov's element in the turn. Volkov turned into the sun and continued to climb, leaving the F-86s unable to follow. After separating from the F-86 pair, Volkov saw a different element of Sabres in front of him, to the left and below, which he then began to pursue. The enemy, spotting the approaching MiGs, went into a left oblique loop. In the third loop, Volkov emerged on the tail of the Sabres and gave his first burst from a range of 1,000 meters. However, realizing that the range was too great, he moved in a little closer and fired a second burst at the Sabre wingman's plane at a range of 600 meters. Then, streaking past the target, he failed to spot any more enemy planes and exited from the combat at the command.

Captain Dokashenko, evading the Sabre attack in a climbing left turn, noticed a pair of F-86s approaching at an angle from the left and below, which were moving into position behind a group of MiGs. Nikolai Dokashenko swung around in a descending left turn to follow the enemy. The Sabre pilots, noticing their pursuers, immediately turned away in the direction of the sea. Dokashenko followed the enemy to the coastline, after which his element exited the combat in a climbing left turn.

The crews of the 2nd Aviation Squadron (Mishakin-Bozhko, Chernozemov-Zelenov) under the command of Captain Mishakin, which was also attacked in the opening moments of the action by the eight F-86s in the area of Taeju, joined the 3rd Aviation Squadron in its climbing turn to the right. Having completed a full circle, Mishakin's flight continued on to the area of Anju, where Mishakin spotted a flight of F–86s 500 to 600 meters below him, to his left and front. He began to pursue them, but having closed to within a distance of 1,500 meters of the enemy flight Mishakin unexpectedly saw another flight of Sabres in front and to the left of him. The Sabres were approaching and already turning to get behind Mishakin's flight. Captain Mishakin halted his pursuit of the first four F–86s and tried to evade the second flight of Sabres through a climbing left turn, but the enemy continued to follow him. He shifted into a climbing spiral to the left to shake off his pursuers, but the enemy continued to follow to an altitude of 11,000 meters, where they finally abandoned the chase. At the direction of the group commander, Mishakin headed back to base with his flight.

The swirling dogfight with the enemy fighters lasted ten to twelve minutes. As a result of the action, the assistant regiment commander for aerial tactics and aerial gunnery Captain Sutiagin downed one Sabre from a range of 400 meters at a target aspect angle of 1/4. Confirmation of the crash of this Sabre later arrived from local North Korean authorities in January. Despite the enemy's superiority in numbers, the entire regiment had actively engaged them in combat. However, the regiment had not carried out its assignment to repulse the enemy ground attack strike, since it had been tied up by the combat with the enemy fighters.[18]

The F–86, downed on 18 December 1951 by Captain Sutiagin fell in an area 2 kilometers south-east of Chasan.[19] The Americans also confirmed this loss: again, a new F–86E (No. 51-2370) from the 51st Fighter Wing's 25th Fighter Squadron fell under the fire from the cannons of Captain Sutiagin's MiG. Its pilot, George M. Pistole, managed to eject from the burning plane and survived.

'Captain Bychkov is to lead the group into battle!'

On 22 December, the entire flight staff of the regiment assembled in formation to hear the announcement of a Decree on awarding pilots with Orders and medals, and the latest round of promotions by order of the Air Force Commander-in-Chief. Major Pulov, Captain Blagov, and Senior Lieutenants Bykov and Shulev all received promotions.

The next day, the regiment flew two combat missions, the first since the clash on 18 December. On the first mission, the regiment group, flying as part of the entire 303rd IAD, was led by Captain Sutiagin. Between 09:47 and 09:53 on this day, radar stations detected up to sixty enemy fighters and fighter-bombers at an altitude of 7,000–9,000 meters in the region of Chinnampo. The enemy was flying nearly due north in groups of twelve to sixteen planes.

The regiment in the strength of eighteen MiGs under the command of Captain Sutiagin took off at 10:00 from readiness level No. 1 to repulse an enemy ground attack strike in the Sukchon–Uiju area. After gaining altitude, the regiment in a column of squadrons was vectored to the area of Sukchon with the assignment to intercept and destroy enemy fighter-bombers.

Flying in the strike group of the division at an altitude of 8,500–9,000 meters in the area of Anju, Sutiagin's group conducted a right turn of 70–80° and began to descend. Dropping to an altitude of 6,000 meters, Captain Bychkov spotted eight F-84 planes below and in front of the group, and informed the group commander Captain Sutiagin of his discovery. Sutiagin immediately led the group toward the enemy. The adversary, noticing the approach of our MiGs, broke sharply right, forcing the six MiGs to overshoot at high speed and a high deflection angle. Pulling up in a climbing turn, Sutiagin led the group around for a second attack.

Closing rapidly, Nikolai Sutiagin with his wingman Nikolai Perepelkin swung sharply around to the left to drop onto the tail of the enemy, and began to pursue them. The Thunderjet pilots were trying to drag the combat to the south over Pyongyang. Sutiagin quickly closed to within a range of 600 meters of the tail-end pair of F-84s, but their pilots saw him coming and broke right. Briefly following the Thunderjets through their turn, Sutiagin drew to within 300 meters of the leader of the pair in the turn, opened fire and then exited the attack in a climbing turn to the left.

Captain Bychkov, following behind Captain Sutiagin's element with his wingman Senior Lieutenant Kramarenko as the third pair in the group, attacked a different Thunderjet element, but opened fire at a great range of 1,000–1,500 meters and a high deflection angle, after which he pulled out of the attack in a climbing left turn. Senior Lieutenant Malunov and his wingman Captain Tikhonov followed Captain Bychkov's element through this attack. There were no repeat attacks since the enemy had managed to escape beyond a no-fly line for the Soviet pilots, and the pilots of the 1st Aviation Squadron headed back to their airbase in a climb.

The pilots of the 3rd and 2nd Aviation Squadrons followed in a column of flights and pairs behind the 1st Aviation Squadron. They encountered the enemy Thunderjets at a high closing deflection angle, but had no time to maneuver for a better shot before the order to return to base arrived from the division command post and group commander Captain Sutiagin.

This brief clash against enemy fighter-bombers lasted for only five to seven minutes, during which Captain Sutiagin damaged one F-84 from a range of 240 meters. The expenditure of ammunition consisted of nineteen 37mm shells and thirty-eight 23mm shells. There were no significant losses inflicted on the enemy, because they managed to retreat beyond the Pyongyang–Wonsan line, which the MiGs were forbidden to cross.[20]

The targets had probably been Thunderjets from the 49th Fighter Bomber Wing, since the Americans later (on 25 December) recognized the loss of two of their F-84Es; most likely, one of these fell from the cannon fire of Captain Sutiagin. In January, confirmation arrived from Korean authorities that on '23 December in the period of 12:00 (Korean time) there was an aerial combat in the area of Unsan, as the result of which one enemy F-84 plane fell; it crashed in the region of Unsan.' Captain Sutiagin received credit for this 'kill'.

On the second mission of 23 December, a twenty-ship formation of the regiment under the command of Major Pulov conducted a dogfight 'on equal terms' with twenty F-86s. Senior Lieutenant Malunov managed to down one Sabre.

After this day, a brief period of relative calm descended over 'MiG Alley'. It was only on 27 December that battles over the area flared up again with renewed violence.

The brief lull was marked by an unpleasant incident. On 24 December, deputy commander of the regiment Major B.V. Maslennikov received his promotion to the rank of lieutenant colonel. Taking advantage of the lull in fighting, the regiment staged a cocktail reception that evening to mark the occasion. During the meal in the pilots' mess hall, one intoxicated pilot demanded a bottle of beer from a Chinese servant, instead of the glass of cognac she had given him. The servant replied that there was no beer. To show his dissatisfaction with the answer, the pilot smashed the glass on the floor. When attending officers demanded that he stop his scandalous behavior, he replied with a rude remark. The division commander, who was present, intervened. The 'beer lover' was strictly punished.

On 27 December the regiment twice took off with the mission to cover the operations of other units of the division. On the second mission at 14:13 in the area of Anju, Major Pulov was leading the regimental group to cover pilots of the 18th GIAP. Captain Shulev and Senior Lieutenant Savchenko aborted the mission because Savchenko's plane was getting no fuel from the drop tanks. The ensuing battle, which involved eighteen MiG-15s and twenty-two F-86s, ended without results.

On 28 December, the regiment again conducted two missions and again a technician let it down. On the second mission between 12:50 and 12:52, when a group of twenty MiG-15s led by Lieutenant Colonel Maslennikov took off to protect a forward airfield, some of the pilots had to abort the mission. Captain Dokashenko and Senior Lieutenant Khrisanov returned immediately after take-off, because the right-hand landing gear of Khrisanov's plane failed to retract, while Senior Lieutenant Savchenko with his wingman Senior Lieutenant Kramarenko also returned early when a drop tank on

Kramarenko's plane ruptured.

The regiment became involved in a scrap with six F-86s, in which Senior Lieutenant Shestopalov was jumped by a pair of F-86s at an altitude of 10,000 meters in an area 25–30 kilometers south-east of Pakchon. The .50 calibre fire from the Sabres caused an engine explosion, and Shestopalov felt a wound to the back of his head, after which he made the decision to eject. He landed safely and was brought in for medical attention. The pilot's health was evaluated by the examining doctors as satisfactory: he had received a light wound to the back of the head and in the lower portion of his left shoulder. Thus the pilots of the 51st Fighter Wing had taken a measure of sweet revenge for the bitter pill of their own losses at the hands of the pilots of the 17th IAP earlier that month. A pilot of the 25th Fighter Squadron, First Lieutenant Paul E. Roach, received credit for this victory.

In a dogfight on 31 December, deputy commander of the 1st Aviation Squadron Captain Bychkov led a group of sixteen MiG-15s against twenty-four F-86s. The group had been scrambled between 14:05 and 14:08 at a signal from the division command post. Captain Sutiagin was supposed to be leading the regimental group, but as he was beginning to accelerate down the runway to take off, oil suddenly began to spray his cockpit canopy. He and his wingman Senior Lieutenant Perepelkin quickly aborted the take-off, turning over command of the regimental group to Captain Bychkov. Senior Lieutenant Chernozemov and his wingman Senior Lieutenant Zelenov also had to abort the mission shortly after take-off because of a rupture in the hermetic seal around the cockpit canopy of Chernozemov's MiG.

Although this battle for the 17th IAP ended without any results, the group successfully carried out its assignment to repulse an enemy ground attack strike and cover the actions of the pilots of the 18th GIAP. The 18th GIAP claimed three F-80s on this mission. The division commander expressed his gratitude to the entire flight staff of both regiments, while Captain Bychkov was singled out for his performance and awarded a bonus of 150 rubles.

Altogether in the month of December, the regiment conducted 554 combat sorties and downed eleven enemy planes, four of which went to Captain Sutiagin's credit. In the monthly political report for December, it was noted that Captain Sutiagin as group leader skilfully directed aerial combat, used good tactical approaches, and that he capably applied Stalinist military precepts. The report further stated that Sutiagin shared his leading combat experience with his subordinates. Thus, in December Nikolai Sutiagin had prepared and given a lecture for the flight staff on the subject, 'The firepower of the MiG-15 and its skillful use in aerial combat to destroy the enemy'.

In December, the pilots Blagov, Khvostantsev, Shestopalov and Polishchuk were written up for the Order of the Red Banner, while Captain Artemchenko was recommended for the title Hero of the Soviet Union. By this time, he had six personal victories to his credit. At the same time, however, the division command noted that some element leaders would engage in combat, but would break it off as soon as the enemy began to use his superiority in the dive.

By the end of December, the flight staff was physically exhausted. There were incidents in the air in December that were directly connected with the deteriorating condition of the pilots:

1. At an altitude of 12,000 meters Senior Lieutenant Kramarenko lost consciousness and went into a spin; he regained consciousness and brought his plane out of the spin only after it had fallen to 6,000 meters.
2. Captain Ponomarev kept slipping in and out of consciousness at an altitude of 7,000 meters while flying in formation, became disoriented, and guided his plane with great difficulty only by following his wingman's movements.
3. Senior Lieutenant Bashlykov while on a mission vomited directly into his oxygen mask and almost collided with the group leader Major Pulov.
4. Senior Lieutenant Polianichko had a heart attack after landing his plane because of exhaustion.

The incident with Bashlykov was a consequence of 'oxygen toxicity': the oversaturation of the organism with oxygen, which appeared after eighty to ninety sorties in almost every pilot. Doctors watched for this and at the first signs of hyperoxia suspended the pilots from flight duty and sent them for rest at a sanatorium, but they didn't always manage to do this in time. More frequently, the situation didn't permit them to take these steps, when the presence of every pilot in the regiment counted.

The year 1951 was the most intense one of the air war that unfolded in the skies above North Korea, but it was also the most productive for the pilots of the 64th IAK. For the first time jet fighters, the MiG-15 and the F-86 Sabre, commensurate in their tactical and technical capabilities collided in massive aerial combats. It was in the year 1951 that modern aerial combat tactics were worked out, and that the technical capabilities of jet aircraft were tested in practice; when electronics became crucial, and methods of signals intelligence and electronic warfare were being elaborated.

Altogether for the year 1951, pilots of the 64th IAK conducted 307 daytime group combats in the air and sixteen individual combats, in which 532 enemy planes of the following types were downed (including two night-time victories): 236 F-86s, 119 F-84s, eighty-two F-80s, forty-two B-29s, twenty-seven Gloster Meteors, eleven F–51s, eight F–94s, three B–26s, three unidentified piston–engine fighter-bombers and one RB–45 (these totals do not include damaged enemy planes). The specific numbers of destroyed F–80s and F–84s in these data are open to question, since our pilots often confused them when making victory claims. Over the same period, the 64th IAK lost approximately seventy MiG–15s in combat or that were later written off due to excessive damage, and twenty–nine pilots who were killed in action or perished in accidents. In addition, another ten pilots were wounded in combat. About thirty more planes received varying amounts of combat damage, but all of these managed to return to base and were restored to service by the technical personnel of the regiments.

By the middle of 1951, the strength of the 64th IAK had almost doubled what it was at the beginning of the year, which had a profound influence on the course of the air war over Korea. The superiority of the United States Air Force and its allies in the sky over North Korea, especially in the 64th IAK's zone of responsibility, was seriously challenged, and the heavy bombing of North Korea with impunity was brought to an end. Even though this sphere of influence and control did not extend across the entire territory of North Korea, the ability of the North Korean-Chinese Joint Air Army and the 64th IAK to contest the control of airspace expanded southward, and presented a genuine obstacle to the successful execution of missions by the United States Air Force and its allies. Yet while the UN air forces maintained their numerical superiority in Korea, it no longer gave them complete superiority in the skies of Korea, which forced the US Fifth Air Force in Korea to change its strategy and tactics in the coming year of 1952.[21]

Chapter Six

The Final Months of Deployment

Recommended for the Title 'Twice Hero'

In the month of January 1952, the pace of the enemy's air operations slackened somewhat. The enemy conducted only one to three mass raids a day, operating primarily as before against crossings, bridges, railroads and main roads, and against local concentrations of troops and equipment. Pyongyang, Unsan, Chasan, Anju, Pakchon, Taechon, and Taeju were the primary target areas.

At the same time, the situation in the air became more difficult for the 64th IAK at the start of 1952. Operating alongside the veteran 4th Fighter Wing, the 51st Fighter Wing had added a second full strength squadron, the 16th Fighter Squadron, equipped with the updated F-86E Sabre, to the already operational 25th Fighter Squadron. One more squadron of the 51st Fighter Wing, the 39th Fighter Squadron, was at this time still in Japan being re-equipped with the more modern F-86E.

The adversary's shift to night-time raids by B-29s and light bombers placed heavy new demands on the 64th IAK. The corps' zone of responsibility continued to grow as the Communist forces continued to construct new airfields in North Korea that required protection.

The flight staff of the 303rd IAD had become worn out in the final months of 1951 by the relentless pace of operations, and many pilots were put out of action by the heavy psychological and physical burdens and sent back to the Soviet Union. The remaining pilots continued to fight in the final months of their assignment to China at the limits of their strength, which explains their poorer results and the rising number of losses. Although the regiments of the division had received ten replacement pilots in November 1951, they had no combat experience and flew primarily as the wingmen of more experienced pilots in the division. In the remaining two and a half of months of combat service, these replacements simply did not have time to assume leading places in the regiments of the division and affect the regiments' productivity in air combat.

The former commander of a flight in the 523rd IAP's 2nd Squadron, Hero of the Soviet Union Senior Lieutenant Dmitrii Aleksandrovich Samoilov, writes the following in a letter to the authors about the mission to China's final months:

In this period, division and corps command began to accuse the pilots of avoiding combat activity as the number of downed enemy planes decreased, while we in turn noticed that we were now facing a different Sabre. It had become more difficult to chase them down or to separate from them in climbs. We were offering this as an explanation for our reduced effectiveness, but the command didn't really believe us. Yet it turned out that they really were a new modification of Sabres. One downed American pilot, taken prisoner by the Koreans, yielded information during an interrogation that they had received new F-86E Sabres, an upgraded version with a more powerful engine.

Moreover, obviously, both the physical and psychological fatigue of the pilots was beginning to tell on our operations. Illnesses began to thin our ranks. In January 1952 the regiment only had enough pilots left to man sixteen MiGs, and by February, it only had enough to fly primarily in a group of eight. On 20 February 1952, only half of the regiment's original complement of pilots that had arrived in China in 1951 returned to the Motherland: sixteen pilots, plus six more who had arrived in the regiment as replacements.

The combat reports for the 303rd IAD bear out Samoilov's words. According to combat rosters for 1 January 1952, the 523rd IAP had twenty-six planes, of which twenty were operational; and thirty-one pilots, of which eight were sick (three of them in the hospital), and eight were on temporary leave. The 18th GIAP had twenty-seven MiG-15s and two Yak-11s, and thirty-one pilots, of which four were grounded by illness, five more were sick and in the hospital, and five were on temporary leave at a sanatorium. The situation in the 17th IAP was somewhat better: it had thirty-two aircraft, two of which were under repair and three lacked hydraulic controls. Of its thirty-seven pilots, four were sick (Shcherbakov, Shestopalov, Komarov and Perepelkin), and five were on temporary leave at a sanatorium (Artemchenko, Masly, Gostiukhin, Kordanov and Polianichko). One pilot, Blagov, was resting in the regiment. Two element leaders, B. Maslennikov and Sutiagin, lacked wingmen. In the 17th IAP, the 1st Aviation Squadron had eight pilots ready for duty, the 2nd Squadron had six, and the 3rd Aviation Squadron also had six.

The New Year began with new air battles in the region of Anju, since war has no holidays. Already on 1 January, pilots of the 523rd IAP had a brief, but fierce scrap with a group of Sabres, in which the deputy commander of the regiment Major G.U. Okhai (the group leader) and the commander of the 1st Aviation Squadron S.A. Bakhaev each downed a Sabre. The regiment returned to its base with no losses.

The first day of January also didn't leave the 17th IAP without work to do: it conducted two combat missions and became involved in two aerial combats. The regiment took off at 14:15 on its second mission of the day to the region of Anju, with a twenty-ship formation of MiG-15s led by Major Pulov. Our group dueled with thirty F-86s in the indicated region, but with no results. Captain Shulev and his wingman Senior Lieutenant Savchenko had to abort this mission because of a nozzle malfunction on the left drop tank on Savchenko's plane.

On 3 January, an order arrived from the Air Force Commander-in-Chief that designated Captain Sutiagin as assistant commander of the regiment. The next day, on 4 January, Nikolai Sutiagin received an early promotion to the rank of major, having spent only three months as a captain.

On 5 January 1952, Sutiagin was recommended for a second Hero's Star for his downing of ten more planes. By this time he had eighteen enemy planes to his personal credit.

This recommendation, like many others, never received approval. A copy of it remains in the personal files of Nikolai Sutiagin. In such instances, the reasons for the paperwork getting snagged somewhere in the military bureaucracy remained unknown.

It must be said that those who decided such matters didn't pamper other pilots who fought in Korea with decorations either. No action was taken on many of the recommendations for combat decorations, which had been forwarded to Moscow for approval by the regiment and division commanders.

Incidentally, another Soviet ace of the air war in Korea, the commander of the 196th IAP Colonel Evgenii Pepeliaev, who had nineteen official victories to his credit in Korea, was also recommended for the title 'Twice Hero of the Soviet Union', but without results. In his book *'MiGi' protiv 'Seibrov'* [*MiGs against Sabres*], Pepeliaev explains the inaction with recommendations for combat honors and decorations in this way:

Returning from the Korean War to the Soviet Union, the 324th Fighter Aviation Division became part of the country's Air Defence forces. Lieutenant General of Aviation Savitsky, being the commander of aviation of the country's Air Defence forces, often came by the airfield at Iniutino with a group of officers to call upon the 196th IAP. He conducted various tests there and analyzed the regiment's combat experience. It was well known to all of us that after our return from Korea, our replacements, the pilots of the 97th IAD, had suffered heavy losses, and the Americans had roamed freely over the Antung base complex. We had received word of this from our former technicians, who had remained in Manchuria after our departure.

General Savitsky never wanted to accept that the Air Defence aviation regiments fought worse than the pilots of the Air Force, so his command tried in every way to belittle the successes of the pilots of the 324th Aviation Division, which had been an Air Force division based in Kubinko. That explains Savitsky's sharp criticisms of the MiG-15. According to him, it was much inferior in battle to the American F-86. Savitsky raised significant obstacles between the pilots of the 196th IAP and the decorations they had earned in their combat work. Of the six pilots recommended for the title of Hero, only I made it through. According to the standards of the Great Patriotic War, many pilots [in Korea] deserved combat Orders for their combat sorties, aerial combats and victories, but they only received Orders of the Red Star. [The Order of the Red Star was the most common decoration of the Great Patriotic War, and it was also awarded simply for long service in the military.] I.N. Kozhedub personally told me that none of the recommendations, which he had written for pilots of the 196th IAP, ever reached higher than General Savitsky's desk.[1]

However, a more likely reason for the absence of a response to the 'Twice Hero' recommendation for Sutiagin was the veil of secrecy – after all, officially the USSR was not involved in the Korean War, while a bust of the Twice Hero was supposed to be erected in his honor for public display in the Motherland, with all the attending publicity that this would create. The entire matter would have received public exposure.

Perhaps there were also other reasons why Nikolai Sutiagin didn't receive the decorations he deserved. It is known that denunciations of him from his native village reached the pinnacle of power in the Soviet Union. They imputed him to be a 'non-proletarian element' – supposedly, the 'son of a kulak' [a prosperous, supposedly exploitative farmer] and so forth. However, General Krasovsky never let any harm come to his top ace. When the matter reached Stalin, the supreme leader issued a command not to touch Sutiagin.

The Year Starts Successfully: Two Sabres in One Battle

The first serious run-in with the adversary of the New Year occurred on 6 January 1952. Groups of MiGs from all five regiments of both divisions of the corps took part in it, as both sides threw reinforcements into the fray. A group of twelve to eighteen planes from each regiment was formed – all the combat-ready pilots from the 303rd and 324th Fighter Aviation Divisions. Our opponents in this engagement were pilots of the 51st Fighter Wing, represented by two squadrons: the 16th and the 25th Fighter Squadrons with a total of fifty fighters.

First to join battle were two groups of MiGs from the 303rd IAD's 18th GIAP and 17th IAP, which had spotted a large group of Sabres, flying in eight-ship formations toward the area of Anju from the south. As the ensuing dogfight raged, two more groups of MiGs from the 324th IAD's 196th IAP and 176th GIAP arrived to finish the engagement initiated by the 303rd IAD's pilots. The pilots of the USAF's 51st Fighter Wing suffered their first major defeat at the hands of MiGs from the 64th IAK in the skies of Korea in this fight. According to records from the 64th IAK headquarters, nine Sabres were downed by our pilots. The losses on our side consisted of one MiG and one pilot: a flight commander in the 18th GIAP, Vasilii Ivanovich Stepanov, who prior to this had scored five victories over Korea. His MiG had been damaged in the course of this massive dogfight. Stepanov nursed his crippled MiG back to the base at Antung, but when landing his plane overran the runway and overturned, killing Stepanov in his cockpit. This was the only loss of the corps, although many MiGs returned from this action with bullet holes in them, but without serious consequences for the pilots or technicians.

The Americans on the other hand recognized the loss of just one Sabre from the 25th Squadron, and its pilot Lester F. Page was listed as missing in action. It is possible that not all of the F-86Es counted by the 64th IAK actually went down and that some of them were only damaged in this battle. However, it is difficult to believe that just one Sabre was lost, as the Americans maintain. Of the nine victories claimed by the 64th IAK in this battle, six were credited to pilots of the 17th IAP, including two to Nikolai Sutiagin, and one each to Pulov, Perepelkin, Kramarenko and Bychkov. Pilots in the 18th GIAP, 176th GIAP and the 196th IAP each claimed an additional Sabre. The pilots of the 523rd IAP remained in the corps reserve.

The 324th IAD was the first to launch on this day from the base at Antung in response to ground radar's detection of approaching enemy formations. Radar was estimating that the several oncoming groups of enemy fighters and fighter-bombers had a total strength of up to 100 aircraft, which dictated a commensurate response by the 64th IAK. So at 09:44, the 17th IAP added to the swarm of MiGs in the air when twenty-two MiG-15s led by Lieutenant Colonel Pulov began to take off from Myaogou.

The 1st Squadron, led by Lieutenant Colonel Pulov himself, was the first to take off with the following crews: Pulov and his wingman Senior Lieutenant Shirokov; the leader of the No. 2 element in Pulov's flight Major Sutiagin and his wingman Senior Lieutenant Perepelkin; the leader of the No. 3 element Senior Lieutenant Shulev and his wingman Captain Osipov; the leader of the Squadron's second flight Captain Bychkov and his wingman Senior Lieutenant Kramarenko; and the leader of the No. 2 element in Bychkov's flight Senior

Lieutenant Miroshnichenko and his wingman Lieutenant Savchenko.

At 09:45, the 3rd Squadron led by Captain Dokashenko began to launch with the following crews: Dokashenko with his wingman Senior Lieutenant Polishchuk; the leader of the No. 2 element Captain Bykov and his wingman Lieutenant Bashlykov; the leader of the 3rd Squadron's second flight, Senior Lieutenant Volkov and his wingman Senior Lieutenant Nikolaev; and the leader of the No. 2 element in Volkov's flight, Senior Lieutenant Khvostantsev and his wingman Senior Lieutenant Khrisanov.

Finally, at 09:46 Major Ponomarev's 2nd Squadron began to take off with Ponomarev and his wingman Lieutenant Bozhko; and the leader of the No. 2 element Senior Lieutenant Fokin with his wingman Senior Lieutenant Komarov.

The squadrons assembled into a full regimental combat formation in the air while making a 180° turn to the right. After climbing to an altitude of 6,000 meters, the regiment was vectored in a column of squadrons to the area of Anju with the order to intercept enemy aircraft there.

The 1st Aviation Squadron with its complement of ten MiGs and the 3rd Aviation Squadron with its complement of eight MiGs comprised the strike group of the regiment's full combat formation, with the 3rd Squadron trailing behind the 1st Squadron at a distance of 700–800 meters. The 2nd Aviation Squadron consisted of only one flight and again flew as the regiment's high cover: it followed 1,000 meters above and 800–1,000 meters behind the 3rd Squadron.

Lieutenant Colonel Pulov's group received the assignment to cover the actions of its neighboring regiments, which were defending against ground attack strikes in the Anju–Sukchon–Unsan region. Arriving in the area of Unsan at an altitude of 9,000 meters, the group banked completely around to the right and began to descend. In the vicinity of Taechon at an altitude of 8,000 meters, the group began to carry out a left-hand turn. During this turn, Nikolai Sutiagin saw four F-86s above him and to the right, which were trying to maneuver onto the tail of Pulov's flight. Nikolai immediately warned the group commander about the enemy. Pulov's flight responded with a climbing turn to the left. While coming out of the turn, Lieutenant Colonel Pulov spotted a flight of Sabres approaching to the left and below him; Pulov went into a descending left turn in order to drop onto their tail. The Sabre pilots discovered that they were being pursued and split into two elements, one of which performed a split-S and dived away, while the other banked to the left. Pulov chose to follow the latter pair through their turn. Catching sight of the closing MiGs, this F-86 element went into a descending spiral to the left. Pursuing the Sabres through the spirals, Pulov gradually closed to within 700 meters of the trailing Sabre and opened fire. The Sabre erupted in flames and plunged toward the earth in a steep dive.

While Lieutenant Colonel Pulov was chasing this enemy element, Senior Lieutenant Shulev's element spotted another pair of F-86s in front of them, which they began to pursue. Vasilii Shulev approached to within 600 meters of the leader's Sabre and opened fire, which sent the Sabre into an uncontrolled fall.

Nikolai Sutiagin, after issuing the warning to the group commander about the enemy, pulled his MiG out of its left-hand turn, let a pair of Sabres pass him from right to left, and then fell in behind them. The flight of Captain Bychkov was covering Major Sutiagin's element from a position above and slightly behind him.

The Sabres noticed that MiGs were following them and went into a descending spiral to the left. After two turns around the spiral, this Sabre pair straightened out, and this allowed Nikolai Sutiagin to close within 600 meters of them. He opened fire on the lead F-86, which sent it spinning toward the earth in a steep dive.

After this attack Nikolai received a warning from Bychkov, whose flight had formed up on the right of Sutiagin's element: 'A flight of Sabres above us and to the right!' Sutiagin issued a command to his group: 'We're going on the attack!' and with a climbing left turn, managed to get behind the Sabres at a distance of 1,000–1,200 meters. The leading pair of Sabres continued straight ahead, while the trailing pair went into a left-hand, descending spiral. As they followed the descending Sabres Bychkov, being inside of Sutiagin, moved in front of his element and began to close on the lead Sabre of the element, which at this moment straightened out and went into a 50–60° dive. Bychkov pulled to within 700 meters of the trailing Sabre and opened fire, and the Sabre went straight into the ground at the same angle.

During the pursuit of the enemy, Sutiagin's wingman Senior Lieutenant Perepelkin lagged behind by 700–800 meters and noticed a solitary Sabre in front of him, which was trying to attack Major Sutiagin. Perepelkin gave the Sabre two bursts as he closed from 400 meters down to 200 meters. After this, the Sabre rolled over to its left, while Perepelkin's MiG streaked past above it and Perepelkin lost sight of his target.

After his attack, Captain Bychkov conducted a chandelle to the left. During the turn, Nikolai Sutiagin noticed a pair of Sabres approaching from the right, obviously intent on attacking Captain Bychkov. Sutiagin opened fire on the lead Sabre from a range of 350 meters, while Senior Lieutenant Kramarenko fired on the trailing Sabre from a range of 600 meters. The pilots reported downing both Sabres. At a signal from the group commander, the 1st Aviation Squadron exited the battle.

The 3rd Aviation Squadron under the command of Captain Dokashenko encountered four F-86s at an altitude of 9,000 meters in the region of Anju, flying to the right and in front of them on a parallel course. At a command from the group commander, Dokashenko began to tail the enemy flight, which noticed the MiGs behind them and reversed course with a dive. After diving, the Sabres pulled up into a steep climb, at the end of which three F-86s banked to the right, while the remaining Sabre went into a descending left turn.

Senior Lieutenant Volkov's flight went after the three Sabres turning to the right, while Captain Dokashenko's flight followed the single Sabre in its descending left turn. This Sabre responded by steepening its dive, and Dokashenko lost sight of it against the backdrop of the terrain. However, at this moment Dokashenko spotted a pair of F-86s in front of him, to the right and below on a parallel heading, which were chasing a flight of MiGs. He eased to the right and shed altitude in order to drop in behind this F-86 element, which caught sight of him and responded with a steep right-hand turn. After circling around once, the Sabres straightened out and then performed a split-S to the right. Captain Dokashenko followed the Sabres into their right-hand turn and kept an eye on them. The Sabres pulled out of the split-S into a climbing left turn, but seeing that they were still being followed, again rolled over and dived away to the south. Dokashenko pursued the Sabres to the edge of the no-fly area, after which his flight climbed away and exited the battle.

Meanwhile Senior Lieutenant Volkov's flight had continued to follow the three F-86s to the coastline, after which it abandoned the chase and returned to the area of Anju, where Volkov noticed a pair of F-86s in hot pursuit of two MiGs. Volkov began to stalk them, but the Sabres caught sight of him and went into a climbing left turn. During this turn, Volkov closed to within 700–800 meters of the trailing Sabre and opened fire. The Sabre flipped over and departed in the direction of the sea. After this, Senior Lieutenant Volkov's flight exited the battle.

The 2nd Aviation Squadron, consisting of four crews under the command of Major Ponomarev, flying at an altitude of 10,000 meters noticed a flight of F-86s in front of them, to the left and below, in an area 10–15 kilometers south of Pakchon. The Sabres were conducting a left-hand turn. Ponomarev with his flight banked left and headed for this target. During the turn Senior Lieutenant Fokin caught sight of another pair of Sabres behind them, to the right and lower by 500 meters, which were moving onto his tail with the plain intention to rescue their comrades from the MiG attack. Fokin increased the angle of his turn and evaded the enemy in a climb. After leveling out of this turn, Fokin spotted a Sabre chasing one of our MiGs, firing at it from a range of 200–300 meters. He went after the antagonist and his wingman Senior

Lieutenant Komarov gave the Sabre a burst to ward it away: the Sabre pilot saw the tracers and immediately went into a split-S and dived away.

Major Ponomarev and his element, following the flight of Sabres, noticed a solitary Sabre attacking a MiG. Ponomarev banked sharply to the right toward this F-86 and gave it a long burst across its front. The Sabre sharply turned up and away to the right in a climb, but then fell into a spin, made three or four revolutions, and then became lost from sight. At this moment, Major Ponomarev caught sight of another Sabre element directly overhead about 1,000 meters above him. He pulled the nose of his plane up into a climb, and approaching the F-86s from behind and beneath, he opened fire at a range of 500–600 meters and gave the tail-end Sabre three medium-length bursts. The adversary conducted a split-S and dived away. After this, Ponomarev's flight received the command to withdraw from the battle, which it then did.

The furious action lasted for twelve to fifteen minutes. During this dogfight, the 17th IAP downed six F-86 Sabres and damaged two more. Indicative of the intensity of the fight, the pilots of the regiment expended 248 37mm shells and 674 23mm shells during it.[2]

This was one of the regiment's most successful aerial combats over the entire period of its combat operations in Korea. Here's how one of its participants, Georgii Tikhonovich Fokin, describes the dogfight:

> On 6 January there was a battle that I can boldly assert was like no other we had experienced in the skies of Korea. Several pages are not enough to give a description of this fight. The point is that at this time, several regiments of the Chinese air force were being introduced to the fighting, and one of our regiments always escorted the Chinese fighter pilots into and out of battle and provided cover for them.
>
> Thus it happened on this occasion too: the 523rd IAP was covering their Chinese 'brothers', which had already returned from their mission and were preparing to land. That's when they launched eighteen MiGs from our regiment and twelve MiGs from the 18th GIAP – a total of thirty MiG-15bis fighters took off then. The Americans also sent two groups of Sabres against us from the 4th and 51st Fighter Wings – they had several dozen Sabres, while we had a total of thirty MiGs against this armada.
>
> Eyewitnesses on the ground later told us that the earth was groaning from the howl of the engines, and their hair was standing on end. We downed eleven enemy planes in this battle, and I'm proud that I also contributed my own bit to this total by shooting down one Sabre.

It must be said that Georgii Tikhonovich Fokin was a little mixed up, which is permissible after fifty years of silence, since the regiment scored fewer victories than he remembered in this action, which doesn't in the least diminish the exploits of the pilots of both fighter aviation divisions that participated in it. In addition, Fokin in actual fact succeeded in only damaging one of these Sabres, not downing it, but he is nevertheless correct – he still contributed his bit to the general victory of our aviation corps' pilots in this clash!

Another pilot of the 17th IAP and participant in this battle, Vladimir Mikhailovich Khvostantsev, informed us about this engagement as follows:

> Somewhere at the end of 1951, a new wing of Sabres arrived in Korea, which was equipped with the most recent version of the Sabre. The pilots of this aviation wing already had combat experience in the skies of Korea. They were even saying that the pilots of this wing had sworn to take revenge on the MiGs. Indeed, in our first encounters with them we suffered losses. The Sabres of this wing were decorated; they had yellow bands on their wings and various kinds of artwork on their fuselages. All this led to our loss of the initiative and sowed a sense of uncertainty in our ranks, and our morale dropped.
>
> Then our division commander Hero of the Soviet Union A.S. Kumanichkin gathered the pilots together and had a conversation with us, telling us approximately the following: 'Either we smash them tomorrow, or they will slaughter us all. I will lead you into battle myself tomorrow.' Indeed, this battle took place. As I believe, seven enemy F-86 planes were downed; our own losses I no longer recall. But from that point on, everything seemed to go in our favor and soon this wing of Sabres suffered heavy losses in combat with the MiGs. Mao Zedong himself congratulated our division on this victory in a telegram, and Kumanichkin read it out to all of us on that evening before a formation of the division.

Within a week, confirmation of the downed enemy planes from this battle arrived from local North Korean authorities for Perepelkin, Kramarenko and Bychkov, and from our own search detachments for Sutiagin.

An episode from the memoirs of Hero of the Soviet Union Mikhail Sergeevich Ponomarev speaks of the experience level of their opponent in the new 51st Fighter Wing:

> On one of the combat sorties with the regiment, while returning from a mission, I noticed in the distance off to one side a single F-86, which was tracking our group. I understood that this was a 'hunter' and that he was waiting for the moment when our group would be passing

through an area where there was no combat occurring – that is to say, when our vigilance would drop and he would pounce on a straggler in the group. I abruptly broke from our combat formation and accelerated to top speed, heading to cut him off, with the intention of getting on his tail. But I miscalculated and cut in front of his nose, putting my plane right under his guns. There was only one way out, and that was straight up, so I hauled my MiG into a vertical climb. The Sabre followed me and opened fire on me at a range of 300–400 meters. Still climbing vertically, I let my plane skid to the right, and in that way his bullets streaked past my left wing. But I knew that his Sabre was heavier than my plane, and that soon he would be unable to sustain the climb. Calculating the moment when this would happen, I anticipated it by a few seconds, then let my right wing drop and allowed the plane to nose over into a dive. The Sabre was already beginning to fall into a dive, and now our roles had changed, and I was on his tail. He maneuvered, while I fired from a range of 600–700 meters. But this opponent was also experienced and danced his plane around so well that I couldn't hit him, and he separated from me in the dive. So in this episode, he had thrown a scare into me, and I had thrown one into him.

Meanwhile the heavy pace of combat operations was not only putting pilots out of action due to accumulated fatigue and excessive physical demands; frequently the equipment was breaking down as well. For example on the morning mission of 7 January, led by Lieutenant Colonel B.V. Maslennikov, Captain Osipov had to abort the mission due to electrical defects: electricity was not reaching the GA-13 switch, thereby disabling a number of devices on the plane. The next sortie took place at 12:54. Its leader was Lieutenant Colonel Pulov, and its mission was to cover the Antung–Myaogou airbase complex. The group returned without having any contact with the enemy. Yet again there were equipment malfunctions: Captain Dokashenko and Senior Lieutenant Khrisanov had to abort the mission, because Khrisanov's MiG experienced a sudden loss of engine power.

There were also non-combat losses among the ground crews. At 20:50 on 8 January, a 2nd Aviation Squadron mechanic, Sergeant Kuz'ma Ivanovich Popov, was accidentally shot and killed by a Private K. from Unit 54954 due to careless handling of a gun.

The next clash with the American pilots of the 51st Fighter Wing occurred on 11 January, when pilots of the 16th and 25th Fighter Squadrons led by their wing commander Colonel Francis S. Gabreski were covering a fighter-bomber strike in the area of 'MiG Alley'. Every regiment of the 64th IAK took part in the effort to repulse this raid, and two major air battles resulted. While the

Soviet pilots of the corps tangled with the Sabres of the 51st Fighter Wing, Chinese pilots of the Joint Air Army attacked the Thunderjets.

Pilots of the 196th IAP, who shot down six Sabres in the two actions, particularly distinguished themselves. Of those six Sabres, Captain I.M. Zaplavnev and Captain V.G. Murav'ev claimed two Sabres each, while one Sabre was added to the score of the commander of the 2nd Aviation Squadron B.V. Bokach and one Sabre was downed by the regiment commander E.G. Pepeliaev.

According to records of the 64th IAK headquarters, a total of eight Sabres were downed on this day. In addition to the six F-86Es claimed by the pilots of the 196th IAP, two more were downed by pilots of the 17th IAP, including Major Sutiagin's next victory over the F-86. Their own losses consisted of only one MiG-15, but one of the top aces of the 18th GIAP, deputy commander of the 1st Aviation Squadron Lev Kirillovich Shchukin, who by this time had seventeen victories (fifteen personal and two shared) to his credit, was shot down. His plane was badly damaged by .50 caliber fire, and fuel gushed into the cockpit and soaked the pilot. Fearing a conflagration in the air, Captain Shchukin jettisoned from his MiG, but was badly injured on landing and sent to a hospital. He took no further part in the fighting.

The Americans claimed four victories over the MiGs, one of which was downed by the commander of the 51st Fighter Wing, Colonel Gabreski. It is possible that three of these victories were over Chinese pilots from the Joint Air Army, two divisions of which (the 3rd and 4th IAD) were operational at this time in Korea, flying in small groups under the cover of Soviet pilots of the 64th IAK and operating primarily against USAF ground attack aircraft.

The 17th IAP became involved in two aerial combats on 11 January. On the first mission, twenty MiGs led by Lieutenant Colonel Maslennikov engaged twenty-four F-86s. Senior Lieutenant Volkov claimed two F-86s in this action, but the results of his cannon fire did not show up on the gun camera footage. This happened because while preparing for the flight, the senior laboratory assistant Senior Sergeant Drozdov had sealed a cassette for the S-13 gun camera that had only 40 centimeters of film inside it, rather than the proper 3.5 meters of film. As a result, the film failed to capture the downing of two F-86s by Senior Lieutenant Volkov, and he was only given credit for one. On 23 January Senior Sergeant Drozdov was removed from his post, while Major Sutiagin's and Lieutenant Colonel Danilov's attentions were drawn to their poor supervision over the work of the photo lab technicians, since this was part of their responsibilities.

After lunch on 11 January, the 303rd IAD's pilots were called upon to make another sortie. A large group of up to sixty enemy planes had been spotted on radar, and pilots of the 17th IAP and 18th GIAP were scrambled to intercept them. First to soar into the sky from the airfield at Myaogou were the MiGs of the 18th GIAP, while MiGs of the 17th IAP began to launch after them at 14:09. The 1st Aviation Squadron took off first with a complement of ten MiGs led by Lieutenant Colonel Pulov. Then with an interval of a minute between each launch, six MiGs of the 3rd Aviation Squadron and four MiGs of the 2nd Aviation Squadron took off. Altogether, the 17th IAP put twenty MiGs into the air. After climbing to an altitude of 6,000 meters, the regiment in a column of squadrons was vectored to the Anju–Sukchon area with the assignment to break up an enemy ground attack strike.

While in the air, Lieutenant Colonel Pulov received information that enemy ground attack planes were in the Anju–Unsan–Taeju region. The group, arriving over Unsan at an altitude of 7,000 meters, failed to spot any enemy planes, after which it conducted a 180° turn to the right and headed toward Anju. In the region of Taeju, Major Sutiagin noticed a pair of Sabres to the left and in front of them, about 1,000 meters higher, moving from left to right as they fired on MiGs of the 18th GIAP at long range. Nikolai Sutiagin and his wingman Perepelkin went into a steep climb, then banked to the right and opened fire on the tail-end Sabre from a range of 550–400 meters: the Sabres ceased firing at the MiGs and departed in a steep dive. One of the Sabres failed to pull out of this dive. Because of low remaining fuel in the tanks, the 1st Squadron conducted a left turn and flew back to base.

The pilots of the 3rd and 2nd Aviation Squadrons were flying in column behind the 1st Aviation Squadron and were keeping formation. The pair of Senior Lieutenant Khvostantsev while making a gentle right turn in the region of Anju at an altitude of 9,000 meters was jumped by a Sabre element from the left and above. Khvostantsev exited from under the attack in a climbing left turn, but the Sabres continued to pursue him. Khvostantsev went into a left oblique loop, and then with a straight loop turned the tables on this F-86 element and began to pursue it: the hunted had become the hunter. Khvostantsev's wingman, Senior Lieutenant Polishchuk, seeing one F-86 break to the right, decided to follow him, and having closed to within 600 meters of the enemy, opened fire. After two bursts from the cannons, the Sabre conducted a split-S to the left and dived away. At this point the signal came from the group commander to head for home, and Khvostantsev's element exited the battle.

This brief action lasted for only two to three minutes, but it resulted in one F-86 downed: Nikolai Sutiagin's twenty-first victory. The regiment successfully carried out its mission.[3]

The pace of activity slowed a bit over the next several days. On 12 and 14 January the regiment flew several missions, but had only one combat against fourteen Sabres, which ended without results.

On 15 January at 08:12, Major Sutiagin led twenty MiG-15s to repulse an enemy fighter-bomber strike. The regiment clashed with sixteen F-86s. As a result of the fighting, Captain Tikhonov downed one F-86 and Senior Lieutenant Malunov damaged another. The regiment had no losses of its own. Nevertheless, the command evaluated this aerial combat as 'passively conducted'.

On 18 January Nikolai Sutiagin twice led a regimental group of eighteen pilots to intercept enemy planes. Both times they tangled in battle with pilots of the 51st Fighter Wing, but these actions ended without results for either side.

At 13:37 on 19 January, Major Sutiagin again led a group of twenty MiG-15s in the strike group of the 303rd IAD to repulse an enemy fighter-bomber ground attack. On this sortie, the pilots of the regiment ran into a group of twelve F-86 Sabres and Major Sutiagin moved to attack the enemy. However, at this moment his flight itself was attacked from behind by a pair of Sabres, and had to conduct a defensive maneuver to evade this attack.

At 14:19 in an area 15 kilometers south of Sukchon at an altitude of 8,000 meters, the leader of the flight's No. 2 element Senior Lieutenant Malunov was attacked from above and behind by a pair of F-86s. As a result of the attack, his MiG received eleven bullet holes in the engine and wing. Malunov immediately had to break off combat and head for home, but was diverted to Antung. En route to that place, his engine stopped: Malunov had to make a forced landing instead in an area 5 kilometers north-east of Antung. His MiG-15 No. 121069 was smashed and had to be written off, but Senior Lieutenant Malunov himself escaped from the landing with only slight injuries. The victory over Malunov was scored by a pilot of the 51st Fighter Wing's 25th Squadron, First Lieutenant Iven C. Kincheloe, Jr. – his first.

After the debriefing, the regiment commander came to the conclusion that the regiment's alertness in the air had been low, as a result of which the lead flight had been attacked by a pair of F-86s and Malunov's plane had been damaged. There had not been fire support between the flights. However, it is impossible to call this mission completely unsuccessful, since the enemy had not been able to avoid losses in the scrap: Captain Shulev had been able to down one Sabre.

Former pilot in the 17th IAP A.N. Nikolaev recalls:

The 1st Aviation Squadron, which was commanded by Captain Artemchenko, fought successfully. I remember Malunov had to make a forced landing, but that's all. Malunov was very unlucky with his wingman. Senior Lieutenant K. flew with him. At first, K. didn't seem to fight too badly. In June, I remember, he even shot down a Sabre –

before I even managed to get my own. I knew this pilot well. He had also graduated from an aviation school for ground attack pilots. We arrived together in the 3rd Aviation Squadron in 1946 and were assigned to Dokashenko's flight. K. spent a long time as the flight commander's wingman. But then in China, he was Malunov's wingman. Well, after his first victory, K. really began to act clever. As soon as a battle erupted, he would separate from his leader at altitude and there he'd linger until the dogfight concluded. Then he'd calmly fly back to base and nonchalantly make his landing. Fedia Malunov wouldn't complain to command, but in our circle, he was very upset with his wingman. So in the end, the Sabres indeed caught Malunov all alone. The 2nd Aviation Squadron also had a pilot like that. Incidentally, K. and I were from the same region. They once even put him in front of the whole formation for cowardice. But then they put everyone on the same level and ended up giving him an Order.

The Ace's Final Victory

Nikolai Sutiagin achieved his twenty-second and final victory in this jet war on 21 January 1952. Here is how it happened.

On this day the regiment only conducted one combat mission, which took place in the afternoon. Twenty MiGs of the regiment took off from their status at readiness level No. 1 under the command of Lieutenant Colonel Pulov as part of the division's strike group to intercept the enemy in the Sukchon–Uiju area. The regiment's own role was to cover the combat of the 523rd IAP's pilots.

The 1st Aviation Squadron with a complement of eight MiGs took off at 14:38, headed by Lieutenant Colonel Pulov. A minute later, six MiGs of the 3rd Aviation Squadron led by Captain Dokashenko were launched, followed by another six MiGs from the 2nd Aviation Squadron under the command of Captain Mishakin. After climbing to 6,000 meters, the regiment was vectored to the Sukchon–Uiju area, flying in the usual column of squadrons.

While heading to the indicated area, Lieutenant Colonel Pulov received a fresh instruction to intercept enemy planes in the Sukchon region at an altitude of 9,500–10,000 meters. Flying in the second echelon of the strike group to the right of the 523rd IAP's group at an altitude of 9,500–10,000 meters, the 17th IAP spotted eight F-86s ahead of them on a parallel course, making a right-hand turn in the area of Uiju. The strike flight from the 523rd IAP banked to the right and moved to close with the adversary. The Sabres, noticing the approaching MiGs, released their drop tanks and performed a descending right turn to meet their opponents.

Major Sutiagin with his wingman Senior Lieutenant Perepelkin, located on the right flank of the formation, closed to within 700 meters of the trailing flight of four Sabres and opened fire on them. The Sabres responded with a steep descending spiral and began to pull away, but then straightened out in level flight at an altitude of 6,000 meters. Nikolai Sutiagin, who had continued to pursue the adversary, spotted a single MiG above and behind him to his left, which was firing on this Sabres flight at long range. The enemy, seeing the tracers, banked sharply to the left. Sutiagin broke off his attack and reversed direction to the right, and immediately noticed a pair of Sabres passing on an opposite heading to his left. So he banked his MiG around to his left to follow. The pilots of this Sabre element, noticing the MiGs on their tail, abruptly reversed course to the right to take on Nikolai Sutiagin's pair in a head-on pass. Sutiagin opened fire at the wingman's F-86 from a range of 700–900 meters, then turned sharply to the right to follow the enemy as they flashed past. Now the adversary was at a disadvantage. When the MiGs had closed to the dangerous range of 700–800 meters, the Sabres began to make a left turn, which placed them in front of Sutiagin's cannons. Nikolai took advantage of this opportunity and opened fire at the wingman's F-86 from a range of 300–260 meters. The Sabre immediately began to trail smoke from its left wing. At that moment, Sutiagin heard the order from the division command post to exit the battle, and headed for his base.

The rest of the group traveled all the way to Pyongyang without encountering any enemy planes, and returned to base at the signal from the division command post. This aerial combat with the enemy fighters had lasted five to six minutes, and resulted in one F-86 downed by Major Sutiagin.[4]

Thus Nikolai Sutiagin scored his twenty-second and final victory in the skies of Korea, and attained a total that remained unmatched by any other pilot of the 64th IAK in the war. In fact, his final tally was not equaled by any of the pilots of the allied regiments of the Chinese and North Korean Joint Air Army, or even any of the pilots of the opposing US and UN air forces! Sutiagin was therefore the highest-scoring ace of the entire war.

On 22 January another change came to the leadership in the 17th IAP. Due to illness, Captain Shcherbakov left his post as commander of the 3rd Aviation Squadron and returned to the Soviet Union. Captain Dokashenko, a Second World War veteran with two victories to his credit, was appointed to replace Shcherbakov.

One of the hardest fights during the 17th IAP's mission to Manchuria occurred on 23 January. On this day, Lieutenant Colonel Maslennikov led a group of twenty MiG-15s to intercept enemy fighters, and became involved in a clash with twenty F-86s. Two Sabres were downed and three more received damage. Captain Ponomarev and Senior Lieutenant Volkov each claimed one of the downed Sabres. The 17th IAP also returned from this dogfight with three damaged planes:

The MiG-15 flown by Senior Lieutenant Polishchuk had three bullet holes in its left and right wings;

The MiG-15 piloted by Senior Lieutenant Bozhko had twelve bullet holes in its fuselage, wing, engine and tail;

The MiG-15 flown by Senior Lieutenant Khrisanov received two bullet holes in one wing.

In this hard fight, the pilots of the 17th IAP were tangling with pilots of the 51st Fighter Wing's 16th Fighter Squadron. The Americans once again deny the losses of any Sabres in this action; instead the pilots of the 16th Fighter Squadron in turn claimed two downed MiGs on this day. Evidently, two of the damaged MiGs were credited to the American pilots as 'certain kills'. Possibly, the pilots of the 16th Fighter Squadron also had planes that were only damaged on this day, but were counted by our side as 'certain kills' – such cases often happen in war!

On 25 January the regiment in a reduced complement, a group of fourteen MiG-15s, conducted two combat missions that resulted in two aerial combats. On the first sortie at 09:20, Senior Lieutenant Bykov downed one F-86. Captain Volkov and his wingman Captain Nikolaev aborted this mission due to a sudden illness of Captain Volkov.

On the second sortie that afternoon, a reinvigorated Captain Volkov downed an additional Sabre. Captain Dokashenko managed to damage another, but in turn, Senior Lieutenant Khrisanov's MiG-15bis No. 1115316 was shot down in the action. It happened this way.

At a signal from the division command post, fourteen MiGs of the 17th IAP were launched to aid Chinese pilots from the Joint Air Army, which were engaged in a hard tussle against Sabres from the 4th and 51st Fighter Wings. However, combat skill and experience were both on the side of the American pilots, who downed eight Chinese MiGs in this dogfight.

At 15:29 in an area 8 kilometers south-west of Pakchon at an altitude of 6,000–7,000 meters, in the process of maneuvering against enemy F-86s, the MiG-15bis piloted by Senior Lieutenant Khrisanov was attacked from above and behind by a pair of F-86s while in a right turn. The Sabre element's lead opened fire on Khrisanov's MiG from a range of 200 meters, and the burst of .50 calibre fire ripped through the plane's cockpit. Rostislav Khrisanov instinctively pulled his MiG up into a climbing turn to an altitude of 10,000 meters, but the F-86 element continued to cling to his tail. A second burst of .50 calibre fire from the lead F-86 caused Khrisanov to lose control over his plane's rudder. His MiG rolled onto its back and Khrisanov made the decision to abandon the jet in this inverted position at 10,000 meters. He landed in an area 10 kilometers south-east of Pakchon. An NKPA unit picked Khrisanov up and delivered him to the hospital in Antung with five fragment wounds in his right leg. The doctors concluded that the pilot's wounds were not serious.

In this battle, the pilots of the 17th IAP had tangled with their old acquaintances from the 4th Fighter Wing. The Americans acknowledge the loss of one F-86A, which crashed upon landing at its base in South Korea because of combat damage.

The days of 30 and 31 January were rest days for the 17th IAP's pilots. However, the ground crews had no break, and spent the time supporting the combat sorties of the 523rd IAP. They weren't resting at division headquarters either. In Order No. 0141 from 30 January 1952, the division commander, reminding Pulov of 'old sins', observed that the combat activity of the 17th IAP had declined in the previous November. It cited cases where the regiment had failed to carry out combat orders. Thus, for example, the order states the following:

> On 21 November 1951 at 11:47, Major Pulov was given an assignment over the radio from the division command post to descend with two aviation squadrons and reinforce the actions of the 18th GIAP's pilots, who were operating against fighter-bombers. Major Pulov did not carry out his assignment, did not reduce his altitude, and did not get involved in the combat.
>
> On 28 November 1951, the assignment was given to reinforce the actions of the 523rd IAP's pilots, who were operating against fighter-bombers. Major Pulov remained at a higher altitude than the 523rd IAP's groups, refused to descend and did not go after the fighter-bombers. As a consequence of the disorganization in his group, [Pulov] permitted the enemy with a force of just three Sabres to tie up his entire group.[5]

With this order, Pulov was warned about being unfit for his position, but such a serious criticism had a quick 'educational' effect and did not prevent the recommendation of Georgii Pulov for the title Hero of the Soviet Union. As regards the failure to carry out combat orders, on the ground it was much easier on the basis of hindsight to judge how one should act in combat. However, the situation in the air could dictate completely different actions at the time of the incident.

The pilots of the 523rd IAP scored one victory in combat at the end of January, losing one MiG and pilot in return. This was the final death of a pilot in the 303rd IAD in this war, though it wasn't caused by combat. Upon returning from a combat mission on 30 January, while landing, the wheels of the young pilot Parushkov's jet struck the top of leader Senior Lieutenant I.I. Iakovlev's MiG after it had already touched down, causing it to veer off the runway and slam into one of the hardened revetments. In the collision, the pilot's legs became trapped by the instrument panel, a fire broke out inside the plane, and the ground crews were unable to free the pilot from the grip of the crushed cockpit. Senior Lieutenant Iakovlev was burned alive in his cockpit. In such a cruel fashion, an excellent pilot of the regiment perished, one who had achieved four victories in the skies over Korea.

In January 1952, the pilots of the 324th IAD conducted their final missions. Already after the combat on 17 January, the 176th GIAP had turned over its MiGs to the 148th GIAP of the 97th IAD, which had arrived in China in December 1951. The pilots of the 196th IAP did the same thing on 20 January, turning over its fighters to the 97th IAD's 16th IAP.

As of 31 January, only four planes remained in the 17th IAP: fourteen of its MiG-15bis had been transferred to the 18th GIAP, and one plane had been lost in an accident while on loan to the 523rd IAP. On 1 February the regiment turned over another of its remaining MiGs to the 18th GIAP, and one to Military Unit 42117. By 2 February, the 17th IAP no longer had any of its own MiGs.

Altogether in the month of January, Nikolai Sutiagin completed twenty-one combat sorties, engaged in thirteen aerial combats and shot down four F-86s, but he conducted his final dogfight as part of the regiment on 2 February. At 16:48, Major Sutiagin led fourteen MiG-15s to intercept enemy fighters. The regiment clashed with twelve F-86s. Sutiagin managed to fix his sights on one Sabre and fired on him, but this time the Sabre pilot was lucky and escaped. However, Captain Dokashenko scored his ninth victory in this dogfight when he downed one F-86. Nikolai conducted two more combat sorties in February, but without any resulting actions. At the direction of corps command, Sutiagin spent most of the time in his final month in China on the ground, sharing his combat experience with the pilots of the 190th IAD's regiments.

On 7 February in connection with the ninth anniversary of the forming of the 303rd IAD, thirty men of the division's flight staff received monetary bonuses ranging between seventy-five and 250 rubles each, but Major Sutiagin among a number of the other pilots received only an expression of gratitude. On 9 February, the technical staff of the 17th IAP, numbering 201 men, was transferred to Colonel Kornilov's 494th IAP of the 190th IAD, in order to support the combat operations of this regiment. The 17th IAP's pilots and ground personnel accepted this decision with regret: they had become accustomed to one another and had hardened together, having spent almost a year with each other in the forge of the Korean War. Yet everyone understood that this was the correct decision – the technical staff had acquired extensive experience in supporting combat sorties, and this should be a benefit to the pilots who had arrived to replace the 17th IAP.

On 10 February, the 17th IAP with a complement of twelve MiGs (by now not their own!) flew two combat missions, and became involved in its final combat against thirty F-86s. Captain Shulev downed one F-86, and this was the regiment's final victory in this war. On the same day, pilots of the fresh 97th IAD, which had arrived to replace the 324th IAD, downed three Sabres without any losses of their own.

That evening, the Political Department held a series of meetings between the arriving pilots and the pilot-Heroes of the Soviet Union of the 303rd IAD's regiments. The mission to China had reached its end.

Captain Bychkov was appointed to command the 1st Aviation Squadron on 15 February, and Senior Lieutenant Malunov became his deputy. On 19 February, Major Blagov was designated as the assistant commander for combat tactics and aerial gunnery in the 523rd IAP, while Captain Volkov took his place as deputy commander of the 3rd Aviation Squadron.

The final combats of the 64th IAK in February 1952 involved only pilots of the 17th IAP and the 523rd IAP; the 18th GIAP was being held in division reserve and took no active part in the fighting. The pilots of this regiment were the most exhausted physically and mentally, since they had been flying combat operations in the skies of Korea a month in advance of the other regiments of the division. The pilots of the 17th IAP and 523rd IAP continued to fly combat missions until 20 February, primarily to share their combat experience with the pilots of the 190th IAD that had arrived to replace them, and simultaneously to cover their initial combat sorties. By 20 February, the pilots of the 303rd IAD had downed a total of six Sabres for the month, three of which were added to the score of pilots in the 17th IAP, and three went to pilots of the 523rd IAP.

To fulfill the directive of the Chief of the General Staff of the Soviet Army No. 65/089 from 17 January 1952 and the commander of the 303rd IAD's Order No. 033 from 23 February 1952, monetary awards were paid out to the flight staff for the combat sorties flown and the downed enemy planes between the period 12 January and 30 February 1952. Two thousand rubles each went to the two pilots who had carried out thirty or more missions over this period:

To the deputy commander of the 18th GIAP Lieutenant Colonel Smorchkov, for conducting thirty-four combat sorties;
To the senior pilot of the 17th IAP Captain Miroshnichenko, for conducting thirty combat sorties.

Altogether, the 303rd IAD had seventeen pilots that met this criterion for combat missions.

For personally downed enemy planes, 1,500 rubles for each plane went to:

Commander of the 523rd IAP Major Os'kin – for one F–86;
Deputy commander of the 523rd IAP Major Okhai – for two F–86s;
Squadron commander of the 523rd IAP Major Bakhaev – for one F–86;
Deputy commander of the 18th GIAP Lieutenant Colonel Smorchkov – for one F–86.

In the 17th IAP, Shulev and Dokashenko received 4,000 rubles each for downing two enemy planes. Sutiagin, Tikhonov, Ponomarev, Bychkov, Volkov and Pulov each received 2,000 rubles for downing one enemy plane.[6]

Altogether in the division, there were nineteen such 'lucky fellows'. After all, there were no such monetary awards for downing enemy planes prior to 12 January 1952! For comparison's sake, at that time the commander of a radar platoon received a monthly salary of 900 rubles; a sergeant, 150–250 rubles; a private, fifty rubles. A pilot received a salary of the order of 2,000 rubles, and a regiment commander, around 3,000 rubles. Thus the monetary award for downing a plane was equal to a pilot's monthly salary.

Chapter Seven

Results and Lessons

Operational Combat Results: Victories and Losses

According to the summary of combat operations between 14 June 1951 and 1 February 1952, the 17th IAP had flown a total of 3,223 hours and 2 minutes on 4,226 combat sorties, including a total of 3,062 hours and 43 minutes on 3,762 sorties to intercept enemy aircraft; and a total of 345 hours and 2 minutes on 444 sorties to patrol over ground targets. Altogether, the regiment engaged in 119 aerial combats, downed ninety-eight enemy aircraft and damaged thirty-eight more (not all the victories had been confirmed at the time of compiling this summary report). On average, each downed enemy plane required an expenditure of 115 shells, including an average of sixty-one 37mm shells and 170 23mm shells.

The following list presents the victory totals in the 17th IAP as of 1 February 1952 by pilot, in descending order:

1. Sutiagin, N.V. – 22 (15 F-86, 3 F-84, 2 F-80, 2 Gloster Meteor)
2. Ponomarev, M.S. – 10 (5 F-84, 4 F-80, 1 F-86)
3. Dokashenko, N.G. – 8 (7 F-86, 1 F6F5 Hellcat)
4. Pulov, G.I. – 7 (3 F-86, 2 F-80, 1 F-84, 1 Gloster Meteor)
5. Volkov, N.S. – 7 (5 F-86, 1 F-80, 1 F-84)
6. Artemchenko, S.S. – 6 (4 F-86, 1 F-80, 1 F-84)
7. Shulev, V.F. – 6 (5 F-86, 1 F-84)
8. Blagov, V.A. – 4 (4 F-86)
9. Bychkov, S.S. – 4 (2 F-86, 1 F-80, 1 F-84)
10. Khvostantsev, V.M. – 4 (3 F-86, 1 F-84)
11. Bykov, A.V. – 3 (1 F-84, 1 F-86, 1 B-29)
12. Maslennikov, B.V. – 3 (3 F-86)
13. Nikolaev, A.N. – 3 (1 F-84, 1 F-86, 1 B-29)
14. Agranovich, E.N. – 1 F-80
15. Bashlykov, V.I. – 1 F-86
16. Bozhko, A.T. – 1 F-80
17. Fokin, G.T. – 1 F-84
18. Komarov, A.A. – 1 F-86
19. Kramarenko, N.N. – 1 F-86
20. Malunov, F.G. – 1 F-86

21. Miroshnichenko, N.F. – 1 F-86
22. Mishakin, N.P. – 1 F-80
23. Perepelkin, N.Ia. – 1 F-86
24. Tikhonov, B.E. – 1 F-86

Over the course of combat operations, the regiment lost seven planes and two pilots.[1] Four pilots had to eject from damaged planes: Senior Lieutenant Bozhko (on 11 September 1951); Senior Lieutenant Kordanov (on 26 October 1951); Senior Lieutenant Shestopalov (on 28 December 1951) and Senior Lieutenant Khrisanov (on 25 January 1952). One more MiG was lost on 19 January 1952 as a result of a forced landing by Senior Lieutenant Malunov. The two pilots killed in combat were Senior Lieutenant Agranovich (on 26 June 1951) and Captain Morozov (on 2 October 1951).

Commander of the 64th IAK General Lobov's Order No. 0027 from 24 February 1952, 'On the results of the 303rd IAD's combat operations', presented updated and more precise combat results (which included the enemy planes downed in February 1952). In particular, it states that twenty-one pilots of the 303rd IAD had scored five or more victories:

Major Sutiagin (17th IAP) – 22
Major Os'kin (523rd IAP) – 15
Major Shchukin (18th GIAP) – 15
Lieutenant Colonel Smorchkov (18th GIAP) – 12
Major Bakhaev (523rd IAP) – 11
Major Okhai (523rd IAP) – 11
Major Ponomarev (17th IAP) – 10
Captain Samoilov (523rd IAP) – 10
Captain Dokashenko (17th IAP) – 9
Lieutenant Colonel Pulov (17th IAP) – 8
Lieutenant Colonel Karasev (303rd IAD) – 7
Captain Shulev (17th IAP) – 7
Captain Volkov (17th IAP) – 7
Major Antonov (18th GIAP) – 7
Major Artemchenko (17th IAP) – 6
Captain Kaliuzhnyi (303rd IAD) – 5
Captain Bychkov (17th IAP) – 5
Senior Lieutenant Stepanov (18th GIAP) – 5
Captain Kornienko (18th GIAP) – 5
Captain Shatalov (523rd IAP) – 5
Major Popov (523rd IAP) – 5

In accordance with General Lobov's 24 February order, Pulov, Shulev,

Dokashenko and Bychkov of the 17th IAP received credit for one additional enemy aircraft each from the February 1952 combats.

Of the division, 106 pilots were awarded with Orders; twenty received two Orders. Twenty-three men of the technical staff were decorated with Orders and medals. The division commander expressed his gratitude to all the men and women of the division.[2]

Tables One and Two break down the effectiveness of attacks conducted by the pilots of the 17th IAP by the range to the target and by the target's aspect angle. As is evident and not surprising, close range attacks at low angles of deflection were the most successful. However, the data shows that it was not simple to achieve such a firing position, as the vast majority of firing was from a range beyond 500 meters, while most of the attacks were at a target aspect angle of 2/4. It is noteworthy that firing from beyond 800 meters did not result in a single downed enemy plane, though it may have served the purpose of forcing an adversary to break off an attack on a comrade.

Various factors, especially including meteorological conditions over the given region of Manchuria and Korea, affected the nature and results of air combat

The Effectiveness of Target Aspect Angle[3]

Target Aspect	0/4	1/4	2/4	3/4	4/4
Number of attacks conducted at given target aspect	61	123	138	90	11
Number of planes downed at given target aspect	29	45	14	10	–

The Effectiveness of Attacks by Range

Range to target, meters	100–200	200–300	300–400	400–500	500–600	600–700	700–800	800–900	900–1000	1000–1100	Greater than 1100
Number of attacks	8	22	35	44	70	51	57	56	54	28	35
Number of downed planes	5	18	23	25	18	7	2	–	–	–	–

operations of both sides. Weather conditions ruled out flying on seventy-one of the regiment's 229 days of combat service, which meant that the weather prevented combat operations on 31 per cent of the regiment's days while based at Myaogou. The number of days with poor weather that prevented flight operations was distributed by month as follows:

June (from 14 June 1951) – 1 day
July – 19 days
August – 20 days
September – 6 days
October – 7 days
November – 8 days
December – 7 days
January 1952 – 3 days

From the data, it is apparent that the months of July and August were the most unsuitable period for combat operations in the region, when around 70 per cent of the days had weather that prevented flight operations.

If you examine these same months by the number of combat sorties flown in each month, the records reflect the following:

June – 230 sorties
July – 208 sorties
August – 311 sorties
September – 604 sorties
October – 592 sorties
November – 853 sorties
December – 680 sorties
January 1952 – 632 sorties.[4]

Note that in addition to these numbers, the regiment had conducted sixteen combat sorties in April 1951, before being re-assigned to two months of additional combat training, and 232 sorties in February 1952.

As is apparent from these data, the regiment conducted its most intensive operations in the period between September 1951 and January 1952. In this period, November was the most active month for the regiment, when it completed 853 combat sorties, resulting in the downing of ten enemy aircraft. However, according to the number of victories, the month of October was the most effective for the 17th IAP, when it scored twenty-eight 'kills' while making 592 combat sorties. Prior to the month of November, the regiment conducted one to three missions a day, but in the month of November, the tempo of the regiment's operations increased to an average of four missions a day.

Certain Lessons and Conclusions

Two Soviet aviation divisions – the 303rd and 324th IAD, which fought in Korea in 1951 – were able to offer effective opposition to the air power of the United States and its allies. The overall balance of aerial combat losses between the two sides in this period testifies to this fact.

Favorable factors for our pilots were:

- the more powerful armament of the MiG-15;
- the fact that virtually all the combats were conducted over 'friendly' territory;
- the relative sanctuary that Chinese territory provided to our fighter divisions' bases;
- the numerical advantage enjoyed by the MiG-15 fighters over the F-86 Sabres.

Factors that operated against our pilots were:

- the lower maneuverability of the MiG-15;
- the absence of an organized system of pilot rotation;
- the lack of pressurized G-suits for our pilots;
- the lack of a search and rescue service;
- the superfluous regime of secrecy.

As mentioned previously, four pilots were forced to eject from their crippled MiGs. Lieutenant Bozhko was hospitalized from 11 September 1951 until 8 October 1951 with an injured lower back, with subsequent treatment in a sanatorium from 10 October to 23 October 1951. Senior Lieutenant Kordanov remained in a hospital from 26 October until 14 December 1951 with second-degree burns of the face, and then spent the period from 16 December 1951 until 13 January 1952 in a sanatorium. Senior Lieutenant Shestopalov and Senior Lieutenant Khrisanov each spent up to ten days in a hospital and received flight waivers and treatment in a sanatorium for up to thirty days.

During the period of the regiment's assignment to Manchuria, fourteen pilots received in-patient treatment in the garrison infirmary for reasons of influenza, otitis, gastritis, and enterocolitis; two pilots were admitted for dysentery. One pilot twice spent time in the infirmary for treatment of a combat wound. Patients that did not respond to treatment in the infirmary were sent on to the hospital for further evaluation and treatment, with subsequent examination by a medical flight commission. Altogether, nineteen pilots spent time in the hospital; four pilots were admitted to the hospital twice.

The illnesses that required hospitalization included acute appendicitis, extensive wounds, hypertrophic rhinitis and deviated septums, high blood pressure, and other problems.

As for the technical staff, personnel sought medical help for gastro-intestinal disorders, gastritis, rhinitis, outer and middle otitis, and there was also a case of encephalitis. After recovering with no complications, this patient was sent to the city of Chita in order to obtain a document certifying his fitness for further military service.

The regiment temporarily lost the service of eight men due to medical reasons, two of whom were absent due to wounds, and four for treatment of injuries after ejecting from their plane. Two pilots were killed in action.

Based upon observation of the health of the regiment's personnel, doctors came to the following conclusions:

1. Each aviation squadron should have a reserve flight, in order to reduce the burden on the flight staff without affecting the pace of operations.
2. A special high-altitude diet for the MiG-15 pilots had no practical significance.
3. A pilot who had conducted fifty to sixty combat sorties in the span of two to three months needed a period of R&R.
4. A pilot who had ejected from his plane required forty to forty-five days of recovery in order to return to normal duties and combat operations.

The experience of combat operations indicated that the authorized strength of thirty pilots for the fighter regiment, without any reserves, was insufficient for the demands of fighter combat in the jet age. The enormous stress of combat leads to the rapid exhaustion of the pilots, who require a period of rest after every three to four months of combat; an even longer duration of combat operations without rest leads to a large number of grounded pilots. There were only a few pilots, owing to a proper regime of rest, nutrition, physical exercise and other reasons, who could endure the high stress of combat operations for up to six months without a break. Thus, for example, squadron commander Major Artemchenko flew combat missions without interruption between 17 June and 21 December 1951, during which he conducted 152 combat sorties and engaged in sixty-four aerial combats, and personally downed six enemy planes.

However, the vast majority of pilots after five months of combat operations were unable to fly combat missions and required time in a sanatorium. All this led to the situation after four to five months of combat operations, where only sixteen or fewer of the thirty pilots on the roster of the regiment were able and available to fly combat missions. The experience of combat demonstrated that it was necessary to alter the TO&E of the regiment to increase the number of pilots, so spare pilots would be available to fly missions and thereby give other pilots a rest, without diminishing the size of the mission.

A fighter regiment needs to have three aviation squadrons of twelve fighters each, plus four fighter aircraft in the regiment headquarters flight, which yields a total of forty aircraft at the disposal of the regiment command. At the same time, each aviation squadron needs to have one reserve flight of pilots, equal to all the other pilots in flight experience and training. In this case, each squadron in the fighter regiment could regularly contribute eight to ten pilots to a sortie with less stress on the pilots, while a regiment would be able to put a minimum of twenty-four fighters into the air for an extended period of combat operations. Meanwhile, the actual increase in personnel on the roster would be insignificant.[5]

The engineer–aviation service successfully coped with their tasks for supporting combat operations. By the efforts of PARM-1 and the technical staff, thirteen MiGs damaged in combat were repaired and returned to service, while two MiGs with combat damage were returned to action by PARM-2. Of these fifteen planes that returned with combat damage, three had one bullet hole, two had two bullet holes, two had three bullet holes, one had four bullet holes, four had five bullet holes, and three had twelve bullet holes. Three planes inoperable for other reasons were put back into service, one by PARM-1, the other two by PARM-4.

During the entire period of service in Manchuria, thirty-nine engines had to be replaced: twenty-seven for overhauls, seven due to manufacturing defects, and five due to combat damage that could not be repaired. It required ten to twenty-four hours of labor to replace the engine on a MiG-15.

PARM-1 made 863 minor repairs to planes, as well as repair work on ailerons due to weakening of the rivets. For the entire period of service, Captain Smirnov's PARM-1 built 3,700 fuel tanks and repaired 759. For his excellent work, senior engineer of the regiment Major Papulov was decorated with the Order of the Red Star and was recommended for a second Order of the Red Star.

Which Division Fought Better?

Analyzing the records of the regiments of the 303rd IAD and 324th IAD, which in a certain sense shared a friendly rivalry with one another, one can see that their results were approximately the same, and that the 'provincial' 17th IAP fought no worse than the 'palace' regiments from the Moscow area. It ranked second behind the 196th IAP in victories, but at the same time, the 17th IAP had the fewest number of losses. It had the highest ratio of victories to

Combat Results of the 303rd and 324th IAD

Division	Regiment	Victories	Heroes of the Soviet Union	Period of combat operations	Losses		Ratio of victories to losses
					Planes	Pilots	
303rd IAD		318		05.51–02.52	43	18	7.4 to 1
	17 IAP	108	4	06–51–02.52	9	4	12 to 1
	18 GIAP	96	3	05.51–02.52	18	8	5.3 to 1
	523 IAP	105	4	06.51–02.52	16	6	6.6 to 1
324th IAD		216		04.51–01.52	27	9	9.6 to 1
	176 GIAP	107	4	04.51–01.52	15	5	8.9 to 1
	196 IAP	109	2	04.51–01.52	12	4	10.9 to 1

losses of all the regiments of both divisions, even if you include the 17th IAP's two non-combat losses among its total losses. Table 3 presents the results of the combat operations of the 303rd IAD and the 324th IAD while in Manchuria during this period of the Korean air war.

Between 1 April 1951 to 20 January 1952, the pilots of the 324th IAD downed in combat a total of 215 enemy aircraft (12 B-29, 118 F-86, 33 F-84, 26 F-80, 8 F-94, 6 F-51, 11 Gloster Meteors and 1 RB-45C). From this total number, 109 went to the score of the pilots of the 196th IAP, while the remaining 107 were credited to the pilots of the 176th GIAP. Seventeen pilots of the 324th IAD recorded five or more victories, nine from the 196th IAP and eight from the 176th GIAP. Their own losses, both combat and non-combat, numbered twenty-seven aircraft and nine pilots. The 196th IAP lost twelve aircraft and four pilots killed, while the 176th GIAP lost fifteen MiGs and five pilots killed.

According to its log-book, in its period of combat service over Korea the 303rd IAD conducted 12,980 combat sorties with a total flight time of 10,685 hours. Of this total number of sorties, 10,906 were made from a readiness status to repulse enemy air raids; 1,726 were patrols over the key railroad bridge in the vicinity of Antung, the hydro-electrical station at Suiho, and the airfields at Antung and Myaogou; forty were 'free hunt' sorties; twenty-two were made to cover Chinese bombers; and 286 sorties were ordered to cover other operations of the Chinese and North Korean air force.

The pilots of the 303rd IAD between 1 June 1951 and 20 February 1952 downed 315 enemy planes: 18 B-29, 162 F-86, 69 F-84, 42 F-80, 16 Gloster Meteors, 5 F-51, and 3 F4U-2 Corsairs; several dozen more enemy planes were damaged. Twenty-two of the division's pilots became aces by shooting down five or more planes. The 303rd IAD's own losses consisted of eighteen pilots and forty-three planes.

Pilots of the 18th GIAP scored ninety-six of the division's total number of victories while conducting 4,088 individual combat sorties. Six pilots of the regiment became aces. Its own combat losses consisted of eight pilots and eighteen MiGs.

Three pilots of the 18th GIAP became Heroes of the Soviet Union. The remaining pilots of the regiment during the combat operations in Korea earned Orders and medals as follows: two men earned the Order of Lenin, forty-four men received the Order of the Red Banner, thirty-two men were decorated with the Order of the Red Star, and twenty-eight men received the medal 'For Combat Merit'.

The pilots of the 523rd IAP achieved 105 victories in the skies of Korea in this war, while losing sixteen of their own planes and six of their pilots. Seven of the regiment's pilots became aces.

The pilots of the 17th IAP conducted 4,186 combat sorties during its eight months of combat operations and scored 108 victories, while losing a total of four pilots (two in battle and two in flight accidents prior to the start of combat service) and nine MiGs (two of them in the air crashes). Nine pilots of the 17th IAP earned the title of ace.

The 303rd IAD's Headquarters flight scored an additional nine victories. In particular, division commander General G.A. Lobov (who later became commander of the 64th IAK) downed four F-80s during combat sorties, while Hero of the Soviet Union Colonel A.S. Kumanichkin, who replaced Lobov as division commander, shot down one F-84. Four more American planes were downed in aerial combat by the division's inspector for aerial combat tactics Captain A.A. Kaliuzhnyi.

Commander of the 303rd IAD Colonel Kumanichkin received the Order of the Red Banner in 1951. Deputy division commander Colonel Karasev was decorated with the Order of the Red Banner in 1951, and the Order of Lenin in 1952. The division's chief of staff Colonel Petr Trofimovich Iurakov was twice awarded the Order of the Red Banner, once in 1951 and again in 1952.

In total, these two Soviet fighter aviation divisions over their ten-month period of service in the Korean War as part of the 64th IAK destroyed 534 enemy planes in the skies of Korea, while losing eighty-two aircraft and thirty-one pilots. These two stellar divisions, which left the corps in January–February 1952, had the top results of all the aviation divisions that passed through

Manchuria under the command of the 64th IAK during the entire Korean War. It was no accident that a constellation of leading jet aces arose, who added glittering pages to the history of the Soviet air force through their combat exploits, precisely in this period and from the roster of these two aviation divisions, the 324th IAD and the 303rd IAD. Eighteen of these jet aces in 1951–52 became Heroes of the Soviet Union. They are: S.A. Bakhaev, G.I. Ges', N.G. Dokashenko, S.M. Kramarenko, G.A. Lobov, B.A. Obraztsov (posthumously), D.P. Os'kin, G.U. Okhai, E.G. Pepeliaev, M.S. Ponomarev, G.I. Pulov, D.A. Samoilov, A.P. Smorchkov, E.M. Stel'makh (posthumously), S.P. Subbotin, N.V. Sutiagin, F.A. Shebanov (later killed in action), and L.K. Shchukin. Yet over the entire war in Korea, twenty-two pilots of the 64th IAK received the title of Hero, which means only four more pilots obtained this highest honor after this period. The successful combat operations of the 64th IAK in 1951 were based upon the skills and heroism of these and the other rank and file pilots, and many shining victories were achieved, which on the whole issued a sharp challenge to the supremacy of the United States and United Nations air forces in the skies of Korea.

The pilots of the 17th IAP before the start of combat operations had on average logged only 15–20 hours in the MiG-15, but by the number of victories, they were in no way inferior to the pilots of the other regiments of the 303rd and 324th IAD, who had significantly more time in the cockpit of the MiG-15. Incidentally, the American pilots had flown many more hours, numbering in the hundreds of hours, in their jets, than had our own pilots. According to the statement of Nikolai Sutiagin himself, on one of his first combat sorties he managed to down an American pilot who had logged more than 900 hours in jets, while he himself at the time had only around fifty hours.

Over 200 men of the 17th IAP were recommended for decorations, and seven men for the title of Hero of the Soviet Union: Pulov, Sutiagin, Ponomarev, Dokashenko, Artemchenko, Volkov and Shulev. In the regiment, regiment commander Major G.I. Pulov, commander of the 2nd Aviation Squadron; Captain M.S. Ponomarev, flight commander of the 3rd Aviation Squadron; Captain N.G. Dokashenko and deputy commander of the 1st Aviation Squadron Captain N.V. Sutiagin received this highest honor. Two pilots were honored with two Orders (one of them was Captain Ponomarev), and twenty-seven pilots received one Order. Senior Lieutenant Fokin was awarded the Order of Lenin. Lieutenant Colonel Pulov, Major Artemchenko, Captain Dokashenko and many others received the Order of the Red Banner.

In comparison, the 17th IAP in the course of three previous years of service in the Great Patriotic War had conducted 5,500 combat sorties and destroyed 155 enemy planes. During the entire period of the Great Patriotic War, six men of the regiment earned the Gold Star of Hero of the Soviet Union, nine men earned the Order of Lenin, ninety-two men received the Order of the Red Banner, and 139 the Order of the Red Star.

The 3rd Aviation Squadron was recognized as the best in the 17th IAP. Its pilots downed thirty-one enemy planes without a single loss of their own, and moreover, there was not a single breach of military discipline in the regiment from the month of June 1951.

Captain Dokashenko's flight proved to be the best flight in the regiment. Dokashenko himself personally downed nine planes, while his flight claimed twenty-two victories. There were also no breaches of military discipline in his flight, and no equipment malfunctions on the MiGs at the fault of the technicians and ground crews.

Of course, Nikolai Sutiagin was the best pilot in the regiment. He not only downed more enemy planes than anyone else in his regiment or division, but also in the 64th IAK over the entire period of its combat operations in Korea.

'G-suit Kolia' – the Secret of His Success

Between 17 June 1951 and 2 February 1952, Nikolai Sutiagin conducted 149 combat sorties, engaged in sixty-six aerial combats, and personally downed twenty-two planes – the top result in the Korean War. His list of victories included fifteen F-86 Sabres, two F-80 Shooting Stars, three F-84 Thunderjets, and two Gloster Meteor IVs. In addition, he damaged several more enemy planes.

What was the secret of his combat success? After all, many other skilled, experienced pilots fought in Korea on both sides.

Firstly, there was Sutiagin's superb physical condition, which enabled him to withstand the colossal loads of 8 to 10 Gs, which were typical for jet combat. As it happened, even the plane's construction could not hold up against such high and continuous stresses in combat – areas of the plane's surface would become deformed. Also not every pilot could withstand a force of more than 8 Gs, when vision constricts and darkens, and the control stick becomes difficult to grip. Moreover, unlike the Americans, our pilots flew without pressurized G-suits (the Americans believed that Soviet pilots had such suits). Nikolai Sutiagin received the nickname 'G-suit Kolia' in Korea.

Secondly, Sutiagin had excellent eyesight, which is a critical factor in aerial combat, when the outcome of the duel often depends on who spots the adversary first. As a rule, he was the first among his group to catch the distant glint or see the distant specks of enemy planes in the air. Excellent vision is also necessary for accurate gunnery, as is evident from the entries in his flight book: his scores for gunnery at both air and ground targets were never less than 'excellent', which were better than any other aspect of his flight evaluations. (In civilian life this also helped him, especially while hunting mushrooms in the woods. Nikolai Vasil'evich surprised everyone around him with the sharpness of his vision: even in his older age, he would spot mushrooms missed by everyone else.) His sharp vision was supplemented by a well-developed sense of depth perception, which developed through constant training and enabled him to assess the distance to a target correctly, and this meant that he could accurately select the best moment to open fire.

Thirdly, an inner feeling of unrealized potential and striving in Nikolai also played a role: after all, he had not had the opportunity to participate in the war with the Germans. So the chance to prove himself came only in Korea. The formal reprimand he received on the eve of his departure to Manchuria also motivated him. Incidentally, trained pilots who had no experience in the Great Patriotic War fought in Korea even better than those with front-line experience in the war against Germany, who now no longer felt the need to prove themselves. Moreover, five years of peace and the new jet technology had somewhat reduced the significance of combat experience.

Fourthly, there was simply the matter of luck, which plays a role in any human affair. Throughout his entire combat service, Sutiagin's plane never received damage and he was never wounded; his MiG never received a single bullet hole, though there were occasions when it returned from a mission with deformations to the airframe, caused by the high stress loads in combat. Even in civilian life, he managed to avoid any flight accidents.

In Korea there was one case, when a plane that Sutiagin was scheduled to fly was at the last moment reassigned to a different pilot, and that pilot experienced an engine malfunction at take-off and nearly crashed. The cause of the engine malfunction might even have been sabotage. It is known that enemy agents worked on our bases: there were cases of attempted food poisoning in the regiments, and attempts to fill cockpits with sedative agents. The Americans were not only hunting our aces in the air. Our pilots were also warned that attempts to abduct Soviet military servicemen were even possible, which would have been a major coup for the American politicians in exposing the Soviet Union's direct involvement in combat operations in Korea.

Once Nikolai had to rush to his cockpit directly from the dining table in response to an alarm; or more accurately, directly from the drinking table on the occasion of one of his comrade's promotion or decoration. Naturally, at that time we still didn't have alcohol-free beer, and the pilots were fully authorized to receive a 'front-line' norm of 100 grams of vodka or other liquor at dinner time. Although the pilots, as a rule, did not abuse alcohol – they understood its negative effects on high-altitude flying – on this day many of the pilots had succumbed. In short, they ran to their MiGs in zig-zags. However, they were lucky: they took off, performed their mission, and returned without any losses. Understandably, such incidents were never mentioned in the official reports.

Incidentally, in the neighboring 523rd IAP there was a case, when early one morning a squadron was launched in response to an alarm, but its commander still hadn't managed to catch up on his sleep. Nevertheless, he stumbled out to his jet at the sound of the alarm. His MiG's crew chief, seeing his condition, switched off the fuel and reported that the engine wouldn't start. The experienced pilot, plainly guessing the cause of the engine problem, pulled out his pistol and began to chase the crew chief, demanding that he start the engine. This time, the squadron commander didn't manage to take part in the mission and a little later he realized that his crew chief had done the correct thing.

There was also a time when Nikolai was almost shot down, not by the Americans, but by his own comrades! A political summary report for the month of August 1951 reveals that in one of the dogfights that month Captain Ponomarev in the cover group had mistaken Sutiagin's element for the enemy, and had fired off his entire load of ammunition at Sutiagin and his wingman, Senior Lieutenant Savchenko. The shells passed above and to the right of Sutiagin's MiG. Later at the debriefing, Captain Ponomarev acknowledged that he had failed to identify one of his own planes from a range of 800 meters and had decided to fire. This case was analyzed with all the squadron commanders, who in turn later went over Captain Ponomarev's error with all the pilots.[6]

Thus, luck doesn't play the last role in flying. However, as has long been said, fortune favors the bold and able!

The Antagonists: The MiG-15 against the Sabre

To a great extent, the high capabilities of the most modern for its time MiG-15 fighter and its next modification, the MiG-15bis, greatly contributed to Nikolai Sutiagin's success. The pilots in the regiments affectionately called it the 'Swallow', or a little more crudely, the 'Cigarette Butt'. The MiG-15 was superior in its main characteristics to all the analogous enemy planes at that time, with the exception of the F-86, which received the nickname 'The Boot' among our pilots due to the semblance of its tail to an upturned boot. The F-86A Sabre was the first American fighter with swept wings, and it was designed as a daytime interceptor. In comparison with the Sabre, the MiG had a better rate of climb and heavier armament, though it was somewhat inferior in horizontal maneuvers, operational range, and in dives. The two planes were approximately equivalent in top speed. The F-86's axial flow turbojet engine gave the plane's fuselage a more aerodynamic form. The American fighter quickly accelerated in a dive and was more responsive than the MiG-15 in coming out of a dive. The F-86 was much heavier than the MiG, so when in danger it would evade the attack with a steep dive at top speed. Incidentally, the Sabre also had wing slats and it was more aerodynamically stable: it wouldn't depart into a spin at critical angles of attack. It also had very effective speed brakes, each one square meter in size, along the sides of its fuselage: the MiG's speed brakes were only 0.4 square meters in size, and were less effective.

Our planes were a bright aluminum, coated with lacquer, while the upper part of the vertical stabilizer above the horizontal stabilizers was painted red. They were easily distinguishable against the backdrop of the sky or the earth, and one could spot them from a great distance. The Americans on the other hand colored their planes differently: the under surfaces of the plane were brighter, while its upper surfaces were much duller. Thus when the Sabres departed in a dive whenever they found themselves in a tight situation, they would quickly become lost from view in the haze. Our pilots very frequently raised the matter of the sheen of their planes, but it didn't lead anywhere. Indeed, only in January 1952 did a team of camouflage specialists arrive, and even then they only began to study the matter.

Here's how a participant of the fighting in Korea, Hero of the Soviet Union Grigorii Ul'ianovich Okhai, characterized his opponents:

> In my view, the differences between our MiG-15 with the VK-1 engine [the MiG-15bis] and the Sabres were as follows: the Sabre was somewhat better in horizontal maneuvers up to an altitude of 7,000 to 7,500 meters. It had wing slats, which enabled it to turn more tightly, and it was impossible for the MiG to lay its gunsights on the Sabre when in a tight turn (the shells would always pass behind the tail). At altitudes above 7,000–7,500 meters, this difference diminished. The F-86 had larger speed brakes than the MiG's, which enabled it to cut speed more quickly when necessary.
>
> For example, at speeds of 900 km/hr and above and at low altitudes of 1,000 meters, the Sabre could conduct a split-S and pull out into level flight just above the deck. But the MiG in these circumstances didn't have enough flap to pull out in time, and it would slam into the ground. Moreover, the Sabre also had an afterburner, which allowed it to boost its speed temporarily; consequently, it could chase down an adversary or escape a pursuer more easily. The Sabre's engine was more efficient and the jet had greater operational range. The Sabre was harder to see against the backdrop of the terrain, and it didn't gleam when lit by the sun like our MiGs did.

The MiG-15's armament was more powerful and consisted of three well-placed cannons: two 23mm cannons with eighty shells of ammunition each and one 37mm with forty shells. The N-37 gun's ammunition load, developed in 1945, consisted of a mixture of the BZT [armor-piercing incendiary tracer] shell weighing 765 grams and the OZT [fragmentation-incendiary tracer] shell weighing 722 grams. The rate of fire was approximately 400 rounds a minute. The OZT shells of the N-37 cannon were set to explode at a range of 1,000 meters, so it was pointless to fire at longer ranges. The N-37 cannon could fire 400–600 shells before the barrel needed replacing, while the N-23 required changing after 1,000–1,200 rounds. Both cannons were very reliable and operated practically without malfunctions. The strike of one shell from the 37mm cannon would create a gaping hole in the enemy plane about one square meter in size.

The F-86 had six heavy caliber machine guns: the .50 calibre (12.7mm) Colt-Browning machine gun with an ammo load of 300 cartridges per gun, which plainly lacked sufficient hitting power against the MiGs. However, the cockpit canopy and pilot's position offered the pilot much better visibility from the Sabre cockpit, especially to the rear, and the cockpit itself was a little wider, which offered more comfort and greater conveniences for the pilot.

A clear advantage of the F-86 relative to the MiG-15 was the superior A-1CM radar ranging gunsight that equipped later models of the Sabre. This gunsight would compute the range to the target and could make automatic adjustments to the fire for the range. MiG pilots had to estimate the range visually, and enter the data into the semi-automatic gunsight manually.

Both the Soviet and American fighters received upgrades over the course of the war. Thus, in April 1951, the MiGs began to be equipped with the more powerful VK-1 engine. This variant was designated as the MiG-15bis. The ejectable cockpit seats were equipped with devices that would automatically open the parachutes at a pre-determined altitude. Later, the MiG-15bis was equipped with a radar apparatus that provided the pilot with information about the aerial adversary.

The MiG-15 jet fighter demonstrated high combat capabilities and great reliability and ease of operation, as well as toughness in combat: it could take a lot of punishment and was relatively difficult to flame. The self-sealing fuel tanks quickly closed any ruptures caused by bullets. The VK-1 engine was also relatively invulnerable. It would continue to run even with some serious damage. Some MiGs received up to fifty bullet holes in combat and safely returned to base. Even at airspeeds of up to 1,000 km/hr, the plane would not exhibit any tears in the surface paneling on return, and even with partial damage to the vertical tail and limited movement of the elevators, the plane remained controllable in flight.

The control cables for the rudder and elevators were the most vulnerable part on the MiG. Out of the several dozen cases of pilot ejection, in half the cases the pilot ejected because of loss of control of his plane. A second vulnerable spot was the cockpit canopy itself, even though the pilots themselves were protected by frontal armored glass and 20mm of armor plating behind them. When the cockpit area was struck, the pilots in the majority of cases would receive wounds from the bullet impacts and from fragments of the canopy glass.

Plainly, the MiG-15's toughness more than once caused the American pilots to err, when they believed that they had destroyed the jet, having riddled it with several bursts from their heavy caliber machine guns. The developed gun camera film would reveal a multitude of bullet hits and lead them to conclude that the plane had been downed, whereas in actual fact the MiG would often make its way back to base, and return again to service after several days of repair.

Ironically, perhaps the weakest point in the MiG-15 was the pilot himself. After taking off, while climbing, and in high speed and high altitude maneuvers, the MiG-15 pilots experienced enormous stresses. Unlike the Americans, they lacked high-altitude flight gear, and only used the KM-1618 oxygen masks. The American pilots on the other hand wore special G-suits that helped them withstand high-G maneuvers. Whenever in combat a pilot had to change altitude abruptly, from 10,000–12,000 meters down to just 100–200 meters, such suits reduced the G-force effects on the pilot, which enabled him to handle typical dogfighting conditions better. We developed G-suits for our pilots only after the war in Korea ended.

Despite its toughness, the MiG-15 had a number of shortcomings in aerial combat:

- the tendency of the plane to roll involuntarily at speeds approaching Mach 1;
- the lack of powerful speed brakes, which would enable the pilot to quickly change direction at all speeds;
- the absence of a two- or three-channel ultra high-frequency radio on the plane;
- the lack of a search radar and a warning indicator to signal the approach of an enemy plane from behind;
- poor visibility from the cockpit to the rear;
- the lack of homing beacons on the lead airplanes of the group commanders;
- a gunsight that did not allow the tracking of rapidly and sharply maneuvering targets;
- the absence of an afterburner on the engine, which could have been used at critical moments, but especially after a loss of speed;
- a limited fuel supply, which prevented extended dogfighting, especially at low altitudes.

To compensate for the last mentioned weakness, drop tanks were put into use, but even they, in turn, had their own problems.

The MiG's internal tanks carried 1,460 liters of fuel. This was sufficient for 2 hours and 6 minutes of flight at an altitude of 12,000 meters. Two spare drop tanks with a capacity of 260 (the normal configuration), 300 or 600 liters had been foreseen for the MiG-15. With two mounted drop tanks, the jet could reach a speed of 900 km/hr and could withstand 5-G maneuvers with full drop tanks, and 6.5-G maneuvers with empty tanks. Flight duration with two 260-liter drop tanks rose to 2 hours and 57 minutes, with two 300-liter drop tanks to 3 hours and 9 minutes, and with two 600-liter drop tanks up to 3 hours and 52 minutes. Operational range without drop tanks was 1,330 kilometers: with two drop tanks of 260, 300, and 600 liter capacity, flight range was extended to 1,860, 1,975 and 2,520 kilometers correspondingly.

The F-86 carried 1,645 liters of fuel in its interior fuel tanks. The Sabre also used drop tanks of 455 or 757 liters of capacity to extend its operational range.

From the start of combat operations it became clear that the Chinese-manufactured drop tanks for the MiG-15 had a number of design and manufacturing flaws:

1. The poor aerodynamic design of the drop tank itself.
2. Weak soldering joints, which led to leaks while the engine was running and the tanks were under pressure, and to ruptures during flights, which would lead to a loss of pressure in the tank and cause the fuel to stop flowing.
3. The tanks were made from poor material (simple sheet metal), which led to corrosion inside the tanks during use caused by the fuel. Scaling from the corrosion inside the tanks would clog the fuel filters, reduce fuel flows, and as a result of this, engine revolutions would drop to 9,000–10,000 revolutions a minute. A signal light monitoring the priming pressure would begin to flash. Such a thing happened on Senior Lieutenant Khvostantsev's MiG-15bis No. 581, Senior Lieutenant Volkov's MiG-15bis No. 499, and Senior Lieutenant Kordanov's MiG-15bis No. 712.
4. The tanks' crude construction meant that they didn't always fit the wing mounts for them, and they were poorly aligned. It took up to two hours of labor to prepare and attach the drop tanks.

The technicians took a number of steps to eliminate these defects. Tanks were checked under pressure and leaks were sealed. Small cracks in the tanks on planes at readiness level No. 2 were cleaned with soap and then covered by canvas patches sealed with a coat of enamel or AK-20 glue. Technicians placed a specially prepared filter for the fuel line leading from the drop tank, which was replaced after each day of flights. The technicians also fashioned special templates for retro-fitting the tanks to line up with the mounting brackets.[7]

There were three cases in the regiment when the drop tanks failed to release:

- Plane 132 – electrical failure of the BD-2-48 clasp;
- Plane 185 – broken clasp springs;
- Plane 190 – electrical failure of the clasp.

There were also two cases when the tanks detached during take-off:

- Plane 177 – pilot Senior Lieutenant Sutiagin;
- Plane 191 – pilot Captain Masly – premature release of the left drop tank when a mounting pintle in the fretwork broke off due to a flaw in the pintle.

Such incidents forced the pilots to abort missions and return to base. Altogether, the regiment dropped 7,884 drop tanks while on flights, which were then located and collected by special search teams for repeat use. PARM-1 repaired and inspected 3,890 fuel tanks.

Their Rescue Service and Our Regime of Secrecy

The Americans had a well-organized search and rescue service, while we had practically nothing similar at all. American pilots who ejected from damaged planes had every chance of being rescued, particularly in the Yellow Sea, because of the well-organized and excellently equipped search and rescue service. The pilots themselves had carefully planned emergency equipment. Each pilot had a portable automatic radio beacon, which served as a locator for a search plane or rescue helicopter.

The Americans' leather flight jacket was like ours, but it had numerous pockets, in which you could stick whatever you wanted. A miniature compass was located in one of the pockets, while other pockets held a variety of other useful items and informational material, such as:

- Guidebooks to the berries, mushrooms, and other plants that grew in a specific region, and which were edible and which were not;
- Fishing tackle, and where different types of fish could be found;
- Instructions on how to make a tent out of a parachute, what uses could be made of the shroud lines, and many other pieces of advice for how the pilot should act in an emergency situation.

There was also a special mirror among the gear, with the help of which the downed pilot could signal his location. On one side of the mirror device, there was a little clear circle, and little crosshairs on the other side. If you aimed the circle at the sun, and centered the crosshairs on an overhead aircraft, then a beam of reflected sunlight would strike the cockpit and face of the pilot, who could then spot the location of the downed pilot.

All this raised the morale of the pilots: they knew that if anything ever happened to them on a mission, a mandatory search for them would begin and that everything possible would be done to save them. However, since aerial combats took place primarily over the territory of North Korea, there were cases when downed American pilots wound up as prisoners, even including a few of their aces. Among them were:

1. The commander of the 16th Fighter Squadron of the 51st Fighter Wing, Lieutenant Colonel Edwin Heller, who had 3.5 victories in Korea and 5.5 victories in World War II, making him an ace.
2. The commander of the 4th Fighter Wing Colonel Walker 'Bud' Mahurin, who had 3.5 victories in Korea and twenty to his credit in World War II.
3. Captain Harold 'Hal' Fischer, who shot down ten planes in Korea.

Altogether during the Korean War, 262 American airmen were taken prisoner. Usually, announcements about the capture of important enemy pilots appeared in the Chinese press (since they often came down in Chinese territory), as in the following example:

> On 23 January 1953, planes of the Air Force of the People's Republic of China downed another American warplane, when it intruded into Chinese airspace in the region of Kuan-tien District in north-east China. This F-86 plane was the second American plane downed over Chinese territory in the past two weeks. The pilot Edwin Lewis Heller bailed out of his plane and was taken prisoner. Heller as a lieutenant colonel served in the 16th Squadron of the Fifth Air Force's 51st Fighter Wing. He is 34 years old, and a squadron commander.
>
> Altogether on this day, four American planes intruded in the region of Kuan-tien District, flying from the direction of Uiju in Korea. After fighters of the Chinese Air Force shot down one of their group, the remaining American planes fled. The downed F-86 carried the number '731' and fell near the village of Pa-chuan-tein-tzu in Kuan-tien District.

Everything indicated in the announcement is correct, save for one fact. Pilots of the Chinese Air Force didn't shoot down Heller: Soviet pilots from the 64th IAK shot down the American ace.

Our pilots never wound up as prisoners. There was an order for them not to be taken alive. Despite the fact that Soviet pilots operated over 'friendly' territory well behind the front lines, there were several cases when pilots went missing in action after ejecting from their damaged plane, or after their plane went down in the Yellow Sea. Of course, there were also cases like that of Senior Lieutenant Stel'makh, who may have been killed by Chinese or North Korean troops who mistook him for an American pilot, which led to the fatal exchange of fire. Other downed Soviet pilots were seized by North Korean civilians, who mistakenly identified them as American pilots and 'greeted' them with harsh treatment. The local population didn't know that Russian pilots were fighting for them. Our pilots began to purchase and wear little pins carrying the image of Mao or Kim Il Sung, and this often helped them in a critical situation in their initial encounter with their 'allies'. Still, the possibility of capture could not be ruled out entirely, which is why the Soviet command placed such tight restrictions on the operations of the Soviet fighter squadrons, and issued the strict order for a pilot not to be taken alive.

Major problems also arose due to the need to observe the regime of secrecy, since the Soviet command took every effort to conceal the participation of the Soviet Air Force in the Korean War, and to prevent the United States from obtaining proof that the Soviet-produced MiG-15 fighters (which were not a secret) were being flown by Soviet pilots. With this aim in mind, the MiG-15 jets bore the emblems of the Chinese or North Korean air forces, and Soviet pilots were prohibited from operating over the Yellow Sea or to pursue enemy planes south of the line Pyongyang–Wonsan (that is, south of the 39th Parallel, although the front in 1951 had stabilized along the line of the 38th Parallel). The Americans wisely exploited these restrictions. They primarily operated close to the Yellow Sea coastline. Put at the disadvantage in a dogfight, they would quickly depart in the direction of the sea. Once over the sea and having regained altitude, the pilot could either make an unhindered withdrawal or choose a suitable moment to re-enter combat.

To avoid leaks of secret information, it was forbidden to write about the war and anything connected with it in letters home. Cameras were categorically banned, especially on the bases, so that there would be no photos of the planes, or even partial shots of them. This is why there is precious little photographic documentation of the life and work of our pilots in Korea, where for three years a death struggle for supremacy in the air went on. The Americans on the other hand, as well as their allies from other countries, photographed and even filmed their pilots and operations to excess.

The matter of secrecy reached the point where the pilots of a regiment (according to the testimony of a veteran of this war A.N. Nikolaev) didn't even know exactly how many planes other pilots in their flight and squadron had downed, not to mention anything about the pilots of other squadrons. Our pilots also had no knowledge at all about recommendations for military honors, neither who, when, or what. As Nikolaev relates:

> The pilot booklets, which contained entries about their combat work, were immediately classified. There was nothing in the booklets to trumpet, and they weren't offered for public consumption: you just flew missions – no big deal; you downed a plane – nothing special; what was there to talk about? A layer of some sort of secrecy coated everything. The regiment doctor, Lieutenant Colonel of the Medical Service Pozdniak, had the full picture. He kept scrupulous notes on these matters: the name of the pilot, how many combat sorties he had flown, how many combats he had fought, what kind and how many planes he had downed, and other information. But as soon as we returned to the Soviet Union, there and then everything and everyone was forgotten. The pilot booklets were immediately seized and we were given new ones, in which just some general information had been written.

The central Soviet and local newspapers of those times kept strictly silent about the participation of Soviet pilots in the Korean War. As we saw above, the downing of UN and American aircraft was credited to North Korean or Chinese pilots, or especially to the so-called riflemen-hunter [*strelki-okhotniki*] anti-aircraft teams organized in each regiment of the North Korean and Chinese armies. These special detachments consisted of eighteen to thirty soldiers, armed with one or two light machine guns, one medium machine gun, two or three anti-tank rifles, a heavy caliber anti-aircraft machine gun or a light-caliber anti-aircraft artillery gun. They were usually positioned 100 to 120 meters away from the ground target they were covering and fired at low-flying enemy aircraft.

For example, here is what correspondent Ivan Gribanov wrote in his article, 'The Korean Riflemen-Hunters of American Aircraft', which appeared in the 16 June 1951 issue of the *Red Star* newspaper:

> ... the 19-year-old non-commissioned officer of the Korean People's Army Kim G U – twice Hero of the Korean People's Democratic Republic – downed three planes in one day. He was awarded the title of Hero. Later he downed three more aircraft. In the span of nine months he has shot down nine enemy aircraft and has become a twice Hero.
>
> From the start of the war to 4 January 1951, all the anti-aircraft units of the Korean People's Army have downed 511 American planes,

> including 53 B–29 Flying Fortresses [sic], 90 light bombers, 254 jet planes, 88 ground attack planes, and 26 fighters and reconnaissance planes …

Yet, of course, it wasn't riflemen–hunter teams, but Soviet fighters, that played the major role in the struggle against the American Air Force.

The excessive secrecy very often complicated not only the headquarters' staff work in the aviation regiments, but also combat operations. Initially, with the aim of concealing the control over missions, efforts were made to implement radio exchanges in the Korean language, using a table of translated expressions between the Russian and Korean languages that each pilot carried in his cockpit. This venture collapsed almost immediately with the predecessors of the 17th IAP, and the 303rd IAD promptly rejected resuming it – in a rapidly changing dogfight, where often seconds make the difference between success and failure, to divert a commander's attention to search for needed commands in a table was an impermissible luxury.

The Americans on the other hand had no need to hide their role in this war, which was widely reported in the press and through other means of mass communication. Photographs of their top aces – fighter pilots like Joe McConnell, James Jabara and Pete Fernandez – never left the front pages of American newspapers. Their fame exceeded the reputation of Second World War veterans, like Francis Gabreski, John Meyer or Robin Olds. The only thing they kept concealed were their actual losses: narrow-minded Americans traditionally take news about the death of their fellow countrymen and American military failures very hard. This partially explains the inflated American claims about the number of victories over the MiGs. In addition, the companies of the American military-industrial complex cannot allow negative news about their best examples of American technology such as the F-86 or the B-29 (which explains the practice of writing off a plane as a non-combat loss whenever possible).

Avoidable Mistakes

Unfortunately, the high command of the Soviet Air Force seemed to ignore the lessons of the Korean air war and failed to adapt its policies to the war's demands. This is plainly apparent from the example of the next shift of fighter aviation divisions, which arrived to replace the 303rd and 324th IAD: the 97th, 190th, 133rd, 216th, and 32nd IAD from the Fighter Aviation branch of the Air Defense Force.

Due to a number of reasons, the newly arrived divisions fought less successfully in Korea. If the correlation of victories to losses of the 303rd IAD was 7.4 to 1 and that of the 324th IAD was 9.6 to 1, then that of their replacements decreased as follows: for the 97th IAD, 3.2 to 1; for the 190th IAD, 1.3 to 1; for the 133rd IAD, 2.8 to 1; for the 216th IAD, 1.9 to 1; and for the 32nd IAD, 1.2 to 1. Of the fifty-four Soviet pilots that earned the title of ace, thirty-nine served in the 303rd and 324th IAD.

Three basic reasons are generally offered to explain the reduced effectiveness of the later divisions:

- The lower level of training of the Air Defense Force's fighter regiments;
- The poorly conceived system of rotating the active units;
- The growing quantitative and qualitative strength of the enemy's air power.

In reality, the pilots of the Air Defense Force fighter regiments had been trained primarily to intercept solitary high-altitude targets, as well as to repulse raids of small groups of enemy bombers on strategic targets in the depth of the country, and little attention had been paid to training for the rapid maneuvering of dogfights. In addition, the pilots trained under numerous restrictions in the interest of crew safety.

There were fewer pilots in these Air Defense regiments that had any combat experience, although the headquarters' flights in the regiments and divisions had a similar number of experienced ace pilots as those in comparable Air Force units. For example, over the entire period of the war in Korea, thirty-six pilots who served in the 64th IAK had become Heroes of the Soviet Union during the Great Patriotic War. In the 303rd IAD, there were four such pilots, while the 324th IAD had two (including I.N. Kozhedub). The Air Defense Force divisions had similar numbers of Heroes from the Great Patriotic War: in the 97th IAD, there were three; the 190th IAD had two; the 133rd IAD had four (including twice Hero N.D. Gulaev), the 216th IAD had five; and the 32nd IAD had four.

Another extremely negative factor was the Soviet system of replacing the pilots fighting in Korea. The Soviets chose to rotate entire divisions and regiments through Manchuria, not individual pilots. Such an approach gave rise to large problems. Complete novices who had never sniffed gunpowder arrived in Manchuria in exchange for combat pilots who had gained enormous combat experience in the skies over Korea, and there was no one around to pass on to them the accumulated knowledge of how to fight and win. All the veterans returned to the Soviet Union together with their squadrons and regiments. On their own, the new pilots had to learn many of the things often through bitter experience that were long known to the veterans, and they had to pay for this knowledge with blood. The pilots completing their service in Korea had only the chance to share their experience with the arriving pilots through speeches and talks, not through joint combat sorties.

This ill-conceived system of rotation led to unjustified losses, especially in the first days after the exchange. That was the way it was, when the 324th and 303rd IAD began their combat operations. It was also how it was whenever new divisions from the Soviet Union arrived to replace them.

The 97th IAD of the Air Defense arrived from the Moscow area first, under the command of Hero of the Soviet Union Colonel Aleksander Grigor'evich Shevstsov, with two of the oldest regiments of the Air Defense: the 16th IAP under the command of Hero of the Soviet Union Colonel Nikolai Fedorovich Kuznetsov, and the 148th GIAP under the command of Colonel Mokhnatkin. Both regiments of the division had distinguished themselves in the years of the Great Patriotic War, defending Moscow and other Russian cities against fascist air raids.

The 97th IAD arrived in China at the end of December 1951, and the pilots of the division received their MiGs from the departing 324th IAD at the beginning of January 1952, together with the entire technical staff of Kozhedub's division, since the 97th IAD arrived without its own technicians and mechanics. The 97th IAD began familiarization flights over the area of combat operations, while pilots of the 303rd IAD provided cover. Its introduction to combat consisted of three to five flights into the area of combat operations (with no combat), and presentations in the regiments of the division by the more experienced pilots of the 324th IAD.

The regiments conducted their first combat sorties on 16 January 1952. On this day the 16th IAP with twenty-eight MiGs made another familiarization flight around the area of operations, during which it encountered sixteen F-86s, but both groups peacefully parted without combat. Both regiments of the 97th IAD were stationed at Antung.

A little later at the beginning of February 1952, another Air Defense division arrived from the Maritime Military District – the 190th IAD under the command of Colonel Kornilov. It had three regiments in its complement: the 256th IAP (commanded by Hero of the Soviet Union Lieutenant Colonel I.I. Semeniuk), the 494th IAP (commanded by Lieutenant Colonel A.E. Man'kovsky), and the 821st IAP (commanded by Hero of the Soviet Union Lieutenant Colonel G.F. Dmitriuk).

The 97th and 190th IAD only participated in combat operations for five months. They suffered heavy losses and were soon withdrawn into the second echelon, and then sent back to the Soviet Union. The pilots of the 97th IAD downed sixty-seven enemy planes in Korea, while losing twenty-one of their own planes and ten pilots. The pilots of the 190th IAD shot down eighty-five enemy aircraft, but lost sixty-four planes and fifteen pilots in combat in return. Only one pilot in this rotation was worthy of the title Hero of the Soviet

Union: Major A.S. Boitsov, who downed six planes personally. In addition to him, only one other pilot of the 97th IAD became an ace: Major A.T. Bashman of the 148th GIAP. In the 190th IAD, all the aces were from just one regiment, the 821st IAP, where a squadron commander of this regiment, Major V.N. Zabelin scored nine victories, while the regiment commander Lieutenant Colonel G.F. Dmitriuk and the regiment navigator Major A.A. Olenitsa had five victories each. The day 4 July 1952 was a fateful day for the 190th IAD, when ten MiGs and one pilot were lost on just one of the division's missions.

The next rotation included Colonel A.P. Komarov's 133rd IAD, and Hero of the Soviet Union Colonel A.U. Eremin's 216th IAD. Colonel G.I. Grokhovetsky's 32nd IAD rounded out the arriving complement for the 64th IAK.

The 133rd IAD of the Air Defense, which arrived from Iaroslavl', included the 147th GIAP (commander – Lieutenant Colonel M.I. Studilin), the 415th IAP (commander – Hero of the Soviet Union Major P.F. Shevelev), and the 726th IAP (commander – Lieutenant Colonel L.D. Goriachko). The pilots of this division over its period of combat operations under the 64th IAK downed eighty-five enemy planes in aerial combat and damaged thirty more. Their own losses comprised thirty planes and sixteen pilots. None of the pilots of this division reached the level of five victories.

The 216th IAD of the Air Defense, which arrived from the Baku Air Defense District, included the 518th IAP (commander – Lieutenant Colonel Litvinenko), the 676th IAP (commander – Lieutenant Colonel V.V. Gol'tsev) and the 878th IAP (commander – Lieutenant Colonel S.D. Dronov). The pilots of this division downed 108 enemy aircraft in aerial combat and damaged another forty-nine. Their own losses consisted of fifty-seven MiGs and fifteen pilots. The most effective pilot in this division was the 518th IAP's Captain M.I. Mikhin, who achieved nine victories and became a Hero of the Soviet Union in 1953. Major N.M. Zameskin with seven 'kills' became an ace in the 878th IAP.

The 32nd IAD of Air Defense from the Maritime District had on its roster the 224th IAP (commander – Hero of the Soviet Union Lieutenant Colonel D.V. Ermakov), the 535th IAP (commander – Lieutenant Colonel Smirnov), and the 913th IAP (commander – Lieutenant Colonel V.A. Marchenko). The pilots of the 32nd IAD downed seventy-nine enemy aircraft and damaged thirty-four. Its own losses amounted to sixty-six planes and seventeen pilots. Captain G.N. Berilidze and Captain B.N. Sis'kov in the 224th IAP became aces, each downing five enemy planes. Major S.A. Fedorets of the 913th IAP became its only ace, downing seven American planes.

On the American side, the rotation of pilots was better considered and more rational. They didn't replace flight staff by entire groups or wings, but by squadrons and individual pilots. If a new squadron arrived in the Fifth Air

Force, it was introduced into the fighting gradually with mandatory, exhaustive study of the area of combat operations, and the tactics used by both sides in the struggle. The process of acclimatization to the combat conditions of war lasted from one to two months.

American pilots left these squadrons only after completing 100 combat missions, or because of wounds or trauma. Therefore a fresh pilot, arriving in one of these fighter or fighter-bomber groups or wings, came under the guardianship of more experienced colleagues, who knew well the situation, the tactics, and the strengths and weaknesses of the adversary. He then passed through a process of several weeks of mock dogfights and intensive study of the area of combat operations, before moving on to a period of flying missions as the wingman of a more experienced pilot, not to engage in fighting, but to observe it from the side. Only after this process was completed did a pilot become an active combat participant. After completing half the necessary combat missions for return to the United States and after participating in several dozen aerial combats, the pilot himself would become the leader of an element or flight, and would in turn train and educate the young pilots newly arriving in the squadron. Unlike the Soviet fighter divisions, for the entire period of combat operations during the war in Korea, neither fighter wing of the United States Air Force was withdrawn from the theater of combat operations; both participated in aerial clashes until the end of combat actions. In this fashion, through their ranks passed the best flying cadres of not only the United States Air Force, but also pilots of the US Navy, Marines, and even British and Canadian pilots, who received a period of training in the 4th or 51st Fighter Wings.

The Soviet command chose a different rotation policy, but it was a mistaken one and led not only to an increase in combat losses, but also to the loss of the air superiority over 'MiG Alley' that had been achieved in 1951.

A no less important reason for our air force's decline of combat effectiveness in Korea was the fact that the enemy's equipment and tactics changed. The next variant of the Sabre appeared in the American fighter wings: the F-86F. Indeed, this plane (with the exception of its armament) was no longer inferior in any way to our MiG. The United States Air Force increased its numbers as well. The tactics of the American pilots also became more aggressive: some of them began to infiltrate Chinese airspace, to search for slow-moving MiGs that were on their landing approach to Antung and Myaogou. Cases of MiGs being attacked near their own airfield while making a landing increased. American pilots in their pursuit of 'easy' booty were ignoring the prohibition of their own command against flying across the Yalu River.

Chapter Eight

After Korea

Return to the Soviet Union

The 303rd IAD's mission to China had come to an end. Before their return to the Soviet Union, many pilots, especially those in the 18th GIAP and the 523rd IAP from the Moscow area, were interested in learning about where they would be going. The division commander gathered the men in the club to discuss this subject. Colonel Kumanichkin, counting upon his personal acquaintanceship with Vasily Stalin, the commander of the Moscow Military District's air force, promised the pilots that the division would be sent to the Moscow Military District, adding: 'Let the entire division piss on me, if we don't go to the West!'

However, his promise was not realized. The 303rd IAD received the order to redeploy to the Far East. This once gave Senior Lieutenant Perepelkin, who had the nickname 'The Count' for his somewhat eccentric nature, cause to insult the division commander in front of the formation. One cold March day on the airbase at Galenki, where the headquarters of the 303rd IAD and one of its regiments were located, the division commander appeared: he was surrounded by pilots in light leather jackets, chilled to the bone by the blustery wind. 'Count' Perepelkin stepped out in front of the other men and raised the question: 'Well, Comrade Colonel? Can we take a piss?' The division commander could only snap back in reply: 'Devils, you'd better stop and think!' However, fate did smile upon Colonel Kumanichkin: in May 1952 he left for Moscow to enroll in the Military Academy of the General Staff, turning over his division to his deputy, Lieutenant Colonel Karasev.

The redeployment of the regiment from China by train took several days, from 26 February to 3 March 1952. On 1 March, the flight staff arrived at their permanent garrison on the airbase at Khorol'. In April, fifty-six officers and 192 sergeants from the 494th IAP arrived in the regiment to replace the 17th IAP's own technical staff, which had been left behind in China.

Once in Khorol', the entire flight staff received a two-month leave of absence. The assistant chief of staff Major Odintsov became the acting regiment commander; the chief of radar services Captain A.A. Eliseev became the acting chief of staff; the secretary of the *Komsomol* organization Senior Lieutenant I.E. Gorbunov became the acting deputy regiment commander for political affairs; and squadron technicians became temporary squadron commanders. The regiment was 'grounded' for two months.

On 17 March Major Sutiagin left on a leave of absence until 22 May. First there was a trip to Moscow for a reception at the Kremlin, where on 29 March among several others he received his Order of Lenin and the Gold Star of Hero of the Soviet Union, the 9,282nd on the list. In the name of the Presidium of the Supreme Soviet of the USRR, Secretary of the Presidium N.M. Shvernik handed him his decoration and Certificate of Merit. Pilots of the 523rd IAP Major G.U. Okhai and Senior Lieutenant D.A. Samoilov received their decorations on this day together with Sutiagin.

Dmitrii Aleksandrovich [Samoilov] shared details of this event with the authors:

> In the Hall there were a lot of civilians, from the Ministry of Finances it seemed, who had been invited to attend the ceremony. Portraits of famous commanders, even some from Tsarist times, hung on the walls of the Hall. We stepped into a smoking room and there we saw Nikolai Sutiagin from the 17th IAP: we approached him and had a conversation. Then we returned to the Hall, took our positions, and began to wait. First a woman stepped out – she announced the procedural schedule for the award ceremony and began to form us into groups for photographs. The three of us wound up in the last group. The woman then asked everyone not to grip Shvernik's hand tightly when receiving the honor. Next a lieutenant colonel stepped out, carrying the certificates and the little cases containing the Orders, and laid them on a table.
>
> Finally Shvernik and Gorkin entered the Hall. Gorkin started to read out the Decree of the Presidium of the Supreme Soviet, while Shvernik presented the Orders and medals. Finally it was my turn. When Shvernik presented me the Gold Star, he asked me very quietly, so that others wouldn't overhear: 'Well, how was it there, was it hard in Korea?' I replied, 'Somewhat.' Shvernik joked: 'By your appearance it doesn't seem that things were too bad. You look ready to go back.' Grigorii Okhai and I, in addition to the Star of the Hero and the Order of Lenin, each received the Order of the Red Banner, while Nikolai Sutiagin only received the Star of the Hero and the Order of Lenin. After passing out the decorations to the groups of individuals, they began to photograph them together with Shvernik, after which the groups left. The group before us posed with Shvernik in a sitting position. But with the three of us, plainly as a sign of special merit, Shvernik proposed that we be photographed with him while standing. At this everything came to an end, and we left the Kremlin.

Nikolai spent several days in Moscow: he visited friends and colleagues he knew who had been back in the Far East. Next there was a trip to Belorussia, to the village of Ianovichi, where his wife and daughter were living at the time. Nikolai was reluctant to talk about his time in China, but his wife and close friends guessed where and why he had received his high honor.

Then there was a trip to his native village of Smagino, and meetings with his relatives and friends. Not one of them knew where Nikolai had been for almost the past year.

Study in the Academy and Assignment to a Training Regiment

Upon returning to his regiment from his leave of absence, Nikolai Sutiagin resumed flying, though it was already known that he would soon be departing for study at the Military Air Academy. On 16 June Major Sutiagin left for Khabarovsk for a mandatory testing and medical screening for admission to the Military Air Academy. After successfully passing the commission examinations, he returned to the regiment on 1 July.

In connection with his departure for studies at the Academy, Major Sutiagin was offered a leave of absence from 5 July to 28 August, so he could rest in a sanatorium in the city of L'vov. However, Sutiagin preferred to wait for word from the Academy at his present post, so he continued to fulfill his duties until 28 July, when he finally departed for the town of Monino, where the Academy was located. On this day, Sutiagin was dropped from the regiment rosters. Senior Lieutenant Gostiukhin became the acting assistant commander for combat tactics and aerial gunnery in his place. Once in Monino, Sutiagin enrolled in the preparatory courses for completing his required education before joining the Academy. The next year, Nikolai became a student in the Military Air Academy's Command Faculty.

Other pilots who had distinguished themselves in Korea studied in the same class with Sutiagin: Heroes of the Soviet Union A. Smorchkov, L. Shchukin, D. Os'kin, G. Dmitriuk, S. Subbotin and A. Vas'kin, who often gathered together to reminisce about their time in Korea. However, they didn't discuss their personal victories; at that time it was considered pompous and impolite to do so. Another conspicuous student in the Academy at that time was the future cosmonaut Senior Lieutenant V. Shatalov.

At first, Nikolai had to rent a room in the village of Zagoriansky; it was only when twins appeared in the Sutiagin family in 1953 that he received a ten-meter-square room in the Monino garrison on Labor Street. The twins, a boy and a girl, were born on 15 April two months prematurely and weighed less than a kilogram each. They were in critical condition: the baby boy was particularly weak, and was twice on the verge of death. Nikolai had to exert a lot of effort to save the twins, and his sister Lidia arrived from Smagino to help take care of the children. Other relatives also frequently traveled to Monino for visits: by some miracle, they managed to find space for everyone in the small room.

Despite it all, Nikolai was not a bad student at the Academy: his grade point average for the first year was 4.38 (out of a possible 5.0); his average increased to 4.71 in the second year of study, and to 4.80 in his third and final year. Nikolai also found time to serve as secretary of the department's Party Organization (he had joined the Party back in April 1946). While at the Academy, Sutiagin also had two short stints on temporary assignment to aviation training regiments where he gained practical experience in commanding their operations.

In May 1956, Nikolai Sutiagin received his next promotion to Lieutenant Colonel. Graduating from the Academy in October 1956, Lieutenant Colonel Sutiagin became the deputy regiment commander for flight training in the 826th UIAP of the Second Central Course for Improving the Officer Staff of the Air Force in Taganrog, Rostov Oblast. The regiment was equipped with the MiG-17 and the MiG-15 UTI, the two-seat training version of the MiG-15. The Central Course was preparing flight commanders and deputy squadron commanders and retraining them on the MiG-17. Its chief was General Anton Dmitrievich Iakimenko, a Hero of the Soviet Union and veteran of the fighting on the Khalkin-gol who had downed seven enemy aircraft there, and who went on to score another thirty personal and shared victories in the Great Patriotic War.

During Sutiagin's time with this regiment, several other pilots with whom he had flown in Korea were also serving in the regiment. One of his friends in Taganrog was pilot S.S. Bychkov, who had been a flight commander in Korea and who had shot down five American planes there. Sutiagin and Bychkov had begun their service together in the Far East and their families had become close friends. Unfortunately, Sergei Bychkov was killed in a plane crash in 1956.

After his long sabbatical from flying, connected with his studies at the Academy, Sutiagin's position with the 826th UIAP enabled him to resume flying, and he hadn't lost any of his skills. In 1958, he won the bombing and aerial gunnery competition staged by the North Caucasus Military District Air Force. Nikolai passed along his vast experience to his subordinates in the training regiment not only in words, but also by personal example. By July 1958, Lieutenant Colonel Sutiagin had become the commander of the 826th UIAP.

In May 1960, the Central Course and the 826th UIAP were terminated, and the pilots of the regiment were scattered among different units. Nikolai Sutiagin received appointment to the storied Eisk Higher Military Aviation School for Pilots' 963rd UAP [Training Aviation Regiment], and that September, he received promotion to colonel. The Eisk School had a glorious tradition. The first Gold Star of Hero of the Soviet Union ever awarded was bestowed to its graduate A.V. Liapidevsky, the polar explorer. Of the seven Heroes who in 1934 had taken part in the rescue of the *Cheliuskin* polar expedition, four were graduates of the Eisk School. For their exploits in the years of the Great Patriotic War, 226 graduates of the school became Heroes of the Soviet Union, while six of its pilots became twice Heroes.

Sutiagin's performance in the training regiment received high praise. Later that year, an article appeared in the district newspaper under the title, 'Hero of the Blue Expanses', written by the paper's military correspondent Major I. Borisov. The article extolled Sutiagin's frontline service to the Motherland, but in keeping with the blanket of secrecy still covering the Soviet Air Force's role in Korea, his combat accomplishments were described as belonging to the Great Patriotic War. The article went on to say:

> In the squadrons, you can hardly find a pilot with whom Sutiagin hasn't flown. One pilot he praises; another, he offers constructive criticism and recommendations for eliminating the shortcomings; a third he calls to account. ... Hero of the Soviet Union N.V. Sutiagin keeps busy. Flights go on, and he flies as well. And how! 'If Officer Sutiagin is in the air,' says navigator Captain Nelipa, 'then the adversary doesn't escape. And if he is over the bombing range, then you know the target will be struck on the first attack.'

A year later, in October 1961 Colonel Sutiagin was temporarily appointed as deputy chief of flight training at the Kacha Higher Military Aviation School for Pilots – one of the oldest aviation training facilities in the country, which over the years of its operation produced many thousands of combat pilots for the country. The School's headquarters was located in Volgograd: Nikolai moved there to assume the posting, but left his family behind in Taganrog since his new position was only temporary. He had received the assignment primarily so he could eventually enroll in the General Staff Academy. Colonel Sutiagin spent less than a full year at the Kacha School, but while he was in Volgograd, there was a special commission working on a draft document, 'Higher Military Aviation School Regulations'. After discussion in all the higher military aviation schools in the country, this document was confirmed by the Air Force commander-in-chief as the basic organizational document for all the military flight schools.

There is an interesting story connected with Sutiagin's time with the Kacha

School. One day, he visited the subordinate 704th UAP in Kotel'nikovo. The purpose of his visit was to conduct a mock dogfight in the MiG-15 UTI for demonstration purposes. Two of the two-seater MiG trainers took off for the demonstration. Deputy squadron commander Captain V.G. Kazashvili was piloting one of the trainers, with Sutiagin located in the rear cockpit. Lieutenant Colonel Shavsha took the instructor's place in the second trainer. After taking off, each of the pilots tried to maneuver onto the tail of the other MiG. Soon, the instructors took over the controls themselves, and squeezed everything they could out of their MiGs. The trainees – experienced pilots both – had never experienced such high G-forces before while flying. The control stick was literally ripped from their fingers and they both nearly lost consciousness. Sutiagin deliberately allowed his opponent to get behind him, but then with a sharp maneuver he separated from his mock adversary and turned the tables on him.

Once safely back on the ground, Sutiagin told the trainee pilots during the de-briefing, 'If you want to survive and to win in combat, you must make use of all the maneuvering capabilities of your plane.' Nikolai eagerly shared his combat experience with his students. However, as many veteran pilots of the Korean War observe, the Air Force didn't make sufficient use of their experience. Everything was kept under strict secrecy for many long years.

Chief of a School for Pilots in Kharkov

In July 1962, Colonel Sutiagin left Volgograd to enroll in the Military Academy of the General Staff. His entire family followed him to Moscow, and they lived in one of the academy's dormitories on Vernadsky Prospect. At the time, the dormitory was almost on the city's outskirts, which made it easy for their cross-country ski outings in the winter time. The woods began just a ten-minute walk from their residence. Sometimes they took their son along with them, but he didn't enjoy the outings very much.

Nikolai Sutiagin also loved to take steam baths. He often visited the Sandunovsky Baths, which was one of the few places where Nikolai would take advantage of his red booklet that contained his Hero of the Soviet Union certificate. This gave him the privilege to bypass the normal line standing outside the bath house. Nevertheless, in general, Sutiagin avoided using his privileges.

Practically every year, Nikolai Vasil'evich would also travel back to his native village of Smagino. His children often went there for the summer to stay with their grandmother. When in Smagino, he would typically be visited by the director of the local collective farm and the district leadership. With the practical nature of rural folk, they used the arrival of their local Hero to try to solve some of their economic problems. While Nikolai Vasil'evich himself didn't like to shake something out of the authorities, and didn't really know how to do so, he willingly tried to help. Indeed, often only his presence was necessary, and the local delegation would find someone to listen to them.

Upon graduating from the Military Academy of the General Staff, Colonel Sutiagin was assigned to take command of the S.I. Gritsev Higher Military Aviation School for Pilots in Kharkov. This school had a rich history from its origin in November 1930. Its graduates included three-time Hero of the Soviet Union I. Kozhedub (a 1941 graduate); with sixty-two official victories in the Great Patriotic War, he was the Allies' 'Ace of Aces'. The school also produced twelve twice-Heroes and more than 230 Heroes of the Soviet Union. The well-known test pilot G. Molosov and the cosmonaut A. Leonov also studied at the Kharkov Higher Military Aviation School.

Under Sutiagin's leadership, the school had two primary, interrelated missions: to produce pilots who had a higher special education and deep theoretical training, who would be known as 'pilot-engineers'; and to train the cadets to fly the new supersonic fighter, the MiG-21. However, the school was not only training fighter pilots. Between the years 1966 and 1970, the school also graduated pilots who had been trained to fly the supersonic Yak-28 bomber.

In the number of aircraft at its disposal, the Kharkov School was comparable in size to the air force of the Kiev Military District, to which the school belonged. The aircraft and equipment were becoming more complex. At that time, the MiG-21 was an ultra-modern fighter; there were still hardly any combat regiments equipped with it. So the command at the school devoted a great deal of methodical work to preparing the cadets to fly the plane, but despite their best efforts, there were serious accidents and flight crashes at the Kharkov VAShP in 1965 and 1966, which resulted in the death of both cadets and instructors. Investigative commissions from higher headquarters, looking into the cause of these accidents, almost always accused the school's leadership of shortcomings in their work. In addition to matters of flight training, Colonel Sutiagin also had to oversee the service personnel and the financial management of the garrison. So there was always a lot of work to do, and Sutiagin rarely had a free day from work.

During his rare hours off, Nikolai loved to do a little fishing. There were not only fish in the local rivers and streams, but also crayfish. Catching the tasty little crustaceans brought Nikolai particular satisfaction, and there was always a subsequent crayfish boil or fish soup to share with friends after such fishing trips. Although now a rather important chief, Nikolai Vasil'evich shunned the external attributes of power, like a dacha or similar privileges. The Sutiagin family lived in one of the garrison's regular housing units, and Nikolai remained a modest and accessible man.

After successfully graduating three successive classes in 1965, 1966 and 1967, in October 1967, N. Sutiagin finally received his promotion to the rank of general. It capped a successful year for General Sutiagin, because there were no flight accidents at the Kharkov VAShP in 1967.

In May 1968, General Sutiagin received a new assignment as deputy commander for combat training and the training establishments of the 69th Air Army, the headquarters of which were located in Kiev. Relatively quickly Sutiagin obtained a four-room apartment on Krasnoarmeiskaia Street – the sixth floor of Building 118. The apartment was not very well designed, but he decided it was better not to wait, since he wanted to bring his family to Kiev before the start of the training year. The Sutiagins shared the same entrance with a rather colorful assortment of people: a family of settled gypsies on the second floor; a KGB colonel on the fourth floor; and the son of Lavrentii Beria, the notorious former head of the NKVD (predecessor of the KGB), who lived on the eighth floor. In September the entire family moved to Kiev with the exception of the eldest daughter Galina, who remained in Kharkov to continue her foreign language studies.

Among General Sutiagin's duties with the 69th Air Army was supervisory responsibility over the aviation training establishments of the Kiev Military District: the Kharkov and Chernigov Schools for Pilots; the Lugansk School for Navigators; and the aviation technical schools – the Kharkov Military Aviation Technical Schools No. 1 and No. 2, the Vasilovsky Military Aviation Technical School, and the Kiev Higher Engineer-Aviation Military School of the Air Force. Sutiagin continued to fly a lot, primarily in the MiG-21. For the year 1969, he logged 92 hours and 21 minutes on 146 flights, of which thirty were at night.

Mission to Vietnam

In 1970, General Sutiagin was unexpectedly summoned to the Tenth Main Directorate of the General Staff. There he was offered the opportunity to go to North Vietnam for a year on special assignment as a senior air force military advisor. Sutiagin was an urgent replacement for a different officer who had been originally selected for this mission, but who had broken his leg while skiing. Nikolai Sutiagin had no real desire to go to Vietnam; he was fully satisfied with his work in Kiev, where new work opportunities were opening up to him. In addition, his wife needed special attention, because she was suffering from asthma, but Sutiagin really couldn't even try to refuse such a proposal. Therefore he gathered his things and left for North Vietnam. The 69th Air Army commander General N.M. Skomorokhov promised to hold Sutiagin's place for him in Kiev.

Once again, almost twenty years later, Nikolai found himself in the Far East, and once again he was struggling against the Americans, this time not as a pilot, but as an advisor to the North Vietnamese Air Force command. Sutiagin's new post was labeled as a consultant to the North Vietnamese commander of the Air Defense Organization and the Air Force of the Vietnamese People's Army: he was the senior officer in the group of Soviet military air force specialists in North Vietnam.

Sutiagin arrived in the Democratic Republic of Vietnam on 15 October 1970. With the knowledge he had acquired in his previous years of service, he capably directed the groups of Soviet air force specialists with the North Vietnamese 921st and 923rd Fighter Aviation Regiments, the A-38 workshop, and the Air Force Military-Technical School of the Vietnamese People's Army. The advisors were working to provide comprehensive assistance to their Vietnamese comrades to raise their combat readiness and improve their combat skills, and to offer theoretical and practical training to the flight staff of the North Vietnamese Air Force.

The work of the Soviet air force specialists had a clear impact on the results of flight training in the North Vietnamese aviation regiments. In 1971, the regiments' aggregate hours of flight time increased by 50 per cent in comparison with 1970, while the hours of night flights increased by 43 per cent. The specialists of the Engineer-Aviation Service ensured the reliable operation of the aircraft. The operational readiness of the fighters in the regiments was 95 per cent, and the hours of flight time per one malfunction in the air increased by 28 per cent. Sutiagin oversaw the first complete inventory of the combat equipment, spare parts and instruments, and tools and supplies during his year in North Vietnam, which revealed the true situation with respect to storing and conserving equipment and supplies, enabled their more rational use, and also allowed for a more objective request for aid in 1972.

Colonel (ret.) Lev Petrovich Poltev, who was a flight instructor with the North Vietnamese 921st IAP at the time, recalls:

> There was a regiment of MiG-21PF fighters at Yen Bai near Hanoi. ...
> At night, the planes were kept concealed in shelters that had been previously built by the French in the nearby hills, and in the morning they were brought to the airfield. There were frequent alarms, both genuine and practice drills.
>
> One of the aircraft holding areas was situated 4 kilometers from the Yen Bai base and was connected with it by an asphalt road, along which the fighters could roll out directly to the runway start if necessary. Twenty MiG-21PF fighters and aircraft of earlier modifications were located on this parking apron under an open sky. In one of the nearby

hills, an enormous cave shelter had been excavated, which permitted maintenance and repair work on up to twenty fighters simultaneously by the assembly line method. The airfield had been subjected to attack, and the runway had been damaged, but this had occurred a little before our time there.

There was a group of Soviet specialists with the regiment, approximately twenty men. Four of the men were pilot-instructors with the regiment, while the rest were technicians and specialists, like radio operators and a doctor. There were also four or five civilian specialists from the 'Banner of Labor' factory, who made adjustments to the MiGs in accordance with arriving technical bulletins. Our primary assignment was to train the Vietnamese pilots and prepare them for night flying. We also flew the fighters after repairs or maintenance work in order to check them out. Another task of our group was to instruct the Vietnamese in the proper technical servicing and repair of the MiG-21.

General Sutiagin traveled out to Yen Bai to check on us once. He was living in the Soviet embassy in Hanoi together with the other top commanders of the advisory group. He gave us a long talk and also spoke with the Vietnamese pilots.

Our pilot-instructors flew no combat missions, but it is difficult to exaggerate their role as military advisors: their 'recommendations' were in fact direct instructions for handling combat operations, especially in the early years of the war. Later, toward the end of the 1960s, the Vietnamese started to fall under the influence of China, which was also providing weapons, equipment, and the training of cadres to the North Vietnamese. Chinese military advisors, who enjoyed great authority among the North Vietnamese, were present in Vietnam while General Sutiagin was there.

During Sutiagin's time in Vietnam, the air war was on a lower level of activity than it was later, in December 1972, when strategic bombers of the United States bombed Hanoi and Haiphong for twelve days in a row. Nevertheless, Hanoi experienced regular air raids in 1970–71. Moreover, less than a month after Sutiagin's arrival, in November 1970 American helicopters and Special Forces landed just 20 miles from Hanoi, in an attempt to liberate prisoners they believed were being held at Son Tay prison.

According to the entries in his flight log, N. Sutiagin conducted thirty-eight flights in the month of January 1971, twenty-eight of which were in the MiG-15UTI, seven in the MiG-17, and three in the MiG-21. In March 1971 he made six flights, four in the MiG-21US and two in the MiG-21PF. The purpose of these sorties was not indicated.

For his year of service in Vietnam, Nikolai Vasil'evich was awarded the Order of the Red Star. In October 1971, Sutiagin returned to the Soviet Union, but he found his position in Kiev was now occupied by someone else: General N.M. Skomorokhov had not kept his word to Nikolai. In the Main Directorate for Cadres, N.V. Sutiagin was offered the position of deputy commander of the 16th Air Army for fighter aviation and air defense in the Group of Soviet Forces in Germany (GSFG). After a short leave of absence, he set off for his new position in Wunsdorf in the German Democratic Republic.

His mission to Vietnam had turned out badly for Sutiagin: he lost his position in Kiev, and more importantly, it undermined his health. His eyesight had begun to deteriorate, which is a very serious matter for a pilot. The heat and high humidity of the difficult Vietnamese climate, as well as the unaccustomed food, had taken a toll on his health. As a result, doctors had banned Nikolai from flying in jet aircraft, limiting him to transport planes and helicopters. Although Sutiagin had some experience flying transport planes, he would now have to learn how to fly a helicopter.

With the Group of Soviet Forces in Germany

The GSFG's 16th Air Army was the most powerful formation in the Soviet Air Force. It consisted of three fighter and two fighter-bomber aviation divisions, each with three regiments, and several independent helicopter regiments and squadrons. The 16th Air Army was equipped with various versions of the MiG-21, and with the MiG-23, MiG-27, Su-7, Su-17, and Su-24 fighters and fighter-bombers; helicopters such as the Mi-8 and Mi-24; and other fixed wing and rotary aircraft.

The 16th Air Army had a two-corps organization: the 'Northern' 74th IAK (headquarters in Wittstock) and the 'Southern' 72nd IAK (headquarters in Wittemburg). The headquarters of the Air Army was located in Wunsdorf, a small village about 30 kilometers south of Berlin. The headquarters of the Group of Soviet Forces was also located there. During the Second World War, the German General Staff Headquarters had been located here, and its buildings and barracks remained in good condition. The Soviet military base at Wunsdorf occupied a large area of approximately 100 square kilometers. It included three cantonments: one for the Group Headquarters, the second for a motorized rifle regiment, and the third for the Air Army's headquarters. About 10 kilometers away, in Sperenburg, was the airfield of the 226th Composite Aviation Regiment, which provided the officer staff of the Group and Air Army headquarters with air transportation.

As the deputy commander for air defenses, General Sutiagin was responsible for directing the combat alert status of the fighter units on German

Democratic Republic (GDR) territory. Each fighter aviation regiment constantly maintained an element or flight of fighters at readiness level No. 1, prepared to take off immediately to intercept targets intruding into East German airspace.

Direct intrusions into the defended airspace were infrequent, but in those years – at the height of the Cold War – NATO planes were constantly making reconnaissance flights along the borders of the GDR, and releasing balloons that carried surveillance instruments. These probes caused the greatest concern, because they were difficult to intercept. There was hardly a day when fighters or helicopters weren't launched on an alert.

General Sutiagin spent most of his time on duty at the air army's command post and making inspection visits to the aviation regiments. He usually flew around all the units in Mi–8 helicopters, and while doing so he often took over the helicopter's controls from the pilot – he had to accumulate flight time each month. When the units began to receive the new Mi–24 helicopters in 1974, he conducted several flights in one.

The young combat pilots often called Nikolai 'Grand-dad' to his face. His subordinates respected Nikolai Vasil'evich for his combat service and his demeanor: he rarely raised his voice, was simple and direct in communications, and lived modestly. In addition, many graduates of the Kharkov Military Aviation School – his former pupils – were now serving in the units as squadron or regiment commanders.

One of the tasks of the air defense system was to monitor and control the flights of military transport and civilian passenger aircraft from the Federal Republic of Germany (FRG) into and out of West Berlin. The exclusive, intensively used corridor had three routes: North – Hamburg; Center – Braunschweig; and South – Weimar. Often, the military and civilian aircraft strayed from the established route. Any intentional or unintentional divergence from the corridor required a reaction from our on–duty interceptors.

Light recreational planes also occasionally violated the airspace. Then an on-duty element or flight would be launched to intercept them. The panicked violators would often hasten to get away, putting themselves at risk from getting caught in the turbulent wash of the jet fighters.

In all fairness it must be noted that our aircraft also provoked NATO's air defenses by conducting flights very near the border. According to the word of pilots who served in the GSFG, they had to perform such flights under the code word 'Pinprick'. An aviation regiment would take off by squadrons; the squadrons would assemble into a column of pairs and fly at extremely low altitude to the airfield at Neuruppin. Over the airfield runway, they would climb rapidly to an altitude of 2,000 to 3,000 meters and then race toward the border. Literally within a few hundred meters of the border, which ran along the Elbe River, our planes would abruptly reverse course and fly away to the east. After a couple of minutes, the next squadron would approach the border and repeat the operation. This little game played strongly on the nerves of the NATO officers sitting in the control stations. This practice was later banned.

Once, General Sutiagin decided to check the ground forces' air defense system himself. The day before, in order to keep his intentions unknown, he had filed a flight request for an Mi-8 helicopter to the northern part of the country. The request was misleading. Instead, he flew in a southerly direction near the national border at an altitude of 25 meters. Not a single radar station spotted him. Then he turned around and flew to the north of the country, and had the same result there. A huge scandal erupted: in the first place, General Sutiagin had failed to inform the command of the Air Army and the Group of Soviet Forces about his plans, but the main thing was the failure of the air defense system to catch the 'intruder'. For this, other commanders responsible for air defense of the Group of Soviet Forces received a real dressing-down.

However, the most unpleasant case while Sutiagin held this post occurred in the spring of 1973, when a technician, Senior Lieutenant Vronsky, stole an Su-7 BKL 'Fitter' fighter. The Su-7 was considered difficult to fly, but Vronsky managed to take off, fly with lowered landing gear for about 20 minutes over GDR territory with afterburner on, and reach West German territory. Fearing an attempt to land the plane, Vronsky ejected and safely came to earth. Several on-duty fighter elements were launched from various bases to intercept his plane, but failed to catch the fugitive.

Many were astonished: how could a completely untrained man manage to take off in an Su-7? It was later revealed that a friend of Vronsky, who was the chief of training in the aviation regiment, had taught Vronsky the rudiments of flying the plane, using a parked trainer. After this scandal, very strict precautionary measures were put into place: it became almost impossible for an unauthorized person to gain access to a trainer; padlocked gates barred access to parking aprons and taxiways; and cables with sharp spikes were manufactured that could be tossed under the wheels of a taxiing jet. However, all these measures came too late.

In 1975, there was another incident that sheds a lot of light on Nikolai Sutiagin's character. The crew of an Mi-2 helicopter crashed near Neuruppin: a commission from the headquarters of 16th Air Army, headed by General Sutiagin, arrived to investigate the crash. All the facts in the case pointed to the fault of the helicopter pilot. In Germany, there were many nude beaches, and our chopper pilots never missed a chance to fly over one. Vacationing Germans had become accustomed to these overflights and no longer paid any attention to them. The pilot of the ill-fated Mi-2 was flying at extremely low altitude, had become distracted by the sights below him, and had failed to notice a low hill in their flight path. The pilot and the helicopter's flight engineer died in the crash. After reporting the cause of the accident, Nikolai Vasil'evich, who had the final word, said:

> We understand that the crew was at fault. But the airmen have already punished themselves. If we place the guilt on their shoulders, then their families will be punished. Their wives will not receive a pension to help offset the loss of their breadwinner. Let's give some thought to how we can get out of this situation.

The engineering service didn't want to write off the crash as an equipment failure, this would seriously ruin their performance measures. As happens in such cases, other services also didn't want to shoulder the responsibility for the disaster. Nevertheless, a way out was found: the investigative commission's final report stated that the helicopter had encountered a weather front, become caught in a pocket of turbulence, and the pilot had lost control. The crew's fault was erased, and their family members didn't suffer.

There was another major incident in 1977, when an Su-7 accidentally strayed 30 kilometers into FRG airspace before being guided back to the GDR. Though this was a serious transgression, neither the young pilot nor anyone in the ground control crew or the regiment or division command received punishment. Referring to this, Major General (ret.) Sergei Andreevich Kalensky, who often collaborated together with General Sutiagin in Wunsdorf, recalled, 'This was General Sutiagin's work style – he didn't look for opportunities to punish subordinates; it was most important for him to analyze the causes of errors thoroughly and to devise measures to prevent similar mistakes in the future.'

Given the relatively small territory of the GDR back then, such incidents were simply unavoidable. Accordingly, even the post of deputy commander for air defense was a very stressful one. Sutiagin also regularly traveled to appear at air defense command conferences hosted by other members of the Warsaw Pact, so he had the opportunity to spend time in other East European capitals like Budapest, Warsaw and Prague. He always returned with souvenirs.

Twenty years after the Korean War, Nikolai Sutiagin also had occasion to meet with the Americans face to face – his duties sometimes took him to West Berlin to conduct negotiations with American, British and French air force delegations. American delegations sometimes included American pilots who had fought in Korea. The western delegations would also invite their Soviet counterparts to receptions on the occasion of their national holidays. In an interview with one of the authors, Colonel-General of Aviation Aleksandr Nikolaevich Zakrevsky described what happened at one of these receptions:

At one of these receptions in West Berlin … an American general proposed a toast in honor of the American Korean War aces, and lavished praise on their pilots and American jet fighters of those times. He offered examples of their prominent accomplishments, such as American pilots who had downed ten or more enemy aircraft.

The head of our delegation, the chief of staff of the GSFG Colonel-General Grinkevich could not long endure this presentation. In order to knock the American general off his pedestal, Grinkevich rose to his feet and proposed his own toast in honor of the attending Nikolai Sutiagin, who had downed twenty-two planes in Korea – many more than the top American aces had managed to score. The Yankees were humbled, or at the very least discouraged, but they joined in the toast and then for a long time afterward sportingly expressed their admiration.

Incidentally, Sutiagin himself always spoke quite highly of the professional qualities of the American pilots. He said they were most worthy opponents.

When not busy with his many official duties, Nikolai liked to relax by doing a little fishing or mushroom hunting. He also enjoyed gathering every Friday with Generals Avdonin, Zakrevsky and Il'nitsky in a little 'generals' bathhouse' at an outdoor swimming pool. The bathhouse was a modest one, but it had all the necessary attributes: a sauna, a bathroom, a hydro-massage Charcot shower, and a leisure room. After work, the little group would gather and socialize over some pickled fish, a little beer, or something a little stronger. Nikolai Vasil'evich always enjoyed pleasant company, though he usually did more listening than talking – he wasn't a glib speaker.

As the term of his service with the GSFG was coming to an end, Nikolai Vasil'evich was offered the position as first deputy commander of an Air Army in Khabarovsk with the prospect of becoming its commander, but he declined the offer. The climate in Khabarovsk would be detrimental to the health of his asthmatic wife Raisa, and Nikolai didn't want to go alone. The Air Force offered him several staff positions, but Nikolai had no fondness for paperwork. Finally, he was offered the post of chairman of the Department of Army Aviation at the Gagarin Air Force Academy. However, the interview with the head of the academy, General N.M. Skomorokhov, was disappointing. Nikolai Vasil'evich learned he would have to write a dissertation, so he declined the position. To be honest, he really just wanted to return to Kiev: he liked the city, the climate was beneficial for his wife, and they had an apartment there. In the end, Nikolai decided to remain where he was and to serve out his term in Germany.

In May 1978, General Sutiagin reached fifty-five years of age and was released from active service, though generals continue to serve in staff positions or in training institutions until sixty-five years of age. Major General of Aviation N.V. Sutiagin had served thirty-seven years in the Soviet Air Force. In that time, he had learned to fly twenty different types of planes and helicopters, in which he had accumulated around 3,300 hours of flight time.

In Retirement

Released from the ranks of the armed forces, Nikolai Vasil'evich returned to Kiev and took up a few household chores and projects, like repairs around the apartment and building a garage. Yet Sutiagin generally didn't particularly care for household duties, with the exception of cooking. It is hard to say where he had learned to cook, but he had a limited repertoire of dishes like Russian cabbage soup and Siberian meat dumplings that he could prepare as well as a professional chef.

With his household affairs in order, Nikolai soon accepted a position in Kiev as the chief of staff of the Scientific Research Institute of Hydrology and Irrigation's civil defense organization. Such a position existed in practically every major State institution. The director and employees of the Institute all regarded Nikolai Vasil'evich with great respect.

In 1980, Sutiagin traveled to Kharkov for the anniversary of the military aviation school there that he had formerly commanded for almost four years. At the time there was still nothing that portended the sad fate of this renowned aviation school, which at the end of the 1990s simply vanished after numerous reorganizations during the epoch of 'great change' that swept the Ukraine. Incidentally, the same thing happened with many other famous aviation schools of the former Soviet Union. The Kacha VAShP was closed, and the Eisk School now trains only operations officers. At the time of writing, only one military aviation school in Krasnodar continues to train the future fighter pilots of Russia.

Nikolai Vasil'evich fell seriously ill in 1984 – on New Year's Eve – and went to the hospital with suspected appendicitis. They rushed him directly to the operating table, but the diagnosis was even more serious than the doctors had supposed. Nikolai had peritonitis, with a subsequent inflammation of the lungs. Over the next couple of years, he had to endure several major operations. The doctors were impressed by his endurance and courage, but they were unable to cure him fully. Then in May 1986, Nikolai Vasil'evich, together with other citizens of Kiev, was exposed to the effects of radiation as a result of the accident at the Chernobyl nuclear power plant. The large dose of radiation adversely affected Nikolai Vasil'evich's struggle with his illness. On 12

November 1986, Sutiagin passed away in the Kiev District Hospital. He was buried with honors in the Baikov Cemetery in Kiev.

Nikolai Vasil'evich's remains lie not on the Central Alley of the cemetery, as was due him because of his Hero status, but in a remote section next to his wife Raisa Onufrievna. This was Sutiagin's last will. By coincidence, another pilot is buried on the other side of Sutiagin's grave: F.P. Suprun, the brother of the famous test pilot Twice Hero of the Soviet Union Stepan Suprun. Not far from their graves lies the well-known Ukrainian movie actor and film director Leonid Bykov, whose famous movie *V boi idut odni stariki* [Only Old Men Go into Battle] remains one of the best films about the heroic pilots of the Great Patriotic War.

These people, modest in life, remained modest after death as well. However, along the Central Alley of the Baikov Cemetery, pompous memorial sculptures for Gypsy barons, 'New Russians' and 'New Ukrainians' are now multiplying ... different times, different values.

Appendix

Technical Characteristics of the Planes Used by Both Sides in Korea

Plane	Engine[a]	Max. Speed, km/hr	Ceiling, m	Range, km	Armament	Nation
Jet Fighters and Ground Attack Planes						
Gloster Meteor F8	2x1590	950	13600	1400	4x20mm 8 rockets	UK
F-80 Shooting Star	2450	900	13700	1220	6x12.7mm 8 rockets	USA
F-84 Thunderjet	2270	960	13500	1040	6x12.7mm 10 rockets	USA
F-86A Sabre	2360	1080	14500	1060	6x12.7mm 16 rockets	USA
F-86E Sabre	2360	1080	14630	1365	6x12.7mm 16 rockets	USA
F-86F Sabre	2680	1100	14600	750	6x12.7mm 16 rockets	USA
F-94C Starfire	2880	1020	15600	2500	4x12mm 24 rockets	USA
F2N Banshee	2x1470	960	14500	1900	4x20mm 6 rockets	USA carrier
F9F Panther	3180	1000	12400	1900	4x20mm 6 rockets	USA carrier
F3D Skyknight	2x1360	930	12200	3200	4x20mm	USA carrier
MiG-15	2270	1050	15200	1300	2x23mm 1x37mm	USSR
MiG-15bis	2700	1076	15500	1200	2x23mm 1x37mm	USSR
Piston-engine Fighters and Ground Attack Planes						
La-11	1630	670	10250	2550	3x23mm	USSR
Yak-11	570	450	7000	1300	1x12.7mm	USSR

F-47 Thunderbolt	2800	740	12500	1950	6x12.7mm 10 rockets	USA
F-51 Mustang	1695	710	13400	2100	6x12.7mm 10 rockets	USA
F-82 Twin Mustang	2x1380	765	13700	2500	6x12.7mm 25 rockets	USA
F4U Corsair	2100	725	13000	2600	6x12.7mm 8 rockets	USA carrier
F7F Tigercat	2x2100	685	11000	1800	4x20mm 8 rockets	USA carrier
AD-4 Skyraider	2700	580	7600	2000	4x20mm 12 rockets	USA carrier
Bombers						
B-26 Invader	2x2360	570	7300	2100	6x12.7mm 2.7 tons of bombs	USA
B-29 Superfortress	4x2500	590	10400	5200	10x12.7mm 1x20mm 9 tons of bombs	USA

[a] For jet airplanes, the number indicates the kilograms of thrust per second produced by the engine; for piston-engine planes, the number indicates the engine's horsepower.

Notes

Chapter One: The Making of an Air Warrior

1. TsAMO, l/d 0802079, l.17.
2. The personal flight log of N.V. Sutiagin, 1941–1947, p. 187.
3. TsAMO, F. 5 iap, Op. 518550s.
4. TsAMO, l/d 0802079, l.19.
5. TsAMO, l/d 0802079, l.20.
6. TsAMO, l/d 0802079, l.21.

Chapter Two: In China the Regiment Prepares for Battle

1. *'Asy Koreiskoi Voiny'* ['Aces of the Korean War'] *Zhurnal 'Voina v vozdukhe'* [Journal 'War in the Air'] No. 13, 2000, p. 6.
2. This officer was responsible for analyzing the gun camera film to determine the results of aerial gunnery: whether or not a target was damaged or destroyed. He was also responsible for collecting and reporting the data from each MiG's flight box after a mission, and for checking the simple self-diagnostic devices in each aircraft before a mission.
3. TsAMO, F. 17 iap, Op. 539850, d. 5.
4. TsAMO, F. 17 iap, Op. 683351c, d. 5, c. 119.
5. At readiness level No. 1, the MiGs were expected to take off within two or three minutes of a launch order, so the pilots were kept sitting in the cockpits with parachutes on, radios switched on, and the engines were kept warm by periodic starting. At readiness level No. 2, the pilots waited in a nearby dugout or ready shack, while the crew chiefs and maintenance personnel remained near the aircraft. At a signal to launch or to assume readiness level No. 1, pilots climbed into the cockpits, switched on their radios, put on their parachutes, and their aircraft engines were started. As soon as the aircraft at readiness level No. 1 launched, readiness level No. 2 aircraft assumed the readiness level No. 1 status, while readiness level No. 3 aircraft moved up to readiness level No. 2. See Dmitriy Loza, *Attack of the Airacobras: Soviet Aces, American P-39s, & the Air War Against Germany* (Lawrence, KS: University Press of Kansas, 2002), note 10, p. 345.
6. TsAMO, F. 17 iap, Op. 152732, d. 4.
7. Ibid.
8. TsAMO, F. 303 iad, Op. 152695ss, d.1, s. 11–15.
9. Editor's note: Whenever work was done on a plane, Soviet mechanics and technicians were supposed to place seals over the panel doors and compartment hatches

once they had completed the service. This was to indicate the completion of work and to prevent unauthorized access to the MiG's key components and systems.

10. TsAMO, F. 17 iap, Op. 683351, d. 5, s. 61–63.
11. TsAMO, l/d 0802079, l. 24.
12. TsAMO, F. 17 iap, Op. 152732, d. 4.

Chapter Three: Combat Operations, Tactics and Routines in the Korean Air War

1. TsAMO, F. 17 iap, Op. 683351s, d. 5, s. 29–41.
2. Ibid.
3. Target aspect angle is the angle between the longitudinal axis of the target (projected rearward) and the line of sight to the interceptor measured from the tail of the target. Aspect angle is used in aerial gunnery for determining the angle of deflection for a firing solution.
4. V.K. Babich, *Istrebiteli meniaiut taktiku* [Fighters are changing tactics] (Moscow: Voennaia Istoriia, 1983), p. 10.
5. TsAMO, F. 17 iap, Op. 683351s, d. 5, s. 16–21.

Chapter Four: An Auspicious Debut

1. Editor's note: In this celebrated speech to the Soviet people after the German invasion of the Soviet Union, Stalin warned of the grave danger hanging over the country and called for the complete and rapid mobilization of the Soviet people in defense of the Soviet Motherland.
2. James T. Stewart, *Airpower – The Decisive Force in Korea* (Princeton, NJ: D. Van Nostrand Company, Inc., 1957), p. 121.
3. TsAMO, F. 17 iap, Op. 539850s, d. 11, s. 2–4.
4. TsAMO, F. 17 iap, Op. 152732, d. 7.
5. TsAMO, F. 17 iap, Op. 539850s, d. 11, s. 14–17.
6. TsAMO, F. 303 iad, Op. 539825, d. 4, s. 111.
7. TsAMO, F. 17 iap, Op. 683351s, d. 6.
8. TsAMO, F. 17 iap, Op. 683351s, d. 5, s. 47.
9. TsAMO, F. 17 iap, Op. 539850s, d. 11, s. 48–49.
10. TsAMO, F. 17 iap, Op. 152732, d. 4.
11. TsAMO, F. 17 iap, Op. 539850s, d. 11, s. 51–52.
12. TsAMO, F. 303 iad, Op. 539825, d. 4, s. 150.
13. Archive of the Moscow District Military Commissariat, city of Kiev, l/d No. 40846 (inv. 11320), l. 17.
14. TsAMO, F. 17 iap, Op. 827056, d. 1.

Chapter Five: The Autumn Marathon

1. TsAMO, F. 17 iap, Op. 539850s, d. 11, l. 98–99.
2. A. Demin, *'V nebe Korei'* ['In the Korean Sky'], *Zhurnal 'Aviatsiia i kosmonavtika'*

[Aviation and Cosmonautics Journal] (No. 10, 2004), p. 35.

3. L. Krylov and Iu. Tepsurkaev, *'Chernaia nedelia Bombardirovochnogo komandovaniye'* ['Bomber Command's Black Week'], *Zhurnal 'Mir Aviatsii'* [The World of Aviation Journal] (No. 2, 1999).

4. TsAMO, F. 17 iap, Op. 539850, d. 11, s. 207–209.

5. TsAMO, F. 303 iad, Op. 152694, d. 1.

6. TsAMO, F. 303 iad, Op. 152695ss, d. 1, s. 24–25.

7. TsAMO, F. 17 iap, Op. 539850s, d. 11, s. 207–209.

8. Ibid., s. 237–239.

9. TsAMO, 1/d 0802079, s. 27.

10. TsAMO, F. 17 iap, Op. 539850s, d. 11, s. 274–276.

11. Ibid., s. 280–281.

12. TsAMO, F. 17 iap, Op. 539850s, d. 11, s. 207–209.

13. Ibid., s. 299–300.

14. Ibid., s. 312–314.

15. Ibid., s. 322–324.

16. Ibid., s. 332–333.

17. TsAMO, F. 303 iad, Op. 539831, d. 1.

18. TsAMO, F. 17 iap, Op. 539850s, d. 11, s. 332–333.

19. TsAMO, F. 303 iad, Op. 539831, d. 1, s. 75.

20. TsAMO, F. 17 iap, Op. 539850s, d. 11, s. 370–371.

21. I. Seidov, *Krasnye d'iavoly na 38-i paralleli* [Red devils on the 38th parallel], 1st Ed., (Kiev, 1998), pp. 160–165.

Chapter Six: The Final Months of Deployment

1. Pepeliaev, E.G. *'MiGi' protiv 'Seibrov'* [MiGs against Sabres] (Moscow: NPP Del'ta, 2000), pp. 25–26.

2. TsAMO, F. 17 iap, Op. 539851s, d. 3, s. 27–29.

3. TsAMO, F. 17 iap, Op. 539851s, d. 3, s. 34–35.

4. TsAMO, F. 17 iap, Op. 539851s, d. 3, s. 68–69.

5. TsAMO, F. 303 iad, Op. 539831, d. 1.

6. Ibid.

Chapter Seven: Results and Lessons

1. TsAMO, F. 17 iap, Op. 683351s, d. 5, s. 9–10.

2. TsAMO, F. 303 iad, Op. 152695s, d. 1, s. 68.

3. TsAMO, F. 17 iap, Op. 683351s, d. 5, s. 58–59.

4. Ibid., s. 8.

5. Ibid., s. 123.

6. TsAMO, F. 17 iap, Op. 683351s, d. 5, s. 123.

7. A. Dokuchaev, *'Virtuozy reaktivnoi voiny. Tekhnika i oruzhi'* ['Virtuosos of the jet war. Equipment and Weaponry'], (No. 3–4, 1995).

Index

NB: Sutiagin is not generally indexed as he occurs passim, with the exception of specific listings such as Flight Rosters, combat victories, etc.